CHEVY/GMC TRUCKS 1973–1987

HOW TO BUILD & MODIFY

Jim Pickering

CarTech ®

CarTech®, Inc.
6118 Main Street
North Branch, MN 55056
Phone: 651-277-1200 or 800-551-4754
Fax: 651-277-1203
www.cartechbooks.com

Edit by Wes Eisenschenk
Layout by Monica Seiberlich

ISBN 978-1-61325-516-2
Item No. SA471

Library of Congress Cataloging-in-Publication Data

Names: Pickering, Jim, 1982- author.
Title: Chevrolet/GMC trucks 1973-1987 : how to build & modify / Jim Pickering.
Description: Forest Lake, MN : CarTech, Inc., [2020] | "CT612."
Identifiers: LCCN 2019053278 | ISBN 9781613255162 (paperback)
Subjects: LCSH: Chevrolet trucks–Maintenance and repair. | GMC trucks–Maintenance and repair. | Chevrolet trucks–Customizing. | GMC trucks–Customizing.
Classification: LCC TL230.5.C45 P53 2020 | DDC 629.28/73–dc23
LC record available at https://lccn.loc.gov/2019053278

Written, edited, and designed in the U.S.A.
Printed in China
10 9 8 7 6 5 4 3 2

DISTRIBUTION BY:

Europe
PGUK
63 Hatton Garden
London EC1N 8LE, England
Phone: 020 7061 1980 • Fax: 020 7242 3725
www.pguk.co.uk

Australia
Renniks Publications Ltd.
3/37-39 Green Street
Banksmeadow, NSW 2109, Australia
Phone: 2 9695 7055 • Fax: 2 9695 7355
www.renniks.com

Canada
Login Canada
300 Saulteaux Crescent
Winnipeg, MB, R3J 3T2 Canada
Phone: 800 665 1148 • Fax: 800 665 0103
www.lb.ca

SA
S·A DESIGN

DEDICATION

To Kristina, Katie, and Emma for always being ready for a ride in a truck.

ACKNOWLEDGMENTS

Building a custom truck and writing a book about the process takes a lot of effort from a lot of people—especially when the project is done on a deadline.

This book never would have happened without the support of the *Sports Car Market* and *American Car Collector* staff—specifically Chester Allen, who pushed me to tackle the project and graciously made time for me to do so. A special thanks to Jeff Stites for his assistance with illustrations, Jeff Zurschmeide for his insight into book production, and Jay Harden, Brian Baker, Chad Tyson, and Chad Taylor for listening to me drone on about C10s for the better part of a year.

For parts information and support, I have to thank Steve Chryssochoos from RideTech, Blane Burnett and Jeff Teel from Holley, Alan Rebescher from Summit Racing, Rick Elam from Baer Brakes, Edward Navarro from Classic Industries, Matt Graves from American Powertrain, Ken Lingenfelter and Mark Rapson from Lingenfelter Performance Engineering, Chris Plump from Wheelpros, Matt Murray from The Eastwood Company, and Shari Arfons from McCullough PR.

Thanks to Alistair Case for his paintwork, Jim Fahey for donating his TIG welding and fabrication skills, Rick Redmond of AIR Automotive for interior assistance, Dan Suldul of Dan's Gears for help with the axle chapter, and Luke Wilson of Wilson Cylinder Head for pointing me the right way with my LS build.

Brian M. Carlson (auction sleuth and American truck specialist) supplied a number of images that I couldn't shoot myself, as did Kevin Whipps—author of CarTech's books on 1967–1972 and 1973–1987 GM truck restoration. Matt Kincaid was gracious enough to let me crash his high school shop class numerous times to shoot images of his turbo 5.3 1978 C10 build.

Thanks to Wes Eisenchenk at CarTech for his persistence and patience and to the whole CarTech team.

Finally, none of this would have been possible without the support and assistance of my wife, Kristina, and my kids. They made time for this project and encouraged me along the way. Last but by no means least, my father, James M. Pickering, was a huge part of this build—and all of my builds. He's an inspiration, an enabler, a problem solver, and the one responsible for setting me on a car-crazy path.

INTRODUCTION

Everybody has a truck story. Mine started in the mid-1980s. That's when my father dragged home a hulk of a 1975 Chevrolet C20. It was a mess of dents under flat Hawaiian Blue paint, and it had been left for dead, claimed by some blackberry bushes that had grown over its smashed-up bed and cab. A fried TH350 had saved it from a life of hauling heavy equipment. My father, a hot rod and muscle car guy turned family man, saw potential.

I was an impressionable little kid when Dad brought that C20 back to life. I remember riding around in it with no bed bolted to the chassis, my eyes just about level to the "Scottsdale" badge on the dash. I remember Dad beating the body straight and laying down a custom two-tone blue paint job in his makeshift paint booth on the side of our house. For years we used it as our family truck. Its cheap turndown exhaust droned when Dad would arrive home from work—our rattling windows announcing with authority that he was home.

That truck was the first vehicle I ever saw restored, and it was eventually the first thing I ever drove. I went on to build a car of my own with Dad, became a mechanic right out of high school and throughout college, and eventually landed as Managing Editor for *Sports Car Market* and *American Car Collector* magazines. All that has taken me to some cool places—and in a very real sense, it all started with that old blue Scottsdale truck.

My story is by no means unique. GM's square trucks have a way of getting into your system and staying there, so it's no surprise that they're becoming more and more popular as specialty vehicles. Hindsight tends to highlight the best of an era; we like to think of simpler days of weekend projects with Dad or Grandpa, back when these trucks were new and riding around on a C10's bench seat was the highlight of the day. When we buy one of these trucks to get back there, the driving experience is, well, all truck: bouncy, kind of slow, and not really that much fun once those rosy memories wear off.

All of that can be fixed, however, while keeping that old-truck feel intact. I'm about to show you how in the following chapters.

There are any number of ways you can build one of these trucks, as they were offered in so many different configurations, from 4x4s to duallies, 3+3s, long-beds, and short-beds. If you want to build a lifted rig for off-roading or rock crawling, the squarebody is a great choice—but for this project, I chose to build a two-wheel-drive single-cab truck for street use. Unfortunately, you won't find much 4x4 information here—but a lot of what I do cover carries over to just about any squarebody you'd like to build, including Blazers and Suburbans.

These trucks don't require much in the way of special tools to tear them down or build them back up, and most of the components are basic, robust, and easy to source if they are missing or broken. You can still find parts in wrecking yards, at swap meets, and on Craigslist very easily. As such, these trucks are a great place to start for a first-time build, and I've tried to gear my writing toward builders who may be new to the process of putting together a custom car or truck. You'll find basic info here as well as in-depth dives on factory systems and upgrades.

To illustrate what you can do with a C10 build, I built a complete truck from start to finish and documented the process. My goal was to produce a truck that's fun and fast while also being safe to use in modern traffic.

This truck needed to be something I could drive every single day of the year if I wanted to, which is key—a lot of performance and style builds come with a great deal of compromise for the look or performance they provide. If you don't like driving something because it's uncomfortable, will you really drive it? To me, building something that is usable is the most important—especially if you want to be able to haul your own kids around in it for those weekend projects, just like Dad or Grandpa did.

It's pretty easy to get classic looks and modern performance out of these rigs. Do it right and you'll have a no-compromise solution that you'll actually want to use—and something that will create fun that you, and your kids, will remember.

The 1973–1987 Chevrolet and GMC trucks are growing in interest among restorers and builders looking for an affordable classic truck to build, and that's driving an aftermarket to produce more and more parts to make these trucks turn, stop, and accelerate better than they ever could have in stock configuration. It's just up to you to get your truck to do it. I'm confident that, after reading the following chapters, you can.

GM's Square Years

GM's squarebody pickups were special when they were introduced in 1973. Their design looked nothing like the trucks that came before—or anything like what was offered from the rivals over at Ford and Dodge. Of course, now, after millions of these trucks were built and let loose on the roads of America, we're all used to seeing them everywhere, most of them working hard as GM intended. But they really were unique back in 1973—the new look was an evolutionary step in truck design that carries through to the newest trucks built today.

This book is all about how to build and modify one of these classic 1973–1987 GM trucks. But before I get to that, it's important to take a look at what made these trucks special in the first place, as it gets to why they're still special today—and why you might consider building one into a modern hot rod. So first, a little history.

An All-New Hauler

The task of designing GM's next gen truck kicked off in 1968—just one year after the launch of the popular "Action Line" 1967 GM pickup.

This new design was called "Rounded Line" by GM.

The Rounded Line rigs were so named due to the extensive use of radiused edges in their design. Features included rounded windshield and side window corners, rounded body lines that allowed wraparound taillamps, and rounded doors that fit high up into the roof, allowing for a shorter-looking cab while simultaneously helping with ease of entry and exit. These trucks had 20 percent more glass than the previous model, a more comfortable, larger cab with flow-through ventilation, a thicker frame, and more.

It wasn't until later that these trucks gained the now well-known "squarebody" nickname, mostly

GM's light-duty trucks roared into the market in 1973. The all-new design was head-turning then and has aged well. Trucks from this era continue to gain in popularity, and they lend themselves well to modification. This custom truck with a stock theme, done by Joe Yezzi's Squarebody Syndicate, was a highlight of SEMA in 2016.

due to their flat, squared-off nose and grille, which became more pronounced with the 1981 design refresh. Generally, it seems that people became so accustomed to the rounded edges that they looked right past them—and they still do today. Thus, the squarebody was born, and the name has stuck, even if it's the exact opposite of what GM's truck designers were going for.

Computerized Design

These trucks were among the first that GM built with the help of a computer. The plan was to increase aerodynamic efficiency, therefore decreasing noise and increasing fuel economy.

All of that was a must, as the American truck market had become extremely competitive by that time. Ford was beating GM in terms of sales and had been for years, and GM was looking to get out in front and take that ever-elusive title of best-selling truck. To do so, they even went so far as to use wind tunnel testing on this new pickup to ensure they could gain an edge—and bragging rights—over the competition. Aero cues included a radio antenna embedded in the windshield glass, which itself had a steeper rake than what was used in the trucks that came before.

It was all a very slick plan, designed to make a quieter, more comfortable, and more efficient truck to put GM out front for the 1973 model-year launch. Over 630,000 were built of all configurations that year. Ford still had the edge, but GM wasn't far behind, especially if you consider GMC's production of a basically identical truck alongside Chevrolet. In 1982, Chevrolet finally took the top slot in sales—with a look that was nine years old at that time.

One Truck for Them All

The 1973-model Chevrolet and GMC trucks hit the market at a pivotal moment for truck design in America.

GM's trucks were fairly simple up until 1941. It wasn't until after World War II that their utility started to be offset by more trim, chrome, and luxury items, such as automatic transmissions.

A booming postwar market boosted that idea—after all, returning GIs wanted new vehicles, and the Arsenal of Democracy was still geared up to produce. But at this point, trucks started to evolve to suit the tastes of a generation that was looking for some style—or more specifically, some chrome to go with their utility. Ultimately, that thought process resulted in the 1955 Chevrolet Cameo Carrier—a truck that wasn't a hot seller at the time but did prove to be the mold for future American trucks in its mix of style, comfort, and utility.

The Carrier featured stylized fiberglass pickup box sides, two-tone paint, and a deluxe interior. That truck introduced car-like style to the truck-buying market, and the trend gained steam through the subsequent years, ultimately resulting in more well-rounded—and higher-styled—GM, Ford, and Dodge trucks.

Good evidence of GM's plan for a slicker overall design is visibly embedded in the original windshield glass of a C10. No need for an aerial antenna here, as the wires were part of the glass itself.

Squarebody trucks can trace their lineage directly to the Cameo Carrier, launched in 1955 as an upscale pickup for the worker who wanted some car-like style to go along with utility. GM sold 5,220 that year. (Photo Courtesy B. Mitchell Carlson and American Car Collector *magazine)*

The days of owners living with a rough-riding rig with no creature comforts were over by the mid-1960s, and by the early 1970s, trucks had become more car-like than ever before. Buyers wanted a rig that would be just as at home hauling hay bales on the farm as it would be heading into town for church on Sunday. GM was happy to give it to them, but it was typically done in an add-on sort of way. The truck underneath those higher options was still fundamentally basic.

After the Cameo, trucks became less for just work and more for work and play—and for whatever else fell in between. Car-like options like power steering, power brakes, air conditioning, and nice interior appointments were the norm, especially by 1973. Of course, you could still have your base-level rubber mat, column-shift 3-speed, and power-nothing that year, but key here for the all-new Rounded Line was that buyers were also getting one of the first trucks effectively designed from the very beginning to be more comfortable and more drivable—with more shoulder room, better visibility, better interior airflow, and less noise.

And of course, you didn't have to stop at the basics on your truck order sheet at your local dealership—and many buyers didn't. Many of these squarebody trucks were well equipped.

Equally important was the quasi–fuel-saving design by GM, especially after the 1973 OPEC oil crisis, which hit right after the introduction of this new-for-1973 truck and its aerodynamically improved body. In reality, most of these trucks still get the same 10 mpg loaded or unloaded that earlier examples did. But it was a good attempt by GM that came at the right time.

Overall, the Rounded Line trucks were the ultimate in comfortable, stylish GM trucks for their time. It just goes to show how they were able to remain in production (with minor running changes) for an unheard of 15 model years.

Plenty of Rigs

What does all that mean for you? If you're looking for one of these trucks (either to restore or to modify) the numbers are in your favor.

There are a lot of trucks out there to choose from, and most of them have good options while still feeling like classic trucks with a classic design. And on top of that, so many were built that they're ubiquitous in Americans' memories—chances are you knew someone who had one of these, or maybe you had one yourself. Reliving that memory and building something modern at the same time is easier than ever before.

Sentimentality is a funny thing, but it's a primary driver of values in the classic car and truck market. Over at *American Car Collector* magazine, we noted that prices shot to the moon on the earlier 1967–1972 Chevy and GMC trucks starting around 2010, ostensibly because of their mix of utility, styling, nostalgia, and comfort. That tide is lifting all boats, and after decades of work-truck duty, more buyers and builders are now starting to look at these more-comfortable but still old-feeling squarebody trucks, too—and the aftermarket is taking notice of that in a big way.

Now, 1987 wasn't the complete end of this bodystyle. Partway through the year, both Chevrolet and GMC released all-new 1988 models on 1/2-ton and 3/4-ton chassis. One-ton trucks, Blazers, and Suburbans continued using the square body through 1991.

If you take all those production numbers and add them up, you get just under 9.8 million trucks sold by GM through the squarebody years. That number does not include Blazers and Suburbans, so in reality, this basic bodystyle was stamped out well over 10 million times.

Thanks to their simple construction and good parts interchange and availability, these trucks are the perfect starting point for a custom project. The trick is finding a good one—and planning out what you're going to do with it.

This 1973 is a 3/4-ton C20 with original paint and woodgrain trim. The slotted mag wheels were a common period upgrade, and they continue to be popular today. The woodgrain has aged pretty well, too. Generally, stock examples such as this are getting harder to find, but they are still out there. (Photo Courtesy B. Mitchell Carlson and American Car Collector *magazine)*

Design Evolution

So you've decided you want to buy and build a square-body GM truck. There are a lot of them on the market today, but there were changes from year to year that might make a difference to you depending on the end goals for your project. Here's a quick rundown of what made each year special and how to identify them quickly.

1973

Truck Production: *Chevrolet:* 633,715 *GMC:* 115,000 (approximately)

This was the first year of the Rounded Line trucks. These are typically easy to spot thanks to the lack of cab drip rails above the doors. Opening the door, even after a light rain, would direct water right down onto driver's and passenger's heads, which was fixed by Chevrolet before the next model year.

Also note that the grille sits inside the nose of the truck slightly more than 1975-and-later models. Its egg-crate design and its inset look has a '55 Bel Air quality to it. GMCs also had a recessed grille but with three prominent vertical divisions.

Also new for 1973 was a crew-cab dually model and a four-door Suburban, which was a first, as the prior model was a three-door. Additionally, the 402-ci big-block V-8 was dropped in favor of the 454-ci big-block.

Until 1987, a C truck was a two-wheel-drive and a K was a four-wheel-drive. A 10-series was a 1/2-ton (five-lug wheel for two-wheel-drive and six-lug for 4x4), a 20-series was a 3/4-ton, and a 30-series was a 1-ton.

This first-year squarebody is a basic Custom Deluxe, which would have a few options from the factory. This would be a great starting point for a project. Note the lack of major rust, at least in the lower fenders and bedsides. (Photo Courtesy B. Mitchell Carlson and American Car Collector *magazine)*

1974

Truck Production: *Chevrolet:* 664,492 *GMC:* 98,000 (approximately)

Rain gutters became optional over both doors. For 4x4 models, the NP203 chain-driven transfer case was available, offering full-time 4x4. Both the Chevrolet and GMC grille carried over from 1973, so visually, these are very similar to 1973s. The rain gutters and recessed grille should give either truck away as a 1974.

This 1974 is a short-bed Stepside fitted with optional bumper guards. GMCs in this configuration were called Fendersides. (Photo Courtesy B. Mitchell Carlson and American Car Collector *magazine)*

1975

Truck Production: *Chevrolet:* 507,795 *GMC:* 97,000 (approximately)

The biggest change of note was a new grille for both models. Chevrolets had larger gridwork with seven vertical dividers. GMCs had just two. Both grilles were mounted more flush with the nose of the trucks. The tailgate design was revised slightly, with brushed aluminum insert panels for upper-level trim trucks.

At Chevrolet, several trim-level changes took place, with the Custom line dropped in favor of Custom Deluxe as the base model. Silverado replaced Cheyenne Super as the top trim, and the Scottsdale line was added as a mid-level trim.

Design Evolution *continued*

HEI ignition became standard. Also, standard were rain gutters over the doors. A folding seatback became optional, and dash bezels were revised slightly at the windshield wiper switch.

Residents in states that require emissions testing take note: Catalytic converters became standard on trucks with GVW below 6,001 pounds, and depending on your state, emissions regulations and testing can limit your performance modification options. V-8 trucks came with engine call-out designations in the grille for the last time, so the newer grille with that "350," "400," or "454" in the lower corner tells you it's a 1975—or at least the grille is—from 20 yards away.

The 1975 model featured an all-new grille, and V-8 trucks retained engine callouts in the lower corner. This truck has earlier amber turn signal lenses installed. Factory would have been clear with amber bulbs. It's also running later wheel covers, probably from an early-1990s Suburban.

1976   Truck Production: *Chevrolet:* 676,142 *GMC:* 155,000 (approximately)

Do you like your Chevrolet engine Chevrolet Orange? This is the last year you'll find it. Inside both trucks, a volt gauge replaced the prior amp gauge. Outside, a new chrome bumper with black rubber impact strips was an option. The 400-ci small-block became an option. Grilles lost engine ID tags but retained eight vertical bars (Chevrolet) and two (GMC), so these are easy to spot too.

The grille in this 1976 is identical to what you'd see in a 1975, minus the engine callout in the corner. That's the quickest way to tell them apart. Note the correct clear turn signal lenses for the year. (Photo Courtesy B. Mitchell Carlson and American Car Collector *magazine)*

1977   Truck Production: *Chevrolet:* 775,720 *GMC:* 163,000 (approximately)

For both trucks, an all-new grille debuted again. For Chevrolet, it had four vertical bars and two horizontal bars. At GMC, the new grille also featured four vertical bars but just one horizontal bar.

The only thing missing here is the center bowtie in the grille, but otherwise this 1977 is generally stock. Note the 1977-only yellow side trim installed here. Some special-edition GMC trucks used this same trim as well. (Photo Courtesy Brett Hatfield and American Car Collector *magazine)*

Internal door parts are different than earlier trucks, so beware when parts swapping. Power locks and windows became optional—a first in the industry—and bucket seats changed midyear, first using low-back units and later using high-back units. This year is the only Chevrolet to use a yellowish-gold stripe in the center of the side trim. A 305-ci V-8 became optional, and all Chevrolet engines were painted blue.

1978 Truck Production: *Chevrolet:* 785,713 *GMC:* 196,000 (approximately)

A 5.7L 350-ci diesel became available in C10s, which is noteworthy only for those of you looking to buy a cheap rig to engine swap. Outside, nothing much changed (other than how woodgrain side trim was no longer available on Chevrolets). Inside, a midyear change saw the addition of a modern-style spade-type fuse box.

This 1978 was restored by GM in a great color combination. Short-bed 4x4s are somewhat harder to find in good condition, as many have been modified and used hard as off-road rigs over the years.

1979 Truck Production: *Chevrolet:* 764,338 *GMC:* 106,504

A new front-end design made its way to both Chevrolet and GMC. It included a chrome bezel that surrounded the headlight, and the hood gained a decorative ridge across the front edge. Also, a new bright trim apron was added below the grille.

A fuel door replaced the exposed fuel filler cap in the bedside, which had been used since 1973.

An optional sport grille was available on Chevrolets, with two horizontal bars and a center bowtie. Heavy-duty truck builders take note: catalytic converters became standard on trucks up to 8,500 GVW, which, as noted before, can limit your build options if your state tests for emissions.

Here are two quick ways to spot a 1979: headlight bezels that extend down into the turn signal area up front, and gas filler doors rather than flush-mounted caps as used in 1973–1978 models. You may find an earlier truck with the fuel filler door; be advised that it might be fitted with a later bed. (Photo Courtesy B. Mitchell Carlson and American Car Collector *magazine)*

1980 Truck Production: *Chevrolet:* 449,971 *GMC:* 102,130

These can be the easiest to spot, as a one-year-only addition of rectangular headlights on Silverado and High Sierra trim trucks can be seen from a mile away. Lesser-trim trucks kept the 1979 design.

GMC offered an optional "Deluxe" front-end treatment with stacked headlamps similar to what was available later in the decade.

A new grille was added to Chevrolet again, this time with 10 vertical bars and 2 horizontal bars. The NP203 full-time 4x4 transfer case was dropped—all K-series trucks had the tried-and-true gear-driven part-time 4x4 NP205.

Another truck milestone: wood bed floors (RPO E81) ceased to be an option after 1980.

Design Evolution *continued*

This truck, owned by Stu Lenzke, is a C10 body on a K30 chassis, but it's all 1980. Note the square headlights and updated grille. This truck is a 350/4-speed. (Photo Courtesy B. Mitchell Carlson and American Car Collector magazine)

1981

Truck Production: *Chevrolet:* 444,547 *GMC:* 97,599

If squarebody trucks can be broken into two separate groups within the 1973–1987 generation, the change-up year is 1981, with a complete front-end redesign that featured new fenders, horizontal side-marker lights, a new grille, and either two or four square headlamps. These trucks were up to 300 pounds lighter than 1980 models. Fuel tanks were moved from the passenger's side to the driver's side. Inside, a new dash with an updated shape eliminated a vertical seam between the gauges.

4x4 trucks were available with the part-time chain-driven NP208 transfer case, automatic locking hubs, and quad front shocks. The 400-ci engine was discontinued, but for the first time, the 454 was available in a 4x4 from the factory.

This was also the last year for the 12-bolt rear end, which was replaced with a 10-bolt for 1982 (although they were phased in and may appear in earlier rigs). A quick look at the nose and the rear axle can tell you if the truck's a 1981.

The squarebody became even squarer for 1981 with updated sheet metal that's most noticeable at the nose of the truck. This one is indicative of a 1990s-style custom—the cowl hood and SS stripes are typical muscle car items. Now that trucks have become muscle car replacements, modifications like this are common. (Photo Courtesy American Car Collector magazine)

1982

Truck Production: *Chevrolet:* 368,778 *GMC:* 109,762

A chrome grille was standard across the Chevrolet line, making 1982s stand out versus 1981 models. Cheyenne models were discontinued, leaving Custom Deluxe, Scottsdale, and Silverado as the available Chevrolet trim levels.

A new 6.2L diesel became available, along with the 700R4 automatic overdrive transmission. The 20 and 30 series trucks lost the 16.5-inch steel rims, which were replaced with 16-inchers—a huge plus for tire shoppers today because 16.5-inch rubber had limited tire choices for years.

A chrome grille and bumper-mounted turn signals show this to be a 1982 C10. This one also has factory-style truck rally wheels. (Photo Courtesy American Car Collector magazine)

1983

Truck Production: *Chevrolet:* 322,134 *GMC:* 105,741

A new grille was the only major change for both trucks. The Chevrolet's grille was mostly blacked-out, and the turn signals were mounted inboard of the headlights rather than in the bumper in 1981 and 1982. The horizontal grille divider bar was painted body color.

GMCs were available with two grilles this year: one with three vertical dividers and one with an additional six smaller ones (used in Sierra Classics). Turn signals were moved into the grille on GMCs too.

The grille is the defining factor of later squarebody Chevrolet trucks. This is a 1983. Note the placement of the turn signals inside the grille rather than down in the bumper. From here until the end of production in 1987, front-end changes were minor.

1984

Truck Production: *Chevrolet:* 410,334 *GMC:* 121,704

The grille design continued to feature upper and lower sections, each with three prominent horizontal bars. Inside, headlight controls, cruise control, and wiper controls moved to the turn-signal stalk on the steering column.

Starting in 1984, the U.S. government bought Chevrolet trucks for its Commercial Utility Cargo Vehicle (CUCV) program. All were diesel-powered and fitted with the TH400 automatic.

This 1984 Blazer features the same grille configuration as the C10. Changes are minor from 1983, mostly consisting of slight interior upgrades. (Photo Courtesy American Car Collector *magazine)*

1985

Truck Production: *Chevrolet:* 430,600 *GMC:* 105,651

A new Vortec V-6 was introduced (the 4.3L) with a 4-barrel carburetor. This engine is basically a 350 small-block without the rear two cylinders. Many parts interchange between the two powerplants.

A new grille for Chevrolet and GMC (again) makes these easy to spot, thanks to Chevrolet's wide body-color division

This 1985 has been slammed down to the ground, and it looks fantastic in its factory color scheme. The wide body-color division in the grille helps identify this as a 1985.

Design Evolution continued

between the upper and lower sections and only one horizontal bar per section. GMC's new-for-1985 grille is mostly blacked out, save for two vertical dividers.

A hydraulic clutch was added this year on 3- and 4-speed trucks and used though the end of the model run.

1986

Truck Production: *Chevrolet:* 414,907 *GMC:* 114,115

For the first time, C10s, 20s, and 30s continued on generally unchanged from the year prior. That makes these hard—if not impossible—to visually differentiate from 1985s. But if you have one of these trucks, that can be seen as a plus: you have twice the number of available parts as other years.

This is a 1986 C20 with a carbureted 454—just the sort of rig you'll find retired from use on a farm or ranch. If you want to be able to tell this apart from a 1985, you'll need to look at the build date in the driver's doorjamb.

1987

Truck Production: *Chevrolet:* 366,882 *GMC:* 57,000 (approximately)

Internally, GM changed the naming conventions for trucks in 1987: the C-series became the R-series and the K-series became the V-series. More noteworthy is the addition of throttle body fuel injection (TBI) engines and computerized ignition controls in some trucks, which allowed for higher compression and more power but has traditionally been somewhat of an obstacle to performance modification.

These trucks had an in-tank electric fuel pump rather than a block-mounted mechanical unit, which is notable for those of you doing fuel injection swaps on the cheap—look for 1987-year tanks.

While heavier-duty versions of the Chevrolet and GMC truck—Blazer and Suburban—continued to use the same general body until 1991, 1987 is generally considered the end of the line for the squarebody GM truck. This one has a few common add-ons, such as a brush guard, bug deflector, and running boards. (Photo Courtesy B. Mitchell Carlson)

Note: Truck-specific GMC production numbers are not available for certain years. Several of these figures are best-guess options, applying other model year production percentages to the overall GMC production numbers for the year. ■

GETTING STARTED

With so many Chevrolet trucks built over 15 model years, you should have plenty of options when it comes to finding the right squarebody truck to build.

But before buying a truck or turning any wrenches, you have to come up with a plan for your project.

Do you want to build a basic driver, or are you looking for a show truck? If you don't already own a truck, deciding on a direction before you choose one to build is smart because the kind of truck you want to build will impact what specific truck you buy. You can waste a lot of time and money by changing direction mid-project or by buying something that isn't ideal for what you ultimately want to do.

Chances are that you've already done your homework and have a style of truck in mind, but if not, Instagram and Facebook are great sources of information on what the current trends in the custom truck market are—from the slammed-low Squarebody Syndicate builds that have taken SEMA by storm to old-school mud trucks on 8 inches of spring lift and TSL Super Swampers.

There's nothing better than shiny eye candy to help you pick a direction for your own build, either on social media or out at a physical car show or Cars and Coffee event. From there, it's all about the parts you intend to swap or modify to get there.

Squarebody Syndicate showed off this truck—Syndicate Series 02—at SEMA 2018. It's a 1975 GMC Indy Pace tribute truck fitted with modern supercharged LS power and all sorts of trick parts inside and out. Look to rigs like this for ideas for your own build.

Setting the Initial Budget

It's vital to have an understanding of what your project will cost, as that will dictate what you do and in what order you upgrade different components.

Consider that the most basic engine build will cost at least $1,500 with machining, and any performance modifications will carry it north from there. Some engines can push $15,000 or more, depending on power levels, forced induction requirements, and any special parts required.

Then there's suspension, brakes, rear axles, and transmissions to add in, as well as other items such as

LS engine swaps are great for performance, but if you're going to install one in your truck, you need to consider all the costs associated with the job, from the mounts through the exhaust, intake, fueling, and the engine itself. A junkyard LS could be run as-is, but if it's a higher-mileage unit, it's smart to install piston rings and rod/crank bearings before you go to the trouble of installing it.

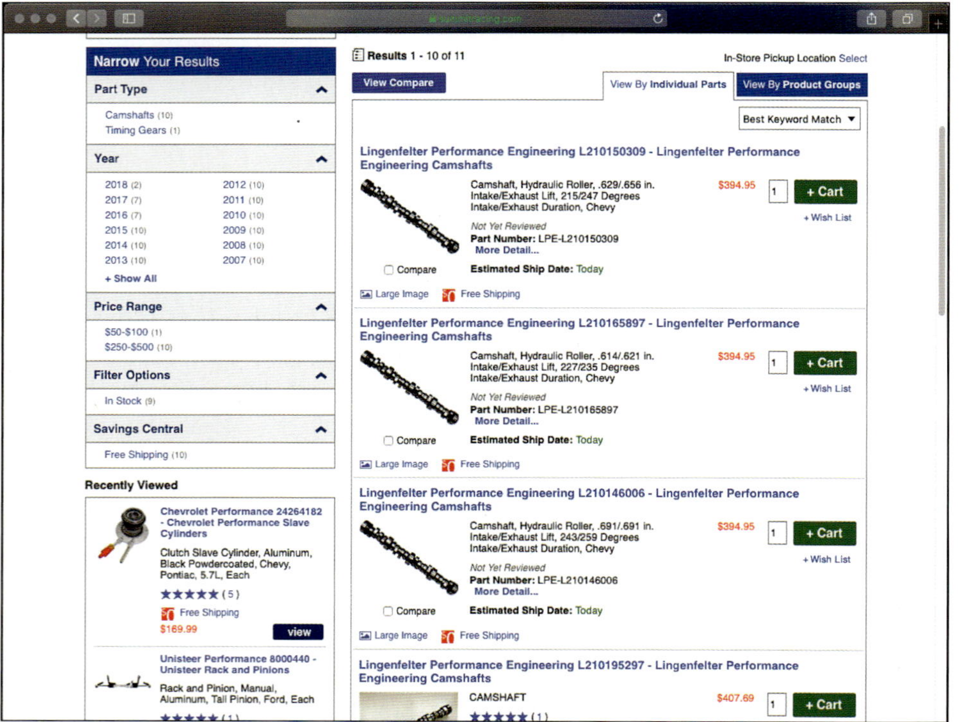

Summit Racing's site is a great place to go dreaming about parts, as it allows you to search by year, make, and model, thus eliminating the parts that won't fit your truck from your search. Summit also has fantastic customer service and ridiculously quick shipping to most parts of the country.

fuel systems, cooling systems, A/C systems, wheels and tires, paint and body, and more. All of this stuff can be cheap or expensive, depending on what you choose to change from stock, and how you intend to change it. Your budget can dictate your whole project or just what you tackle first—everyone is different—but at the very least, it can help you plan out what changes you're going to make and when.

Don't let any of those costs scare you off from your project. After all, these trucks work great with both stock and aftermarket parts, and you'll be able to budget your way into the rig you want if you plan things in advance. Plus, if you plan accordingly, you can build a truck in stages and continue to drive it while you work, which will let you enjoy the truck and help spread out the burden of paying for it.

The very first thing I do with a project is make a list of must-have items. From there, I take a trip over to Summit Racing's website (www.summitracing.com) to price out the items I can't live without. That helps me set up my plan, as it puts real numbers into play and makes me really consider what it's going to take to build the truck I want versus the truck I can afford. For most of us, the truck we end up with, at least at first, will be a compromise between those two things.

Tools and Workspace

You're going to need a clean, well-lit, dry workspace to tackle your project. A single-car garage is enough for most builds, but the more space you can come up with, the better. Having a lockable, dedicated space for the project really helps here, as a bunch of the projects you're going to take on will likely require the truck to be down for days or weeks on end. Being able to walk away from your project truck for several days can really help if you run into a frustrating issue that isn't simple to resolve. Time away from the problem can give you a fresh perspective on how to solve it, and having the truck in a safe, dry place during that time is a real plus.

Additionally, a few other must-have items include a solid work bench with a good vise, a good set of jack stands and a sturdy floor jack, a storage area for the items you remove from the truck, a dedicated shop vac,

Build Theory: 1979 C10 Project Truck

You have a lot of options when it comes to the style of truck you wish to build. For me, having something that can be driven regularly without fuss is paramount.

I built a 1972 K10 prior to the project truck in this book, and with that rig, I left everything mostly stock, from the engine through the suspension and brakes. Driving it daily was a lesson in how much the world has changed since 1972.

Modern traffic with OEM truck brakes—even factory discs—was a challenge. I had spent years of my spare time building and painting this rig, so having people thoughtlessly pull out in front of it—and barely being able to stop in time—made commuting a hair-raising experience.

With that in mind, I came up with a better plan for the C10 project truck featured in this book.

The goal here was to have a leg up on the other commuters in every single area of the build, from suspension through brakes and power delivery. For the Kia, Nissan, Toyota, and Honda crossover commuters of the world, a little plastic bumper damage isn't that big of a deal. For you, the C10 builder, who just spent a bunch of time and money on his or her truck—a rig that doesn't have any modern safety systems integrated into it—the stakes are higher. Handling, power, and braking need to be better than what you'll find in an average modern daily driver.

So, to make the most of the experience, I mapped out and completed as many fundamental upgrades as possible, all of them documented in the following chapters.

Keep in mind that you don't need to run massive brakes or an LS engine to have a great-driving C10, but those things certainly help! ∎

A good workspace is important for your project. A two-car garage is ideal, as it will allow you to tear down a truck and still have room to work around it regardless of what the weather is doing outside.

and a solid air compressor to run air tools—pancake units for home construction need not apply.

As for other tools, you'll want good screwdrivers, punches, hammers, pry bars, and a full set of both SAE and metric wrenches and sockets.

Why both sets? Because partway through construction of these trucks (around 1977), GM started to shift from standard fasteners (3/8, 3/4-inch) to metric (10, 18 mm). Many of these trucks have both types sprinkled throughout with the metric fasteners originally painted blue. Of course, over the years (and under the grime), that paint has faded away, and you'll drive yourself mad wondering why none of your wrenches will fit on those tie rod nuts before you realize that they have metric heads instead of standard.

A wide array of tools certainly helps when it comes to truck disassembly, but it's not required. That said, it really does help to have some odd bends, shorties, and line wrenches. If you're tearing your truck all the way down, you'll find uses for all of the tools you have.

Good lighting is also very important. I've had great luck with LED garage lighting sourced from Home Depot. For this project, I installed six 4,500-lumen 4-foot-long LED lights in my garage, which work great to give consistent lighting, day or night. You can't fix what you can't see!

A good compressor will have at least a 20-gallon tank, should be rated for constant duty, and should deliver a good amount of CFM to run air tools. The IR Garage Mate is a great option for DIYers because it's compact and runs on 110 volts, yet it has enough power to run air tools all day long.

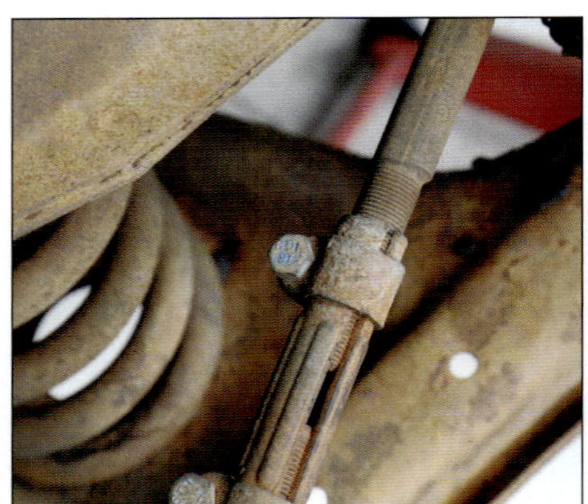

In the transition from SAE to metric fasteners, GM thought they'd be helpful by painting the metrics blue. If you're lucky, some of that blue paint will still be in place. Otherwise, prepare for a guessing game every time you need a wrench or socket. These tie rod end adjuster nuts are metric (probably 13 mm, which is equal to 1/2 inch).

A generic repair manual is helpful in a lot of ways, and so is GM's factory assembly manual for your specific year of truck. These are available for most model years through suppliers such as Classic Industries or at your local swap meet. Consider these as required reading before you tear into your truck.

Here's the C10 subject of this book on the day I bought it. It's completely stock and in decent shape, although it looks semi-rough on the outside. It's a 350/ SM465 4-speed truck with dual tanks and factory paint. An early owner clearly kept this truck indoors for years before it was sold to someone who beat it up.

A few missing trim pieces, some minor body damage, and a bunch of dirt hides some of this truck's potential—but if you can see past all that, trucks like this are prime candidates for modification.

Beyond that, the most important tool you can have is a good service manual for the year of truck you choose. A book like this will include most of what you need to know about the mechanicals of your truck and can assist in showing you how things come apart, which is not always immediately clear.

Certain years of truck have GM's *Chassis Service Manual* and *Body Service Manual* available from places such as Classic Industries. These books include wiring diagrams and also illustrate the locations of all the body bolts—again, very important information to have before you start pulling things apart.

Finding a Rig

With 9.8 million of these trucks roaming the roads, there are a lot of choices out there when it comes to a basic project. But while all of these trucks were created more or less equal (options and equipment notwithstanding), their lives over the past 30 years most certainly were not.

There are a lot of places to hunt for a squarebody, but I've found local paper classifieds, Facebook Marketplace, and Craigslist to be good sources. For Craigslist, searching a variety of terms can net good results from *Silverado* to *Chevy Truck* to *C-10* and *C10*, or even *C=10*. You'd be surprised what you can find that way— the truck I bought for this book is a 1979 short wide with 105,000 miles on the clock and basically a rust-free body. It was listed as a C=10 on my local Craigslist, which apparently kept a number of buyers from seeing it.

Deals are out there if you're willing to look for them and are willing to jump on them with cash in hand as soon as they pop up. The lesson is that if you're shopping, be ready to pull the trigger at any time—from midday during the week through evenings and weekends too—otherwise you might miss out on a good deal.

Rust

How do you know a deal when you see one? It's all about condition, and one of the main issues you'll face in a squarebody Chevrolet or GMC is rust.

These trucks are susceptible to rust in a number of places, some of which can be challenging to fix. Places to check include over the rear wheel wells on either side of the pickup box, under the hood at the body seam that runs horizontally behind the distributor, both rocker panels (under the doors), the lower front fender corners (front and rear), and the lower cab corners, floors, and kickplates. You

Don't let mechanical issues slow you down on your initial purchase because chances are good that you'll be modifying your truck's drivetrain anyway. I drove this truck home with my belt tied around the clutch pedal because the clutch wouldn't return on its own. That issue likely scared off other buyers from this rust-free rig.

The seller of this C10 claimed the engine was a remanufactured Targetmaster engine, but after removing an inch of grime from the block stamping behind the alternator, it proved to be the original engine. This is indicative of what you'll find under most C10 hoods: a smogger-era 350 with flaking blue paint, lots of grime, and some good options like power steering, power brakes, and maybe even A/C, as seen here.

Rust will form where dirt and moisture collect. The bedside above the wheel is a common rust area, so be sure to check here (both inside and out) for bubbling. Complete bedsides are available from the aftermarket for extreme cases, but you need to consider the cost in time and dollars to address this type of problem before you buy.

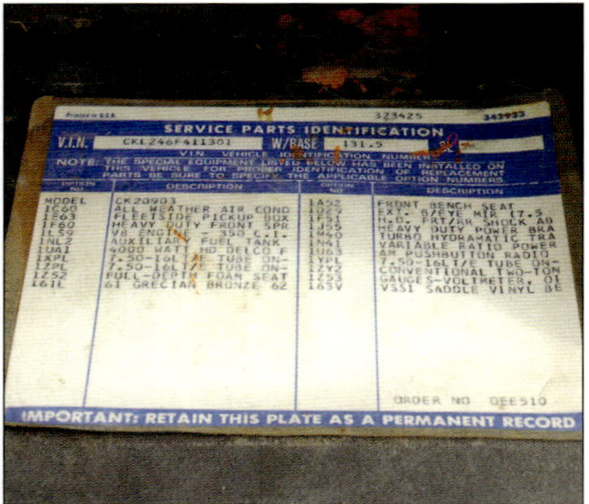

GM's service parts identification sticker, or SPID, is a great way to check out what your truck had as original equipment. This sticker is either in the glovebox or stuck to the passenger-side inner fender, depending on assembly plant and year of manufacture. It will list all the GM option codes, along with a short description, which will tell you everything from the original engine size to the truck's original color. If you want to know what your truck was from new, the SPID should tell you. (Photo Courtesy B. Mitchell Carlson)

The lower sections of the cowl on either side, below the A-pillars, tend to collect leaves over time, and they hold moisture and rust out the cowl, kick panels, and lower rear corners of the front fenders. Cleaning these out isn't challenging once you have the front fenders off the truck, and it should be done to prevent more rust in the future.

Another common spot for rust in a squarebody is the seam between the two panels that make up the cowl. Pine needles, leaves, and dirt make their way down into the cowl and can start it rusting, which then pokes through on the engine side, just behind the distributor.

Years of swinging the door open and slamming it closed will wear out any door hinge, and the C10 is notorious for this. If, when the door is open, you find any up-and-down movement in it at the hinge, you have worn pins and will need to address them. Extreme cases require a healthy slam to close and will have inconsistent gaps and trim lines. Note the cab trim here, as opposed to the dirt mark where the door trim used to be.

Here's another indication of bad door pins: a worn striker, ground down by the door latch over time. This will need to be replaced, and the door latch inside the door will need to be inspected for wear as well.

Tailgates are stout in these model years, but they will bend when subjected to too much weight, and that was common when these trucks worked for a living. This tailgate is straight, which is good, as original-equipment units in good condition are getting harder to find—and more expensive. Reproductions are available, but they typically aren't as heavy-duty as OEM units.

Reinforcing the steering box area is a good idea, especially in 4x4 models. This plate welds in place and helps to beef up the frame area around where the steering box mounts. These are available from several aftermarket suppliers, or you can simply make your own out of plate steel and weld it in place. (Photo Courtesy Joshua Jackowski)

might also find rust in the tailgate as well, specifically at its base.

Rust typically starts in locations that collect mud or leaves, which hold moisture and rot out the metal. Look for bubbling under the paint or visible holes in these areas. Keep in mind that a small bubble or hole usually indicates a much larger problem underneath, so factor that into your plans when looking at possible project trucks.

These trucks tend to collect leaves below the A-pillars. Junk falls down into the cowl and water then flushes it down through holes in the body on either side—but the openings at the bottom don't tend to let anything other than water out easily. Any truck you find—if it's been stored outside—will probably have stuff packed in the cowl drains. This leads to rust in the lower fenders, behind the front tires.

It's also smart to check any and all of these areas with a magnet, as

Bondo can hide a lot of rust issues. Be skeptical of any freshly painted rigs, particularly if they're just primed. Bondo can hide a lot of problems for a short amount of time, but a fix that wasn't done right won't last forever.

Frames tend to be fairly stout in most locations (aside from the U.S. Rust Belt, where all bets are off), but it's wise to check for structural rust or pitting there as well. Climb around under the truck and try to get a visual of all these spaces before you pull the trigger.

As always, it's best to find a rig that lived a long life in a dry climate, away from salt air or salted roads. Craigslist postings in these areas can be a good place to start. Remember that it may be cheaper in the long run to road-trip to a dry part of the country for a solid truck versus buying one that's close and rusty.

Common Issues

Some of these trucks are pushing 50 years old. You will find issues in even the most minty untouched example.

Both driver and passenger doors on these trucks tend to sag over time thanks to worn door hinge pins. The fix isn't too challenging, especially if you plan to remove the front fenders as part of your build. Check for this by opening each door and then attempting to lift up on it to see if it moves. Worn pins can also make a door hard to latch. I detail this fix in chapter 11.

The steering box area of the frame is relatively weak, and over time, it can crack and cause the steering box to move around slightly (or even fall off in extreme cases). Any looseness here will make the truck feel like it's wandering down the road. Look for cracking around this area. This isn't a deal-breaker (as it can be fixed by welding and reinforcing the affected area), but it's best to find a truck without this issue. You'll see this more with 4x4 rigs.

The rear of the frame is also known for stress cracking, specifically around the shock mounts. This

At least half of the 1973–1980 trucks you find will have a bent hood or a replacement hood, and the ones that still sport their original, flat hood will have well-lubed hinges to keep it that way. Typically, once bent, there isn't much you can do to save a factory hood.

A C10's fuel lines are exposed to the weather via the gap between the cab and the bed, and there are rubber sections that connect each tank to the truck's hard lines. It's wise to replace these rubber connections on any new-to-you truck, especially if they look old or original.

Closing the Hood

On 1980-and-earlier rigs, always close the hood from above, pushing down and back toward the cowl. Pulling down on the hood from the inside lip will often result in bending the hood right in the middle, ahead of the hinges. Later rigs had a redesigned hood and hinge setup that largely corrects the issue. It's really easy to cause a lot of damage to one of these earlier hoods by being careless, so be careful! ◼

is usually found in trucks that hauled a lot of weight over the years, which (if we're honest) is most of them. If the truck's bed shows evidence of hauling heavy loads, specifically at the bed floor, it would be wise to get a good look at the frame in this area before buying.

Hood hinges are a weak point in these trucks as well, but the issue is a fundamental one—these trucks' hoods are wide and heavy, and the geometry of the hinges can cause the hood to bend in the center when an unsuspecting owner tries to slam it shut.

Another issue to be aware of has to do with fuel lines. The side saddle tanks used on these trucks are connected to steel fuel lines on the frame with sections of rubber hose.

The lines are basically inaccessible with the cab and bed in place, and over a span of years, the rubber breaks down and can eventually crack.

Typically, this cracking manifests in a hard-start condition, as the fuel pump sucks air from the line and can't properly prime the carburetor. If starting fluid gets the engine going, and it seems to run fine after that, this is the likely culprit. The fix is to drop the tank (or tanks, as some trucks came with duals) and replace the rubber lines that run from the metal lines on the frame to the tank's sending unit. This isn't a big problem, and in fact, it can score you a deal on a truck if you find a solid example with a no-start condition related to the lines.

Checking the Engine

Checking over the engine is wise, even if you don't plan to use it in your build. After all, a good-running 350, 400, or 454 can be sold to offset the price of other items, such as an LS swap.

Look at the oil on the dipstick—make sure it's relatively clean and full. Try to hear and see the truck cold-start to look for smoke from burning oil. Bad valve seals or rings are common in higher-mileage trucks. Leaky valve seals are typically easier to spot when the truck is cold, while worn rings will smoke all the time.

Also be sure to look at the coolant to make sure it's both full and clean. On a cross-flow radiator like the ones

Working for a Living

Squarebody trucks are only now starting to be appreciated, and that's a good thing for buyers looking to get into the market before prices move up and make rigs harder to acquire. The flip side is that most of these trucks have lived hard lives up until very recently, and their condition tends to show it.

These trucks were worker bees—working for a living has been their entire purpose for most of the past 30 or more years. As such, you're likely to find a wide range of issues and damage in these trucks that you'll have to correct, and if you're limited by time, space, or budget (as most of us are), you have to be smart about the truck you buy so you can enjoy the process. This is supposed to be fun.

If you buy the first truck that rolls along, you may end up spending more time than you care to on things like rust repair. That's great if you like rust repair, but if you'd rather be installing an LS motor and driving your truck, cutting up a floor to replace rusty rockers might be enough to stall your project and kill all your fun. Picking the right rig to start with is key. Be realistic about your skills and wait for the right rig to come along. It will. ■

Even years after they were new, squarebody GM trucks are still working for a living—which is great for buyers, as these trucks have not transitioned into being considered collectors' items quite yet. The price of entry is still relatively low, especially for 3/4-ton versions, yet aftermarket parts supply is ramping up. It's a great time to buy.

Don't expect a truck you find to be minty fresh—after years of hauling and outside storage, it won't be. But the parts you'll need to get it back in shape are now easy to come by.

This 1976 from the Ray Lambrecht Chevrolet Collection has only 4 miles on it from new, but it still needs everything, including a new hood, as it has the classic C10 bend from frozen hinge pivot points. Is a truck like this really worth a premium for those low miles? It depends on your goals. (Photo Courtesy Jay Harden and American Car Collector *magazine)*

used in these trucks, the level should be a few inches below the cap. Check for overheating, and be sure to check the passenger-side floor for evidence of a heater core leak.

Inspect the engine for rear main seal leaks too (oil dripping from between the rear of the oil pan and the flexplate or flywheel) and listen for any strange noises or rough running. Some of these trucks (specifically those built in the mid-to-late 1970s) had soft camshafts from new. It's somewhat common to see them go flat, which will result in either an intake or exhaust valve not opening as it should, creating an audible chug at idle. Fixing this typically requires a complete rebuild, as all that metal from the cam will have run through the engine's bottom end bearings.

You're bound to find leaks from automatic transmissions and the 12-bolt rear end, as leaks are typical of pretty much all GM products from the era. But fortunately, they're simple to address, so again, don't let them scare you away.

Obviously, any issues you find are fixable, but ideally you'll find a rig with fewer problems to fix. That will result in more usable parts for you—and better stuff to sell to augment your budget, which will help you buy the parts you want.

Should You Care About Low Miles?

Finding a good truck is important, but what about a low-mile example?

In 2011, Ray Lambrecht, a long-time Chevrolet dealer in Pierce,

Nebraska, sold his collection of Chevrolets. Ray had been known for keeping the inventory he never sold at the dealership, and as such, he had a field full of Chevrolets from the 1960s, 1970s, and 1980s—most of which with fewer than 20 miles on the clock. But they'd been stored outside.

One of these rigs, a 1976 K10, had just 4 miles on the clock. It had never been sold. But over the years, it had weathered just as much as any other K10 sold in 1976. So, while it had a great story, ultimately it needed just about everything a 100,000-miler would have needed. Yet, it sold for $20,000—many multiples of the price of a local used rig you might find on Craigslist.

Low miles can be worth a lot of money to someone interested in restoration—as was likely the case for the Lambrecht 1976—but for those of us planning to swap out parts to make a truck into a more modern version of itself, there's no point in spending the added premium for a truck with a great story or low miles. The only benefit you'll find is in the ease of disassembly and presence of whatever original components and wiring you intend to reuse—but the premium may not be worth it.

The Lambrecht truck may be an extreme case, but once you start looking, you'll find all kinds of trucks in all kinds of conditions for all kinds of prices. Remember this: if you're just going to remove the parts, who cares if they're original? Instead, the smart money is on a relatively rust-free example with miles on the clock, or maybe even a blown (or missing) motor or transmission, depending on your budget and your plan. But again, it all comes down to your goals for your truck.

THE TEARDOWN

GM's squarebody trucks are simple to disassemble. You'll find only a few different sizes of nuts and bolts used throughout, and the fastener locations are easy to access in most situations. Generally, if you can change your own oil, you should be able to tear down a C10 pickup without much trouble.

The teardown is important because to build your custom rig, you need to start with a solid foundation.

Yes, you can build a truck in stages while you're still driving it, but when it comes to working on the suspension, engine, transmission, fuel system, and more, modification is a lot easier with the sheet metal (and truck bed) off the truck and out of the way.

When it is time to remove components, such as the hood, tailgate, bed, fenders, and doors, it's helpful to have an extra pair of hands to help. Parts can be heavy and awkward, and the last thing a truck builder wants to do is have to fix something that he or she dropped because he or she underestimated its weight or fumbled it due to its odd proportions.

One other thing to consider: A truck is never smaller than it is when it's fully assembled. Each part you remove is going to take up space, and if you're not going to be using it

When it comes to disassembly, it helps to stick to your plan, as you may not need to tear your truck completely apart to achieve your goals. Then again, if cleaning and painting the frame is part of your plan, prepare for a major teardown that will probably take several days—or weeks—to accomplish.

Remember that your truck has been assembled (and working in the elements) for 40-plus years. As such, you're going to encounter rust at the fasteners. Your best bet to free things up is a few cans of PB B'laster, which works miracles in lubricating otherwise hopelessly rusted threads. This stuff defies gravity by climbing up the threads of a bolt and works wonders on otherwise-stuck fasteners.

Bagging and Tagging

A truck has thousands of little nuts, bolts, and screws holding it together. Will you really remember what bolts went where in six months when you're reassembling? Sure, if we're only talking about a few. But if you're dealing with any more than a handful, you need to bag and tag.

All you need to keep small parts organized is a box of small plastic sandwich bags and a fresh Sharpie permanent marker. Each set of bolts or small pieces you remove should get its own bag, with a tag written directly on it that explains what the hardware is and where it goes. This way, you won't lose anything—and it helps keep parts you've cleaned organized and ready for reassembly. Do this and you'll thank yourself later, rather than scrambling around, looking for the proper-size fasteners that you once had and somehow misplaced. ■

Bagging and marking parts may seem like a waste of time with Ziploc bags, but it is one of the most important and simplest tasks you can do. It'll be vitally important when you go to reassemble parts, so you won't lose track of fasteners that might otherwise end up missing.

again right away, you'll need to have a good spot planned out for it—preferably well out of the way of your workspace so that you don't trip over it and damage it while you're working. This is especially true for the hood, doors, tailgate, fenders, and bed.

Pickup Box Removal

Removing the bed makes working on the rear suspension, fuel system, brakes, and exhaust a lot easier.

You'll need a couple of friends to help, but these boxes are only held to the frame of the truck with a handful of long bolts and 3/4-inch nuts, fastened from below. A 1/2-inch-drive ratchet with a long extension and a deep-set socket is all you need to tackle the job, along with some rust-penetrant spray for the nuts, as they've likely been untouched since the truck was built.

Getting a squarebody tailgate out of the way doesn't require any tools. Simply remove the straps by opening the tailgate, pulling up on each of them at the joint so they bend up instead of down, and work the square end off of the peg on the tailgate.

With the tailgate about halfway open, there's a window on the passenger's side built into the hinge that will allow you to pull that side up and out. Then, you can pull the gate off the truck at an angle.

Four Phillips-head screws hold each factory taillight in place. Underneath, the factory taillight housing assembly is screwed to the body, with the wires to run the taillights fished down into the bed and plugged in behind the rear bumper. Removing all this prior to removing the bed is a smart thing to do—especially if you intend to replace components later or plan to store the bed on its end.

This step bumper was a lot heavier than it looked, so I loosened the four mounting bolts at the frame, removed all but one, and then placed a fabricated wood block underneath it as a place to set the bumper once we slid it out of place. With that last bolt removed, I wiggled it off the frame and onto the block.

GM was kind enough to make bed removal easy, at least in terms of the factory wiring harness. All you need to do is unplug this connector, which is located up under the rear of the truck, around the center of the rear bumper. You don't have to remove the wiring and taillights from the bed to get the bed off the truck, but it's not a bad idea, just so you can inspect their condition before reassembly.

The bed is held to the frame with eight bolts: four at the front and four at the rear. These drop down from above and are kept from spinning with square heads, much like bumper bolts. It's smart to spray each of their threads from below with rust-penetrating spray before attempting to loosen their nuts. The size is 3/4-inch.

My bed had never been off of the truck, as evidenced by the factory-applied thread sealant still visible at the end of the threads. Note the square head and square hole that keeps the bolt from rotating in place—although it isn't always effective, particularly on rusty rigs. Beware of using pneumatic tools here, as a free-spinning bed bolt that's hogged out that square hole can slow your progress. Hand tools are best for this job.

Before you can remove the bed, you really should remove the tailgate. This isn't a requirement, but it makes everything lighter.

The bumper should come off next, and I like to remove the taillights as well, but it's not required. What is required is the tailgate wiring—the harness that runs the brake lights, turn signals, and trailer wiring, if equipped. This harness can be unplugged behind the rear bumper.

With the bolts loose and pulled out from their seats, the last thing

Several 10-mm bolts hold the fuel filler necks to each bedside on my 1979 short wide. Removing these will free up each filler neck, and all you'll need to do is push them back and down before attempting to lift the bed off of the frame. Underneath, these connect to each fuel tank with 90-degree-bend rubber hoses.

With the bed out of the way, you have great access to the frame and all the underbed components, including the fuel tanks, driveline, rear axle, and more.

With the eight bolts removed and the filler necks pushed out of the way, the bed is free to move. Also, note that I removed the rear wheels and set the truck down on a block of wood under the center of the rear differential. Doing this makes the bed easier to remove, as you won't have to lift it over the tires to get it off. Having it closer to the ground also helps. Two people can carry a short-bed (one on each side, lifting from the wheel well at the center).

At this point, the bed is free, and getting it off the truck is just a matter of muscle. Beware of setting it down on the ground, as doing so could damage the paint. A better bet is to have either a few wood blocks or sawhorses ready as stands to hold the bed off the ground. Since a bed is heavier and more awkward than it looks, plan where you're going to go with it before you try to move it off the frame.

Hood Removal

With most C10 projects, you'll find that access is key, and pulling the hood off the truck provides both better light and more room to work around the engine compartment. There are only four bolts that hold a squarebody's hood to its hinges. I've found that it's easiest to leave the hinges bolted to the fenders and just remove the four bolts that hold the hood to those hinges.

Two bolts hold each side of the hood to the hood hinge. If you're going to reinstall the same hood on the truck using the same hinges, you can use a pencil or small Sharpie to mark the hood hinge location at the hood underside, which can help when reinstalling a hood. There are numerous points of adjustment here; that can eliminate one.

to consider is the fuel filler neck (or necks, in the case of a truck with dual tanks). These are fixed in place with small bolts that need to be removed before the bed can come off. These are connected to each fuel tank with a rubber hose, so they bend out of the way fairly easily.

An extra pair of hands here is invaluable. Pushing up slightly on the hood helps to keep it in place while removing the hood hinge bolts. Also, note the foam padding placed at each corner of the hood, as it will slide down on its hinges once the bolts have been removed. The foam protects the paint on both the truck's cowl and the hood.

The hood hinges are affixed to the fenders with three 9/16-inch bolts, and again, they're adjustable in several different directions. If you're simply removing the hood to pull the engine or transmission, then there's no need to remove these hinges from the front fenders. If the original hood is going back in place, leaving these alone will maintain most of the up/down closed-hood adjustment.

Sixteen bolts hold each front fender to the truck on this 1979. Be sure to look at the nose adjacent to the headlights and inside the engine compartment next to the core support, as there are several bolts hiding in those locations. Factory thread size is 5/16 x 18 for the smaller bolts and 3/8 x 16 for the larger ones. Remove the front bumper before you try to remove a fender.

However, keep in mind that the hinge bolt holes are elongated to allow the hood to adjust forward and back when it's closed. As such, the hood will shift down toward the cowl once you loosen those mounting bolts, and you'll need to realign it when you go to reinstall it.

Grille and Front Fender Removal

The grille and headlight buckets are held in place with small Phillips-head and Torx-head hardware that's simple to access. Poking around the grille area with a good, crisp screwdriver is all you'll need to do to get the grille and headlight trim off the truck. But again, keeping all your hardware organized is key.

The front fenders are held in place with two different sizes of bolts: 1/2-inch and 9/16-inch in the case of this 1979. Your best bet is to have both a ratchet with a short 3-inch extension and a pair of box-end wrenches ready, as you'll probably need both.

Some builders choose to leave the fenders, core support, and grille assembled and simply remove the entire unit from the truck in one piece. This is also straightforward to do, but it's a lot more bulky and will require a bigger storage spot. I've also found it to be a little more challenging to remove individual components, such as a fender, once the front clip is off the truck. As such, if you're planning to take the front clip apart for any body work or rust repair, I suggest taking it apart in pieces rather than

removing it as one complete unit.

Most front fenders will have a number of adjustment shims from the factory—and maybe several if there's ever been any accident damage repair in the truck's history. If you intend to use your factory fenders at reassembly, you need to be sure to keep track of these shims and remember which ones go where.

Starting at the back and working forward is a good way to make sure you get to all the bolts before trying to remove the fender, and they're relatively easy to spot. Your most challenging ones will likely be the row where the inner fender meets the outer fender, as they've been exposed to the elements for years and may

Inside the doorjamb (just below the windshield) is where you'll find the rear upper fender bolt. There are likely shims here, used to space the fender out from the cab and align the door and fender. Don't lose them, and don't mix up where they go. You'll need them later.

Just down from the doorjamb bolt is the upper fender bolt, found under the hood at the base of the cowl on either side. This is a good bolt to loosen (but leave in place) because it can hold the fender on the truck as you work around it to remove all the other smaller hardware.

With the headlight trim removed, you can see where the lower front valance bolts to the front fender. There is also a bolt behind the turn signal housing as well. All these need to be removed to get the fender off the truck.

The lower valance needs to come off if you intend to remove both fenders and the core support—and if you're doing an engine and trans swap, you'll want to do that. Just a couple bolts hold it in place.

In addition to the numerous 1/2-inch bolts holding the fender in place, you'll also find wiring looms that are held in place with plastic connectors that fit into holes in the fender. These clips can be easy to break, so be careful when removing them—a simple pinch with a pair of pliers will remove the clips from the fender without damaging them. You'll be able to pop them back in place later. If your wiring is crispy, reproduction harnesses are available from several aftermarket suppliers, including Classic Industries.

With all the bolts removed, the fender will lift off. This is a moment of truth for those of you with suspected non-rusty rigs, as the lower inner sections of the cab will be visible—especially the rear, where junk tends to collect and rot out metal. Mine was surprisingly solid for an outdoor-parked Oregon truck.

Take special care around the battery box on the passenger's side. Battery acid leaking down from this location over the years can do a number on the sheet metal underneath—not to mention the fasteners that hold it in place. If you find a few severely rusted bolts in this area that simply won't budge, you'll have to get creative to remove them—an air hammer with a chisel end worked for me. This original inner fender needs to be replaced due to rust.

be rusted in place. There are several small bolts that hold the fenders to the lower valence as well—don't forget to remove them. They're easier to see with the turn signals removed from the truck.

Once everything is free, the fender should slide right off. If it's loose but won't give, you've missed a bolt somewhere and need to check again around the radius of the wheel well, inside by the core support, and underneath the truck at the rear of the fender.

Watch for rusty areas at the lower front and rear sections of the fender, and beware of rust at the lower fender-mount bolt, which threads into the fender from the cab. I've seen the captured nut break free and spin freely due to rust, which can be a real pain to resolve, as it won't let you remove the bolt. As a rule of thumb, if you can't get a bolt to turn with moderate force, stop and evaluate the reason why before you cause a problem that will be hard to correct.

This is where a rust penetrant such as PB B'laster can really pay for itself; it's better to soak a bolt with penetrating oil and wait for it to do its job than to break a bolt or the welds holding the captured nut to the fender.

The inner fenders are held to the frame in much the same way—several bolts at the rear, up into the cab, and a row along the core support. Then they slide up and out of the truck. Again, watch for rust underneath the battery location.

Engine and Transmission Removal

There are two ways to tackle engine removal: pulling just the engine or pulling the engine and transmission together as one assembled unit. It's generally easier to remove the pair together, but the engine will be a lot heavier and potentially more awkward to move around with the transmission attached (especially if it's a cast-iron SM465 4-speed, which weighs about 175 pounds).

Prepping for the job

Take your time and prepare accordingly for engine removal. Getting the

Draining Coolant

GM trucks from this era don't tend to offer a straight shot from the petcock to your drain bucket—typically part of the frame is in the way, which will cause coolant to rain down in several spots. Solve that problem with a small section of 3/8-inch rubber fuel line pushed over the petcock end and run down into your bucket. ■

Prepping your work area is key because any time you take on an engine removal, you're going to make a mess. An old tarp is a good place to start, as it can catch most of what you end up dropping. Also note the collection of buckets, as coolant tends to rain down from several locations throughout this process. The more methods you have to catch it, the better.

If you're pulling a motor, the one tool you can't do without is a solid engine hoist. If you borrow or rent one, be sure to check that it functions as designed, with a jack that goes up and down properly. Also be sure to check all the assembly bolts—several of the ones on this borrowed unit were just hand-tight, which could have led to trouble when the 350/SM465 cast-iron 4-speed was swinging from the end of the boom.

Old coolant hoses tend to glue themselves in place after years of heat cycling under tight clamps. The easiest way to remove these, assuming you're not going to reuse them (and you shouldn't), is to use a razor blade or utility knife to cut a slit from the base of the hose up to the end of the metal tube that it's clamped over. Then, simply grab the hose and twist. It should pop right off.

engine out is a potentially messy job depending on how fast you want to go, but a lot of the mess can be contained if you plan ahead and try not to rush.

Coolant, transmission fluid, and power steering fluid can find ways to escape and end up all over your workspace—so it's best to have some oil and coolant control measures in place before turning wrenches and making a mess of your project and your work area.

Start by draining the engine coolant from the radiator. In addition to the radiator petcock, there are also two drain plugs located on either side of a small-block engine above the oil pan mount. Pulling either one of these plugs will drain the engine block of coolant—although waiting to do this until the engine is out of the truck can help you avoid a big mess.

Disassembly

Before going for the engine and transmission mounts, you need to remove the battery and upper and lower radiator hoses, the heater hoses, the engine grounds, the fuel line at the fuel pump intake, and any vacuum lines routed to emissions equipment such as charcoal canisters.

Where Do You Take Old Fluids?

Engine work produces a number of different oils and fluids, some of which can be tough to dispose of properly. Antifreeze tends to be the most challenging, as it's poisonous, and you'll end up with several gallons of it when you drain a radiator and engine block.

Just about any parts store will take used oil—and some trash companies will even take it at the curb with your weekly garbage, provided that it's in a sealed, labeled container.

Antifreeze is a different story, but there are places that recycle it. Your local dump is a good resource, as many facilities offer hazardous material recycling for a fee. Some places don't charge.

Whatever you do, don't just pour it into the ground, as it can easily make its way into groundwater sources, which is bad for everyone. ■

Once the radiator and A/C hoses are out of the way, the core support can come off, giving much better access to the engine for removal. This is required if the transmission is coming out with the engine, as lifting both over the core support is likely going to be too much for your engine hoist (not to mention dangerous, as that's a lot of weight to be lifting that high). Two bolts are all that hold the core support to the frame.

Just about everything is disconnected from this engine, from the power steering lines through the fuel pump, emissions canisters, brake booster, HEI power wire, throttle cable, and more. Note that I did not remove the belts, as there wasn't much point. Keeping this engine complete was key for me because once it was removed, it was listed for sale on Craigslist to fund several key LS conversion parts.

GM was kind enough to leave two hook locations on these trucks' intake manifolds, which were used to lower the engine in place during assembly. They're perfectly placed for engine removal. A final once-over is all it takes before starting the lifting-out process. Once the weight is barely off of the engine mounts, the mounting bolts can slide out of place.

Some GM trucks of this era have a removable transmission cover inside the cab (the "hump") that is helpful to remove if you're pulling the engine and transmission together. That way, you can guide the transmission out from inside the truck while your other set of hands jacks up the engine hoist and pulls the assembly out over the front of the frame. Automatic trans trucks are simpler: you 4-speed guys may need to lift at an extreme angle to get the tall shifter boss of the SM465 manual transmission to clear the firewall.

Don't forget the throttle cable, oil pressure sender wire (at the back of the block), coolant temperature sender wire (in the driver-side cylinder head), automatic transmission shift linkage, transmission cooler lines, speedometer cable and vacuum modulator line, battery cables (at the alternator bracket and starter motor), and other starter wires. Be sure to mark what everything is with tape and a ballpoint pen—especially the wiring—as that will ease your reassembly later.

Last but not least are the exhaust manifolds, motor mounts, transmission mounts, and driveline. The exhaust manifolds will be rusty, and their mounting bolts may take time to remove from the cylinder heads. I tend to leave them in place and simply unbolt the exhaust at the collectors. Again, PB B'laster is your friend here. Soak the threads and let them sit before trying to turn any fasteners that look rusty or have been heat cycled as part of the exhaust system.

The transmission mount is held in place from below with two large bolts, while the engine mounts use two long bolts with nuts. Loosening all of these is the final step before taking weight off the engine with the engine hoist. Then, all that's left is to pull the motor-mount bolts out. After that, your engine is free to be pulled out of the truck.

Cleanup

Your truck's frame is covered in 40 years of grease and grime. Now's the time to tackle getting it cleaned up, as it'll never be easier than it is with the engine and transmission out of the way.

A good, strong degreaser works wonders here, as does a pressure

With the bed, hood, front fenders, core support, and engine/transmission all removed from the truck, you basically have just a frame, suspension, and a cab to work with. This is the perfect starting point for a custom project—but only after you take the time to clean it. With so much access afforded with all those parts out of the way, this is a great time to get out the degreaser and fire up your pressure washer.

Super Clean is a powerful degreaser that you can usually find at your local grocery store. Using it straight, from a spray bottle, will provide the best results, but beware that it might burn your skin if you use it at its full strength. Spray it on, let it sit for a while, and then pressure wash for best results. Note the tarp, again placed to catch any large bits of grease and grime that might drop off of the frame.

Much like the engine hoist, a good pressure washer is key to removing as much grime as possible. Your truck's had decades to accumulate road grime and oil sludge on its frame and underbody, and you're trying to eliminate all of it. When it comes to pressure washers, the bigger the better. This industrial unit is capable of 3,300 psi. Renting something similar will save you time and will do a decent job of cleaning your frame.

Once the degreaser has had time to work, pressure washing the worst areas should result in a generally clean starting point for your project.

Door Hinge Bolt Removal

Each door hinge has a bolt that passes through from inside the truck, up behind each kick panel under the dash. These need to be removed to pull the hinges completely off the truck—but each side has an access hole under the dash, typically covered up on the passenger's side by a plug and the wire for the dome light switch. Pulling the rubber plug should give access to the bolt head—but be sure to positively retain your socket, either with tape or with a locking socket extension because if you drop it down inside the body, it's gone. ■

washer to help loosen up the grime. Going after the large sections with a putty knife and a rag can eliminate a lot of the buildup, especially under the engine mount locations and the rear axle. Then, liberally apply degreaser, let it sit and work, and pressure wash.

Once dry, you should have a clean, disassembled rig ready for chassis paint, suspension work, engine work, and more.

Keeping water out of the interior, at least as much as possible, is important if you intend on saving and reusing any of the components or wiring inside the cab. With pressure washing done, door removal is the next task.

Removing the doors, similar to the fenders, is also straightforward, and it's a lot easier to accomplish with the front clip off of the truck. If you have worn door hinge pins, and you likely will, door removal will also make the repair job a lot easier. I discuss that in chapter 11.

The door is adjustable in every direction. It's pinched in place at the hinge with six bolts: three 9/16 bolts at the upper hinge and three more at the lower hinge. If you're planning to pull the doors just to replace the hinge pins and bushings, you can just remove the bolts on the door side of the hinge and leave the hinges bolted to the truck.

Pulling the doors, as with the hood, is easiest with two people: one to remove bolts and one to hold the door in place. Unless your truck has

Bolts holding the door to the door hinge are much easier to reach with the front fender off the truck. This way, they can be loosened with the door in the shut position, using the latch to help keep the door more or less in place while you work. Still, as with the hood, an extra set of hands is very helpful.

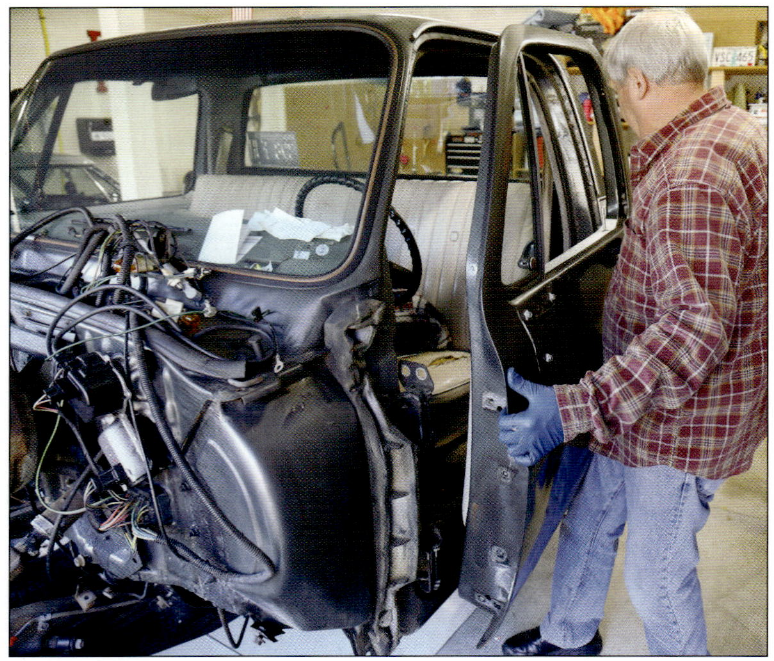

With the upper and lower bolts removed, the door is free from the cab. Rolling the window down can help you manage the door in two ways: first, it allows you to lift it by the upper section of the door frame above the glass; second, it shifts the weight of the entire unit down lower in the door frame, which makes it slightly easier to manage if you're lifting it alone.

Hinge pins are a notoriously wear-prone area on squarebody trucks. Years of operation wears grooves in the pins and deteriorates the pin bushings, both of which allows for play in the hinge and makes the door clunky and hard to latch. With the door removed, check for play by lifting up and down on the hinge. Repair kits are cheap and easy to install once the door is out of the way. I cover that in chapter 11.

power windows and locks, you'll have no wires to disconnect prior to lifting it up and away from the body of the truck.

Final Cleaning and Paint

The point of all of this is to get the truck down to a basic level for suspension, brake, and engine upgrades. Of course, all this can be done with the body panels intact, but it's a whole lot easier to accomplish suspension work, engine swaps, and brake and fuel line installs if you're not trying to work around other components such as the engine, fenders, and bed.

Another plus to all of this is the ability (with everything now out of the way) to paint your basic frame before you start making modifications or installing other parts. This isn't the sort of thing you can do easily, say, once you've installed an exhaust system or nice powdercoated suspension components.

Now that everything is pressure washed, all that's really needed (depending on your level of rust) is a quick once-over to remove any residual grease with a heavy-duty cleaner, such as lacquer thinner, before you can prime and then paint.

If your truck is particularly rusty, you might consider using a product such as POR15 or Eastwood's Rust Encapsulator for the frame rails. Either way, the time to do it is now, when you have the best, easiest access.

Then, once it's dry, you have a great, clean starting point for modification.

You can achieve good results with spray paint if you plan, clean, and prep appropriately before you start spraying. This means a good cleaning with a pressure washer, a grease removal after that, and removal of any components you don't want painted, such as fuel lines or brake lines—or in my case, the factory leaf-spring hangers for the rear suspension. This paint is Rustoleum 2-in-1 paint and primer in Satin Black, which you can find at Home Depot.

SUSPENSION

There are many different upgrades that you can make to a classic GM truck. But the most visible, and one of the most important, is your truck's suspension.

Why suspension? Because first impressions matter and getting your truck's stance just right is key to both overall appearance and handling.

Changing up suspension components typically achieves the largest benefit for the time and money spent versus any other type of modification. For that reason, even if you don't plan to do anything else to your stock rig, suspension mods should be on your list—and they should be some of the first things you tackle.

Front Suspension

GM's two-wheel-drive pickups used a tried-and-true independent A-arm and coil spring system up front that carried over in its fundamental design from the 1967–1972 C10s that came prior. Only some of the 1973–1987 parts interchange with the earlier trucks, but the basic design carried over when the new body was introduced in 1973.

The two-wheel-drive system uses both an upper and lower A-arm, a coil spring, and a spindle that's mounted to the A-arms on an upper and lower ball joint. Some trucks came equipped with a sway bar to control body roll, but many did not.

This system works pretty well for stock applications, offering a decent ride and acceptable handling, which is why it was used throughout the production life of the 1973–1987 trucks.

Even the heavier-duty 3/4- and 1-ton trucks used upgraded versions of the same basic 1/2-ton layout, albeit with heavier-duty parts and a subsequently stiffer ride, especially when running without a load.

Common wear parts here are shocks, suspension bushings, and ball joints. Springs can sag over time as well. The trouble with all of that is wear happens at a gradual pace, so longtime owners typically don't notice issues until they've become pronounced.

There isn't much that's stock about this C10's suspension—in fact, it's probably not running any OEM suspension components underneath to get this rocker-on-the-ground stance. Suspension mods like this are great for style and performance—carefully selected aftermarket components can give you both.

Bone-stock C10 front suspension has a lot of room for improvement. Fortunately, these systems are generally easy to modify, as they're modular—you can unbolt the entire system from the truck, including the front crossmember.

After 30 or 40 years of duty under your truck, the front suspension is going to need some attention—high miles or not. Whether you go stock or aftermarket with the parts you replace is up to you, but while GM's system is good, what's available in the aftermarket (specifically for trucks that are bound for the weeds) is better.

At the very least, if you intend to use any of the stock front suspension components, all of the parts should get a really good once-over to look for excessive play, visible wear, and possible damage. All rubber bushings should be replaced either with stiffer

Taking Apart OEM Front Suspension

Two things make front suspension removal a bit of a challenge. First is the tapered fit of the ball joint and tie rod end to the spindle, and second is the coil spring itself.

Your truck's ball joints and tie rod ends have a tapered fit where they mount to the spindle. By design, the weight of the truck helps to seat this taper—and the truck's been sitting on them for years—so getting them to break free can be tough.

Also, the coil springs can be trouble. They store a lot of energy, even when the truck's unloaded, so they must be treated with respect when you're removing them. Safety needs to come first here, as springs have been known to injure people by flying out of their pockets if compression is released suddenly without some means of spring containment.

There are several ways to get your C10's front suspension apart safely, and the best method really relies on whether you intend to use your factory parts again. ■

1 *Jack up the front of the truck and support it by the frame, aft of where you'll be working. Make sure it's high enough for this job: a good rule of thumb is to raise it up high enough that the lower control arm will just contact the ground when it's swung straight down. Then remove the wheel, brake line, brake caliper, and front shock, then the tie rod end. For the tie rod, remove the cotter pin and then loosen the castle nut, but don't remove it fully, as it will serve to protect the tie rod's threads and will keep it in place after the taper pops loose.*

polyurethane or new rubber components. Getting to them will require removal of the control arms (and coil spring), and while they're off the truck, your best bet is to also replace both ball joints, as coil springs can be a pain to work with, and you'll have the system apart already. Put all that in your budget.

It's also important to note that this suspension system is a common swap for earlier trucks—particularly 1960–1966—as it more or less bolts in place in those earlier rigs and updates how they handle. It's also popular among 3/4- and 1-ton builders who want five-lug conversion parts. If you intend to swap your truck to aftermarket components, take note of that, as you can likely sell the OEM 1/2-ton equipment to offset the cost of aftermarket parts.

Rear Suspension

Starting in 1973, GM standardized rear suspension systems for light-duty trucks. Gone were the long trailing arm coil spring setups that had been optional in earlier rigs. Instead, GM's new "Load Control" system became standard, using a variable-rate multi-leaf spring pack to suspend the rear of the truck. Staggered shocks (one in front of the axle and one behind) were used to help control wheel hop.

With this system, a live axle is held in place with a pair of conventional leaf springs on either side. The springs are fixed to the frame at the front and rear with rubber isolation bushings (and extensions at the rear), and the axle is fixed to the underside of the springs with U-bolts, plates, and nuts. GM used variants of this system on everything—from first-gen Camaros through the most modern 1/2-ton pickups. The springs both control the ride of the truck and locate the rear axle in the correct place.

3 With the coil spring compressed slightly (if your engine is out of the truck, as mine was, you may need a spring compressor for this) and a floor jack under the lower control arm, remove the cotter pin from the lower ball joint and loosen the castle nut that holds it in place. Again, don't remove the nut fully. Break the taper free as you did with the tie rod—it will clunk as it falls to the loosened castle nut, which will retain the spring.

2 If you have access to an air hammer with a pickle fork end, it's your best bet for attacking a stubborn taper. Insert it between the tie rod and the spindle and rattle away until the joint pops free. You can also use two hammers to break the taper fit free. Place one hammer on one side of the spindle, next to the taper, and the other on the opposite side, and then swing away. Each impact from the first hammer will cause the second to recoil and hit the opposite side. After some effort, the taper should pop free. Don't be afraid to hit it hard.

4 Raise the jack under the control arm until the castle nut is loose again, then remove the nut. Lower the jack slowly and your spring should come out safely.

This C10 has already had an axle flip completed. From the factory, the rear axle mounts underneath the spring, not above it. Note the proximity of the axle to the frame rails. The next step here will be C-notches to make clearance for the axle throughout its range of motion.

The leaf-spring eye bushings are a common wear point, usually more from age than use. Polyurethane replacements are available if you intend to reuse your leaf springs, but they do tend to be noisy. Stock rubber replacements are generally the best bet for nonperformance applications. Originals generally need to be pressed out.

This system is simple, robust for towing and hauling, and cheap for GM to produce, which explains why it became the standard system across the truck line.

Common wear points here are few, other than shocks and rubber spring eye bushings. The springs themselves can wear and lose their arch over time, which will be visible as a tail-dragging stance. This is typically seen in trucks that spent a lot of time overloaded.

Upgrades

All trucks from this generation—regardless of their capacity—tend to ride rough when running without a load in back. It's particularly noticeable in the heavier-duty models.

It doesn't have to be that way with your custom C10. You can have a good ride quality, good load-handling capability, and good-looking stance by using the right combination of aftermarket parts.

The best low-buck fixes to your truck's age and factory-designed shortcomings are a set of modern high-performance shocks and a sway bar.

Aftermarket shock technology has come a long way in the past few years—shocks such as RideTech's H-series are adjustable for rebound, which is great for dialing in the exact feel you'd like to have from your suspension system. If you only make one change to your otherwise-stock suspension, it should be a shock like this. (Image Courtesy RideTech)

Shocks

Shocks are commonly overlooked as the cause of—and solution to—many ride-quality issues. Simply swapping out your old shocks for a new, modern set with performance valving, or an upgraded adjustable set, will make a big difference in how your truck feels on the road. The shock is the heart of a suspension system, and replacing shocks is relatively cheap. A modern monotube unit with adjustable settings will do wonders for an otherwise-stock C10.

Sway Bar

Another smart move is to add a front sway bar. Many trucks didn't have them from the factory, which leads to heavy leaning in the corners. A sway bar is basically a torsion spring that links the two sides of the truck's suspension together, helping to keep body roll to a minimum. The thicker the bar, the less roll the truck will experience when pushed into a corner. This is a case where bigger is better.

Rear sway bars are also available, and they go a long way in making a squarebody ride flat through the cor-

---

GM trucks are comfortable, but they weren't designed with handling performance in mind. Sway bars help to limit body roll in the corners and make more use of today's better tire technology. This is RideTech's StreetGrip sway bar, designed for use with a squarebody's factory A-arms. (Photo Courtesy RideTech)

Drop springs are a cheap way to the weeds, but unless you spec them out properly for your truck's weight, they can cause ride issues. This spring has been combined with a drop spindle to compound the drop to approximately 5 inches lower than stock. (Photo Courtesy Kevin Whipps)

ners. Rear bars work best when paired with a front bar—but you don't absolutely need to run a rear bar in most C10 applications. However, if you want to maximize your C10's potential, it would be smart to install both a front and rear bar.

Getting Low

Dropping your truck's altitude can be done in a number of ways, with both positive and negative results. In addition to a more aggressive look, lowered trucks have a lower center of gravity, and as such, they have the potential to handle much better than factory. The key word there is potential. Picking the right parts is key in maintaining—or improving—ride quality over stock, and there is a lot of room for improvement on what the factory considered adequate in 1973.

In the old days, some builders would simply take a torch to a front coil spring and heat it until it sagged to the desired ride height. This is by far the worst way of achieving the goal, as it compromises the truck's handling in unpredictable ways. Don't do it under any circumstances—and if you find a set of springs in your truck that have been heated, ditch them for something better. The cost will be negligible considering the safety lost through running heat-warped, collapsed springs.

Cutting coils has also been popular for years. This was the go-to solution for builders on a budget, as it was as easy as pulling the spring, finding a high-speed cutting wheel, and removing approximately one full coil of the spring for every 2-inch drop in ride height. But again, compromised spring rates resulted, which often led to all sorts of handling issues—especially on bumpy roads or in panic situations.

Unfortunately, there's no magic bullet here for getting low on the cheap without some negative trade-offs. Maintaining a good ride requires parts designed to do just that, and in the long run, the best bet is to use new parts engineered for the job.

Drop Springs

Simple drop springs are an effective, inexpensive solution. They're available from a number of different manufacturers, and they all function in the same way: up front, a shorter spring with a slightly stiffer spring rate shortens the distance from the bottom of the lower control arm to the frame (where the spring sits), thus lowering the truck's ride height. The increased spring rate stiffens the ride, which helps keep the front suspension from bottoming out due to the shorter length of the spring.

Out back, dropped leaf springs typically have less arch, and sometimes fewer leaves in the spring pack, and they can be paired with drop shackles or lowering blocks to achieve the desired drop in the rear to match the front.

Coil spring rates are typically measured in pounds per inch, and for linear springs, the rating works just the way it sounds. A spring with a rate of 1,000 pounds/inch will deflect 1 inch with 1,000 pounds of weight on board. A 500-lb/inch spring will deflect the same inch for every 500 pounds, and so on.

Springs that are progressive rather than linear offer a rate that stiffens as load increases, which can be a good choice for performance applications. They offer a softer ride around town but will feel like they tighten up when subjected to harder cornering.

It's important to know all of this because if you go with drop springs in your C10, you'll want to pick a spring that offers the right deflection for your application; too high of a rate will be bouncy and unforgiving, while too low of a rate will wallow and tend to bottom out easily. You'll need to have a good idea of how heavy your truck is before you can pick which springs to use—and consider that, as a truck, more weight is going to be concentrated up front. Most spring manufacturers can make a recommendation for you based on your specific details: engine, transmission, other modifications, etc.

The plus here is cost: front springs like these tend to be about $150 per pair for front coils, and they usually drop the ride height about 1 to 2 inches.

Drop Spindles

Drop spindles can be used with either stock or dropped springs, and they're probably the most effective low-buck method for getting a lower stance. These are new castings, much like your original spindles, designed to raise the wheel closer to the upper ball joint and farther from the lower ball joint, lowering the effective ride height in the process. They fit to your factory ball joints and tie rod ends, and they have provisions to mount factory disc brakes.

These work well because they

Relocating springs requires cutting a notch for clearance in the lower section of the frame rail. To do that, a C-notch reinforcement kit is a must, as the frame will be weak without it. (Photo Courtesy Kevin Whipps)

don't alter the vehicle's basic suspension design past where the wheel, brake hub, and wheel bearings ride with respect to the ball joints. As such, you get a factory ride while gaining a lower look. This, paired with a drop coil, can net you 5 inches or more of drop in the front, which tucks the front tires into the front fender wells pretty well.

That's a huge plus for the $250 or so you'll spend getting there.

Axle Flip

In the rear, the best overall system for getting low on the cheap is an axle flip and frame C-notch.

In the factory rear suspension

Relocating the rear axle above the spring pack nets a drop in ride height without changing anything else. Kits are available to do this, typically consisting of a new axle locater that indexes off of the original above-axle perch and long U-bolts to affix the axle over the top of the spring.

setup used on these trucks, the rear axle is mounted below the leaf springs. With a flip kit, the axle is removed from the truck and then reinstalled above the leaf springs rather than below them, which (like the drop spindles up front) effectively lowers the truck's rear ride height. That height can be controlled even further with the addition of lowering blocks that space the axle up and away from the spring, lowering the rear of the truck even farther.

Axle flip kits tend to require cutting out two sections of frame (one on either side) to make clearance for the axle tubes to tuck up inside.

Aftermarket C-notch kits come with reinforcing plates that sandwich around the cut area and are either bolted or welded in place. This stiffens the area of the cut and restores the truck's strength in this area— particularly important for impact safety, and for those of you who are still looking to haul loads in the back of your truck after the drop. A truck with a properly installed C-notch will be just as structurally sound as an original that's never been cut.

If a C-notch isn't enough, you can also cut the frame clean off and install a kicked-up section of replacement frame (known as a bridge) where the rear axle sits, which will let you

Drop spindles are the industry standard for getting low without adversely affecting handling characteristics. Other than where the spindle sits with respect to the upper and lower ball joints, these units use mostly stock geometry.

Getting Low with the Squarebody Syndicate Formula

Joe Yezzi knows a thing or two about getting the right stance out of a squarebody Chevrolet or GMC—he's the man behind Squarebody Syndicate, which has taken the aftermarket by storm with its influential SEMA trucks and stock-look custom builds. Getting the right altitude out of a C10 has taken some trial and error, but he's built a formula that works well.

To get the truck level from the ground to the fender trims, he uses McGaughy's MCG33153 2½-inch drop spindles for HD brakes, MCG33128 2-inch lowering coils, MCG1350 front shocks, MCG1850 rear shocks, and MCG33152 C-notch to facilitate hauling items in the bed after the drop.

Out back, he swaps the axle over the spring using McGaughy's part number 33156 and only uses three of the factory spring leaves. Additionally, 1/2-inch lowering blocks, 2½ inches wide, get the truck sitting level.

This is close to a 5.5/7-inch drop, which really changes the overall look of a C10 compared to its sky-high original stance. For a basic setup that just looks right, it's hard to go wrong here. Check out Joe's current projects at squarebody-syndicate.com, and if you're looking for all of these parts in one easy-to-source location, go to Switch Suspension (www.switchsuspension.com) and order part number SWIGM73SB-SHD for trucks with 1¼-inch front brakes. ■

This low-mile 1974 C10 is a great example of a truck that needs an altitude adjustment. Stock ride height works well for a basic hauler, but there's a lot to be gained in both style and performance by getting down lower. (Photo Courtesy Kevin Whipps)

With the Switch/Squarebody Syndicate parts installed, a C10's stance is much improved. The center of gravity is also lowered, which boosts handling as well. This kit is an effective, basic way to get a little closer to the weeds. (Photo Courtesy Kevin Whipps)

lower the truck even more. Be advised, however, that doing so will require extensive pickup bed modifications, including raising the bed floor to make room for the new, taller frame rails.

Complete Suspension Kits

Is image really everything? Your truck's look is certainly important, but if you think about it, that slammed stance is only one part of a much greater equation. How does the truck handle? How does it ride? All of these things together will dictate how much you actually use the truck you're spending a bunch of time and money to build, and that's vitally important.

If "better than it was" isn't good enough for the ride quality in your C10, you'll need to leave the factory-style suspension components behind and install something a little more modern in their place. Whether it's coilovers, air suspension, or just redesigned geometry for better handling, there are plenty of options out there for your truck—but you'd be smart to look at a complete, well-engineered suspension kit that's been designed to function as a unit.

A number of aftermarket companies, such as RideTech, QA1, and Total Cost Involved (TCI Engineering), make kits for the 1973–1987 Chevrolet and GMC truck—all of which will significantly change the way a truck handles.

Complete kits are available at a number of different price points and with a variety of options to suit your style and budget. Consider how you intend to use your truck before you go out and buy the biggest, baddest system available. You may find that a simple drop spring and axle flip kit is really all you need. That said, you do get your money's worth out of well-engineered suspension.

Coilover Conversions

For those serious about both stance and handling, one of the best options is to convert the factory front and rear suspension to a modern coilover setup.

A coilover shock operates more or less just like a standard shock, but it has a threaded body that is surrounded by a coil spring that's retained by two adjustable collars. The lower collar can thread up or down on the shock body, which lengthens or shortens the installed height of the coilover. Tighten the collars and the truck will sit higher. Loosen them and it drops lower.

These units are compact, linear in design, and height adjustable. Higher-end units are also adjustable for compression and rebound, which

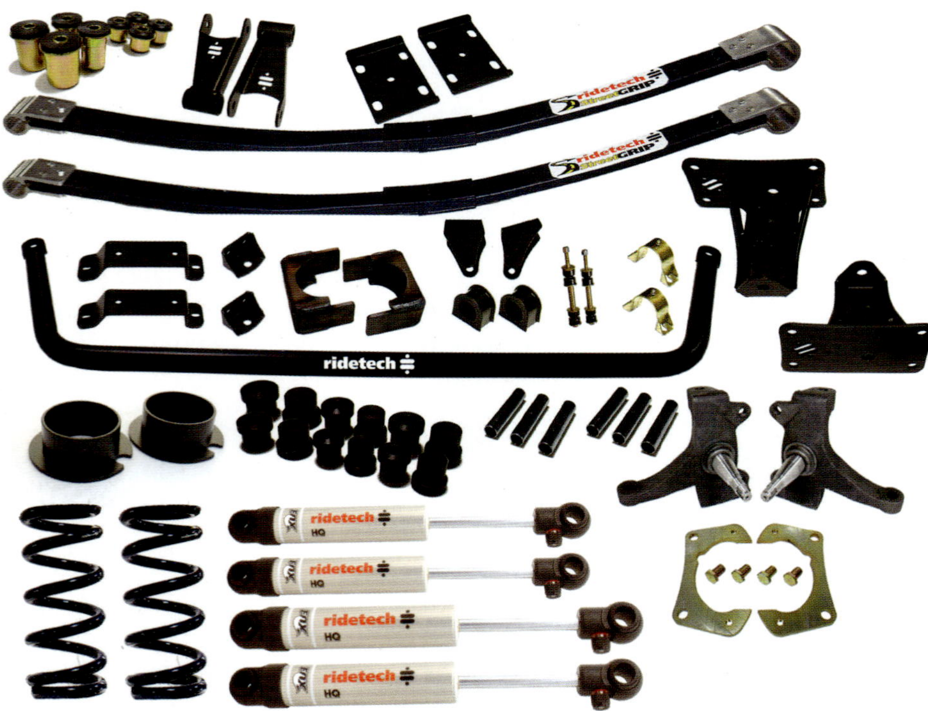

Handling problems can be avoided by using a matched kit of parts, such as RideTech's StreetGrip system, which is a good alternative for a C10 that needs a lower overall ride height and sportier overall handling characteristics. It comes complete with lowering springs, shocks, taller ball joints for better suspension geometry while cornering, thicker-than-stock front and rear sway bars, new Delrin bushings, and all the related hardware for installation. (Photo Courtesy RideTech)

Coilovers are popular among custom car builders, as each one is a spring and shock in one compact lightweight unit. They allow for a bunch of adjustability in terms of ride quality and height. (Photo Courtesy RideTech)

Why Upgrade to a 4-Link?

GM's simple leaf-spring rear suspension system works fine in stock applications, but it's not optimized for anything other than hauling loads and keeping an axle in place at a stock ride height. As mentioned before, in stock form, the C10's rear suspension is bouncy when unloaded, and it's not well suited for any kind of performance application—especially when you also consider that a truck that's been customized isn't likely to be carrying much (or any) weight in the bed.

Changing the spring rate of a leaf spring also changes its ability to keep the axle where it's supposed to be—from side-to-side motion to axle wrap and hop under acceleration. In short, trying to get a better ride out of a C10 via a softer leaf spring can lead to other handling issues because of the design of leaf spring suspension.

A 4-link breaks out the two tasks that those rear leaves are doing—the rear axle is located properly with a 4-link design regardless of the spring chosen, so any spring rate, from soft to stiff (or even an air spring) can be used without ill effect, giving even better adjustability and ride while maintaining decent hauling capabilities. ■

GM used 4-link suspension systems on its A-Body (Chevelle, GTO, and 442) and B-Body (Impala and Caprice) from the factory. They offer a better ride than a leaf spring, and several companies now make bolt-in systems for C10 pickups. This one is from RideTech.

gives you complete control over how each corner of the truck will react under both hard driving and lighter cruising.

Coilover systems typically require custom upper and lower A-arms up front and a 4-link conversion out back. For a truck that may see track time as well as street driving, this is the ideal setup. It's also much easier to service than the factory system, as the springs are contained within a coilover setup, so you can remove and install them as modular units without worrying about a factory coil spring hitting you in the face.

Coilover systems require spring selection, just as you'd need to do with drop springs. Again, knowing your specific truck's weight will help you determine exactly what you need. If you have any questions, contacting the manufacturer of the coilover is your best bet in making sure you get the right parts.

There isn't much downside to a coilover conversion for the C10 other than cost, which can vary significantly based on the components used. You can piece together a kit on your own, or you can pick a well-engineered system and bolt it on. Either way, coilovers offer a lot of benefit for someone looking for tighter, more adjustable handling for a C10.

Air Suspension

Finally, for C10 owners who want the ultimate in adjustability, air suspension has become the gold standard.

For years, air suspension was an exercise in compromise. Ride was traditionally harder to control with air springs, and while the ability to drop height at the touch of a button was cool, early systems didn't offer much in the way of performance, at least not where ride quality was concerned. Shock technology, and the construction of air springs themselves, has evolved considerably, and now mushy handling with air ride is a thing of the past. In fact, air suspension now gives world-class handling when properly set up.

Fundamentally, air springs use pressurized air to control ride height. This gives you the ability to raise and lower the truck by controlling the amount of pressure in the springs. That means you can lay your truck down low at a car show, or (at the touch of a button) raise it to a safe freeway ride height. For the C10 owner who wants to have the best of both worlds in terms of looks, there's no better option.

As with any suspension system, the shock is the heart of it all, as it's the one component that's sole

Air springs offer total adjustability over ride height and spring rate, and they've been in use in semi trucks for decades. A properly engineered air suspension system is ideal if you're looking to build a lowered C10 pickup.

purpose is to control and dampen motion. The spring, be it an air bag or steel coil, is just there to support the weight of the vehicle.

That said, a properly inflated air spring is by nature progressive in how it acts under load, meaning it will tighten more when it's compressed, such as when pushed into a corner. That, combined with the right PSI and the right adjustable shock, is just

Air Pressure Versus Height

Air suspension is all about adjustable ride height, and that up-and-down capability is what sells most owners on losing their coil springs and adopting air.

Height-only systems are available, and they're relatively inexpensive. If your only goal is a show rig, something like that will work. But consider this: Most ride issues with air suspension systems come from running too low a pressure in one or more springs, and a height-only system can't warn you of that problem. Add to that the fact that cross-loading—where two diagonally opposed springs run significantly higher pressures than the other two to achieve ride height—is a common problem. Just because all of your air springs are sitting at the same height doesn't mean they're running the same PSI. A basic height-only system can't warn you of this.

What's the problem? Well, weird ride feel is one. A more serious issue is in the panic stops or swerves. In a panic situation, your suspension will need to react, and you'll end up with uneven control due to dynamic forces and varied effective spring rates because of wonky pressures in one or more springs, caused by measuring only height.

An air spring is a pressure vessel, not unlike a tire. When's the last time you measured your tire's inflation using a tape measure? The same is true for an air spring. Pressure is key—more so than ride height. But both variables are important.

The solution here is to measure both pressure as well as height, and both RideTech and AccuAir now offer complete kits that do just that. ■

RideTech's RideProX digital control system uses pressure measurements to tune spring rates and can compensate for load. This system replaces the traditional switch and gauge setup, instead working in the background to automate—and improve—the process. (Photo Courtesy RideTech)

RideTech's RidePROHP system adds on to the RideProX system with height sensors at each wheel. Together with the pressure readings for each air bag, the electronic control unit (ECU) has a greater picture of where the truck is sitting, so it can compensate for load and leveling. For the best performance in an air suspension system, something like this is key.

the thing to make a C10 into a corner carver that can also drop its frame to the ground.

Just as important as the air spring and shock is a robust air control system, ideally with a large tank and dual compressors for quick fill-ups.

Downsides here are cost and complexity, as running an air suspension system requires the springs themselves, usually aftermarket control arms in front and a 4-link conversion in rear, an air compressor, an air storage tank, valves and lines to control air pressure, and wiring to power and control it all. You can build your own system or buy a complete kit that will bolt into a C10—but expect to be paying four figures at least for a basic kit, and more for something specialized.

For many owners, the positives outweigh those negatives—all you need to do is go to a car show that features custom trucks and you're sure to see a rig on bags, likely aired down to where part (or all) of the frame is sitting on the ground. It'll be easy to spot: it'll be the one with all the people around it.

Installing RideTech's Air Suspension on a C10

Upgrading your C10's suspension may seem like a daunting project, but it's not that challenging if you take things slowly and approach the front first and then the rear. RideTech's C10 kits are designed to be easy to install by a DIYer, and that makes them great choices for owners who prefer to do their own install work. Here's how it all works.

Front Suspension Installation

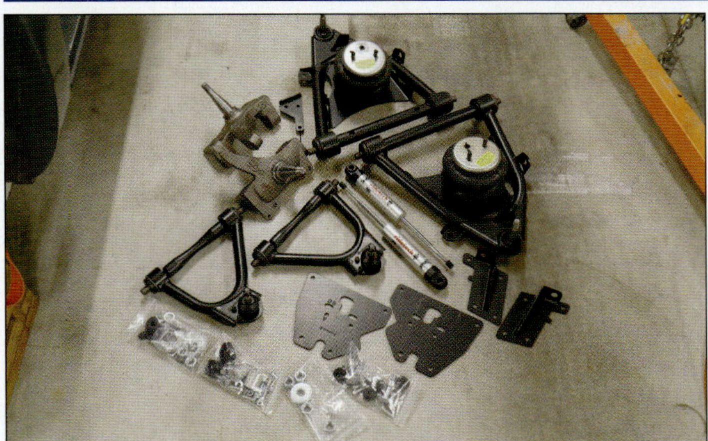

1 *RideTech's front suspension system consists of custom StrongArm control arms, Classic Performance Products (CPP) drop spindles, CoolRide air springs, shock absorbers, and all the required mounts and hardware. It's a high-quality kit with precision-machined, powdercoated components—and it comes with everything you need for the job.*

2 *If you haven't already torn down your factory front suspension, see the steps on pages 38 and 39. The air bag needs to sit where the original coil spring was, but it's not long enough to sit inside the spring pocket in the frame. RideTech's kit comes with this heavy-duty steel plate, which bolts to the underside of the crossmember and serves as the upper mount for the air spring. First, it needs to be clamped in place. Then, you can use it as a template to drill four 3/8-inch mounting holes.*

3 *Once the crossmember holes are drilled, the plate needs to come back off (as the spring must bolt to it), and there's no easy access to the fasteners once the plate is on the truck. This is also the time to install the air line fitting in the top of the spring. You must use some thread sealant here, such as Teflon tape, to prevent leaks. The spring bolts to the plate with flat washers and nyloc nuts.*

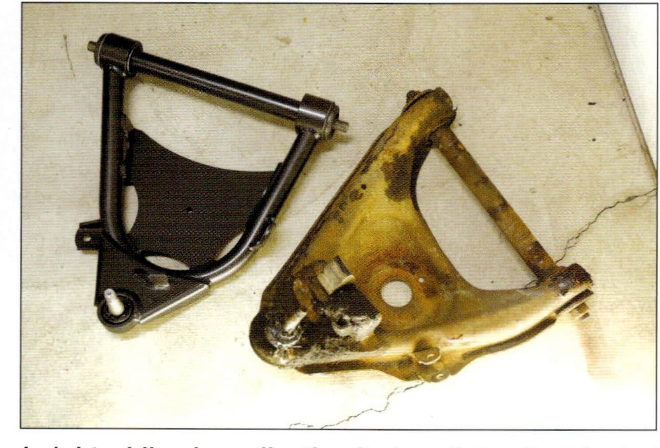

5 *The StrongArm tubular lower control arm is a stout piece, designed specifically for air spring use. Compared to the stock stamped steel control arm, it's a major upgrade: RideTech has updated the fore and aft position of the ball joint to adjust for lower ride height while also adjusting its length to allow for better camber adjustment—no need for a huge pack of shims to achieve proper camber with these arms.*

4 *With the spring mounted to the plate and the air line fitting installed, you can bolt the assembly to the crossmember using the supplied hardware. This is also the time to run the air line—I chose to run mine inside the crossmember to avoid heat from the engine above and road hazards below. As the supplied line is plastic, be sure it isn't rubbing on anything that might wear a hole in it. Use rubber grommets wherever it passes through the frame and rubber fuel line sections sliced lengthwise, slipped over the line, to isolate it from potential hazards.*

6 *The lower control arms mount exactly the same way that the originals did, even using the same hardware. A hole in the cross-shaft of the arm centers on a dowel located in the center of the forward mount. It's helpful to have an extra set of hands here: one person to hold the arm in place and one to install the U-bolt mounts and lock nuts. Once the arm is fastened to the frame, use a 3/8-inch bolt, flat washer, and lock washer to bolt the air spring to the control arm from below.*

7 *The control arm bushings are held in place with large, flat washers and locknuts. These need to be installed and snugged up with the suspension ride height at mid-travel.*

8 *Next is the upper control arm, which mounts using the factory hardware. Be sure to reuse the factory alignment shims here—you'll need to have the truck aligned once you've completed the swap, but putting the upper control arm shims back where they were should get you close.*

9 *RideTech's kit uses a CPP drop spindle for the C10, and it installs just as the original did: castle nut for each ball joint, torqued to 50 ft-lbs (upper joint) and 90 ft-lbs (lower joint). Then turn to the next alignment hole for installing a cotter pin. These spindles, when using the appropriate supplied bracket, support the factory disc brakes with the HD rotor and caliper—the HD rotor is 1¼ inches wide.*

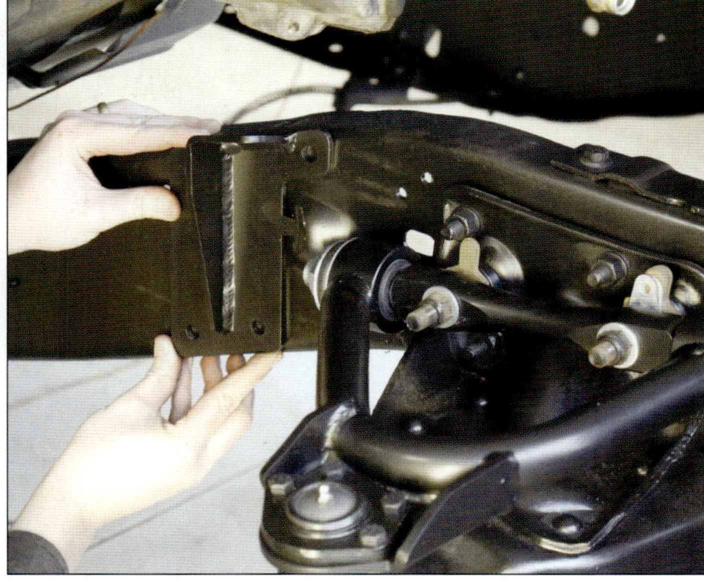

10 *The shock mount bracket bolts to the frame using the original shock mount hole as an index to locate it in the correct place. Installing it requires drilling four more 3/8-inch holes and bolting it in place with the supplied hardware.*

11 *The heart of RideTech's Cool-Ride front kit is the HQ-series shock. It's a monotube shock with a large internal piston for efficient oil flow and cooler operating temps for consistent performance. It also has adjustable rebound with 26 clicks of adjustment for dialing in the right feel.*

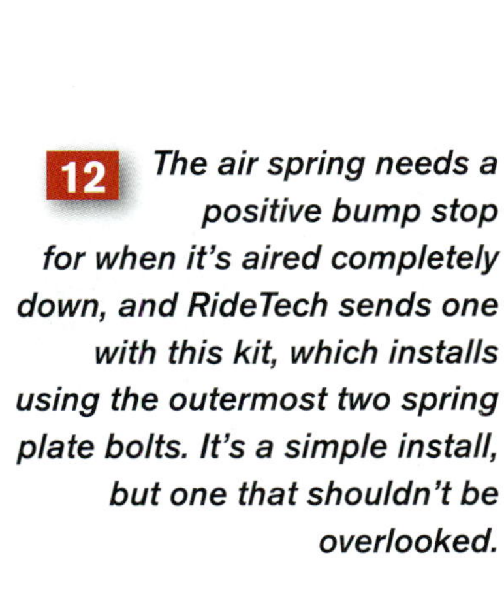

12 *The air spring needs a positive bump stop for when it's aired completely down, and RideTech sends one with this kit, which installs using the outermost two spring plate bolts. It's a simple install, but one that shouldn't be overlooked.*

14 If your truck had a factory sway bar, it will need to be removed, and so will the original brackets, which are riveted to the frame. This truck didn't have a sway bar, but all the C10 frames were drilled for them, so the mounting holes for the MuscleBar are already there.

13 Factory sway bars don't work with the RideTech front suspension system, but the MuscleBar does. It's a massive 1½-inch sway bar with special end links designed specifically to mount to the StrongArm control arms. It comes with all the required mounting hardware, including special brackets that bolt to the frame.

15 The MuscleBar uses Delrin sleeves inside poly bushings. The Delrin is harder than rubber and softer than polyurethane, plus it is self-lubricating, which means no noise. The Delrin liners slip over the end of the MuscleBar, and the poly bushings then fit over them.

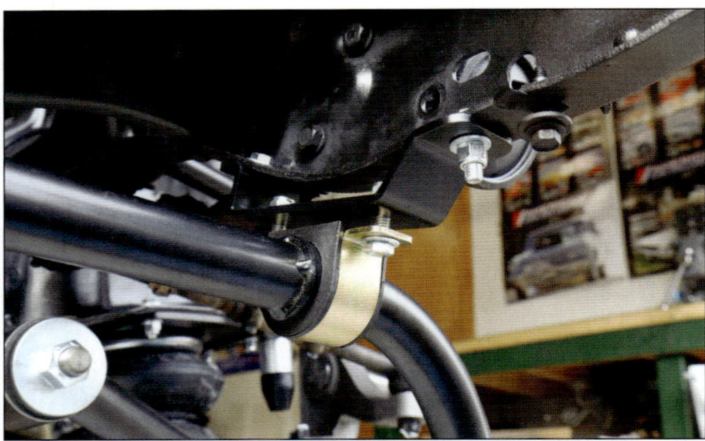

16 Bolting up the bar is as simple as turning a few wrenches, but it's important to leave everything loose until after the sway bar end links are installed on the lower control arms.

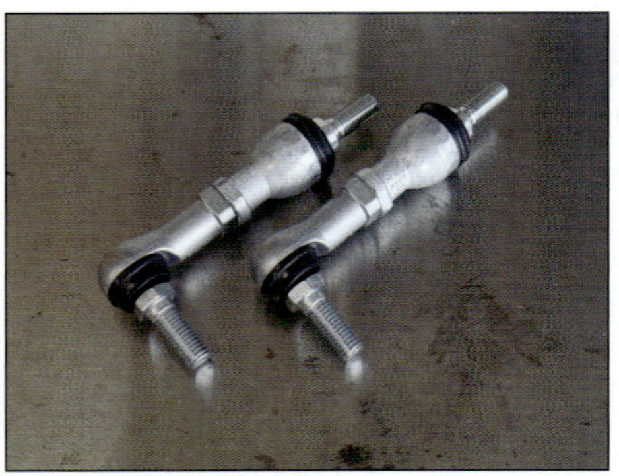

17 The PosiLink allows the truck's ride height to vary while maintaining the sway bar's effect over the front suspension. These feature a sealed joint at the top and bottom to allow for changes in ride height.

18 The PosiLink bars install with the threads pointing toward the center of the truck. They fasten with nyloc nuts torqued to 65 ft-lbs. Note the steel plate that I fabricated to locate the A-arm end of the Level-PRO sensor for the RideProHP system. It simply bolts to the bottom of the sway bar end link bushing, with the control rod snaking around the sway bar and tie rod end.

4-Link Rear Suspension Installation

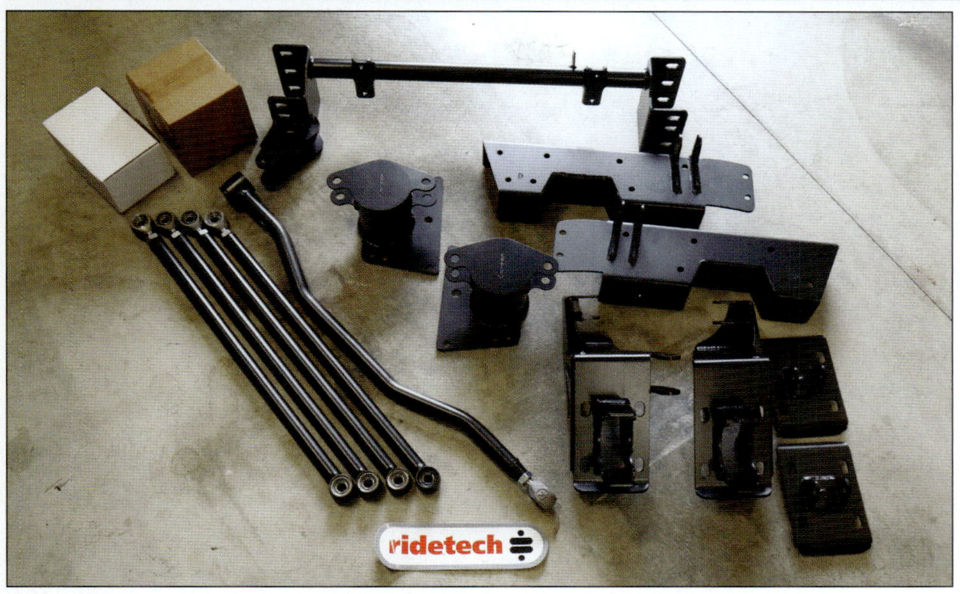

1 RideTech's bolt-in 4-link kit is very well built—stout enough for miles of use and big power applications. It's precision fit for squarebody C10s and features adjustable end links, which allow for tuning of pinion angle. It also comes with special spherical joints that resist binding, and it can be fitted with a rear sway bar as well. No axle modifications are required, making installation easy.

2 If you haven't already removed the pickup bed, now's the time to do it. See pages 27 and 28 for tips on that job. Then the rear axle and springs need to come out, which is as simple as unbolting everything and moving the pieces out of the way. PB B'laster and an impact wrench make quick work of it.

3 With the axle and factory springs out of the way, the spring hangers are next to go. These are riveted to the frame from the factory using a bunch of steel rivets.

4 There are several ways to remove rivets. RideTech recommends using a cutoff wheel to pie cut the heads of the rivets, then either hit them with a hammer and chisel or with an air hammer. I find drilling them out to be most effective, starting with a center punch, a small pilot hole drilled just past the frame level, and then following up with a larger bit, approximately the same diameter as the rivet shank. Then hit them with an air hammer. The heads break off and the remnants can be driven through the frame with a punch and hammer.

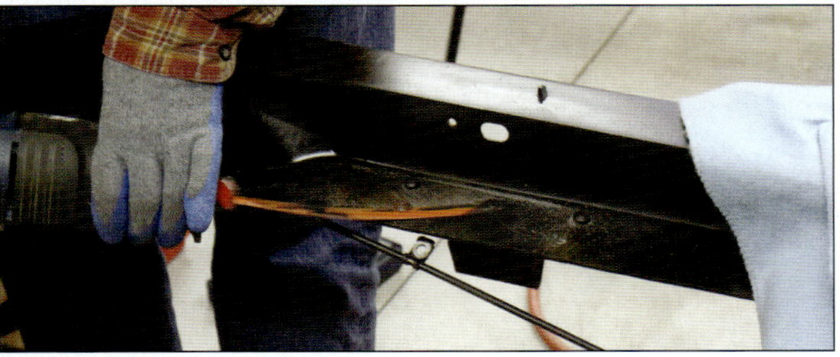

5 This kit requires the installation of a C-notch, which means you'll have to cut the frame rail. On this 1979, two axle bumpstops were in the way, so they needed to go as well. A reciprocating saw is another good option for rivet head removal, especially where a drill won't fit.

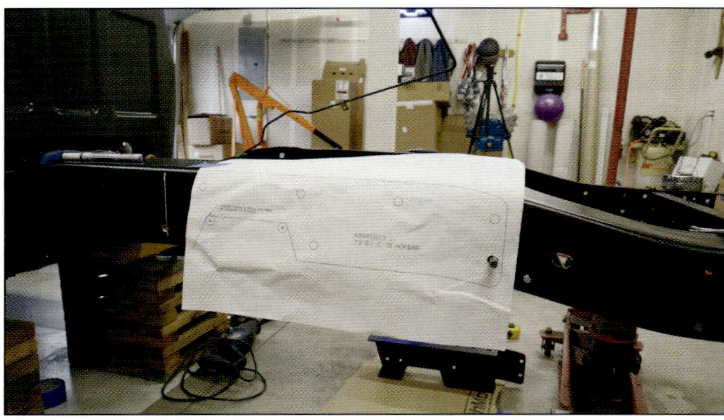

6 *The instructions come with a handy template for C-notch placement. This template is intended to index off the rear lower hole, which is cut out here. The hole is factory punched in C10 frames. With this template in place, center punch and drill two 1/2-inch holes to serve as the corners of the C-notch, then mark the frame where it needs to be cut. The holes serve as corners for the cut, which lessens the possibility of stress cracking in this area.*

7 *A reciprocating saw is a quick way to cut the frame, following the marks transferred over from the template. The cut should be as straight as possible—but you'll need to clean up the edges with a grinder before fitting the C-notch over the frame.*

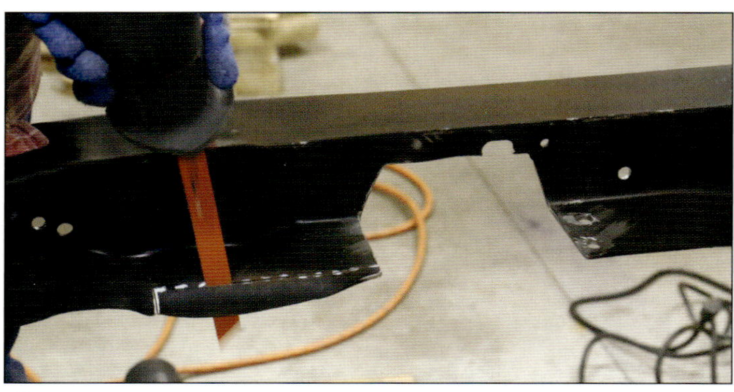

8 *Some C10 frames have a flare at the driver-side rear that will keep the C-notch from mounting flush. You could attempt to flatten it out, but it's easier to cut off the protruding section with a reciprocating saw. The marked section here has to go before the C-notch will fit.*

9 *With the frame properly cut and clearanced, the C-notches can slide into place. They typically fit tight, but a big rubber mallet will seat them in place. With the index hole bolt installed, you can center punch and drill the remaining holes with a 7/16 drill bit, install the supplied bolts, washers, and Nyloc nuts, and then torque to 50 ft-lbs. There are also two bumpstops that need to be installed in the C-notch at this time.*

10 *Once both C-notches are installed, the upper crossmember can go in. It slides in, bolting up to the bottom of the lower frame and below each C-notch. Six more holes need to be drilled per side, then it can bolt in place. Torque is 50 ft-lbs.*

11 *These 4-link mounts install using the same holes that the factory front leaf spring mounts used, although all but two of the holes need to be drilled out to 7/16. These mount with the tabs pointing forward. Torque on the mounting bolts is 50 ft-lbs.*

12 *RideTech's kit uses several brackets that bolt to the factory rear axle housing and use the original leaf spring bracket to locate the axle and attach the 4-link bars and air springs. The upper plates feature a pin that centers them on the OEM spring pad, just like a set of leaf springs.*

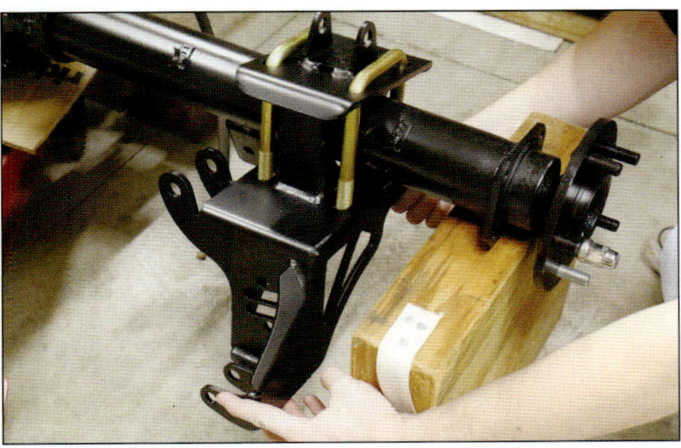

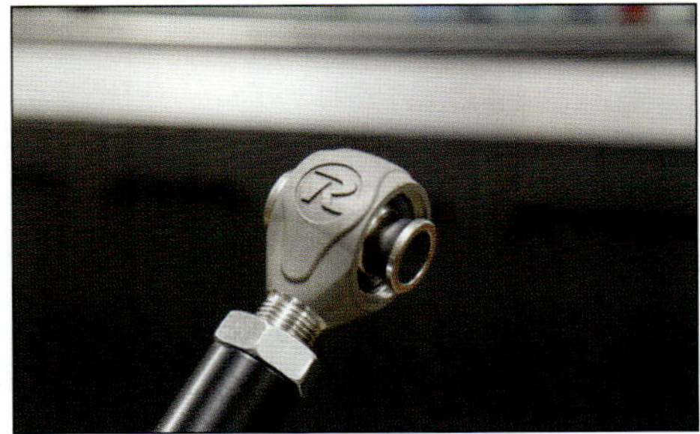

13 *Then, up from below comes the remaining section, with the lower spring/shock mount and lower 4-link mounting tabs. Large 15/16-inch nuts and washers come in the kit. Torque is 60 ft-lbs, done in a crisscross pattern. Right and left are different—but like everything else in the RideTech kit, they're marked as such with "D" for driver and "P" for passenger. The passenger's side has an extra mount for the Panhard rod.*

14 *RideTech's C10 4-link kit uses R-joints—specially designed rod ends that feature a spherical stainless steel ball, composite RXT10 self-lubricating cage, and spring-loaded keepers that keep it all together inside a stainless steel housing. These are self-cleaning and articulate easily—no bind, no noise, and long life regardless of conditions. Two spacers install in each joint, then the joints can be installed on the truck.*

15 *The 4-link bars locate the axle in the truck, and they're adjustable for pinion angle should that be required in your application. All four are the same, but all four should be attached at the front mount first, then at the axle housing. Don't tighten any hardware until all four bars are installed—then tighten enough to eliminate any gaps.*

16 *An adjustable Panhard rod is the final piece in the 4-link puzzle. Its job is to keep the rear axle centered in the truck throughout the up-and-down range of motion of the rear axle. It does this by bolting to the upper crossmember on the driver's side and the lower spring mount on the passenger's side. As shipped, the setting is 33½ inches, but it can be adjusted to center up the rear axle in the truck from side to side. Installation is simple: the poly bushing goes in the crossmember, with the R-joint placed at the axle side.*

18 *Two notches need to be cut in one of the pickup bed's crossmembers to make clearance for the C-notch. The cuts need to be approximately 5 inches wide and are about 7 inches from each fender well, located at the crossmember above each rear wheel. A cutting wheel makes quick work of it, followed with a quick shot of spray paint to eliminate the possibility of rust.*

17 *RideTech's Shockwave is an air spring and adjustable shock in one compact package. Installation is a no-brainer: bolt in, torque to 75 ft-lbs.*

RideTech AirPod and RidePro HP System Installation

1 *The AirPod is a stand-alone weather-sealed air management system. This one includes a 5-gallon tank, dual compressors, the RideProX/HP ECU, and all the required wiring in a plug-and-play weathertight unit. It also just so happens to be approximately the same size as a factory C10 short-bed fuel tank. All of these parts are available individually, but the AirPod makes installation a breeze.*

2 *The AirPod can be mounted just about anywhere and at just about any angle— although the air valves should not point down. You could mount it in the bed of the truck, but if you're looking to keep the bed as usable space, the next best spot is in one of the two factory fuel tank locations. Using basic steel strap, fabricating a mounting bracket is simple. I used the rear fuel tank mounting holes already drilled in the frame and drilled two new holes for the front mount, then welded the pieces together with a few triangulating braces.*

3 *A quick shot of primer and paint over the mild steel protects it, and the AirPod can be mounted to the bracket using 3/8-inch hardware.*

4 *Spacing here is important—you need clearance for cab motion, but you also need the unit to sit higher than the lowest section of frame rail, as well as the rocker panel of the cab. There is enough room for all of that if you measure carefully while building a bracket. One major plus is service-ability: three plugs and four air lines are all that stop you from removing the entire unit from the truck.*

5 *This system is wireless, meaning the control functions are handled via RF frequency rather than by a hard-wired controller for clean-looking final installs. The wireless control unit (WCU) needs to be mounted inside the cab where it's accessible, as it's also equipped with a port for laptop tuning. The kick panel is a good location, since it's close to where the wire will need to pass through the firewall.*

6 *The connection from the ECU under the truck to the WCU in the cab is a hard wire, and the plug is rather large. You'll need to either find a hole in the dash to run the wire through or drill your own. This truck had a factory 4-speed, and the original mechanical linkage hole was perfect. I made a metal cover, drilled a large hole in it, and then ran the wire through it, using a large grommet for protection. The wire continues on the inside of the firewall and connects to the ECU on the AirPod.*

7 *The main power wire (red) connects to constant power at the battery (with an added 40A in-line fuse within 18 inches of the battery), while the yellow wire connects to ignition hot under the dash. Finally, a terminated ground strap connects to the frame under the truck. Be sure to remove any paint or rust between the ground and the frame.*

8 Finally, run the air lines for each spring. You'll need a special plastic tubing cutter here, as the connections need to be as straight as possible. The air lines simply push into the connections at the spring and at the AirPod. Be sure to use grommets where they run through the frame, and wire ties to hold them away from hot exhaust or any moving components. Remember: a broken or worn-through air line is a flat corner of your truck. Take your time here and isolate these lines appropriately.

9 If you're installing ride-height sensors, now's the time to do it. They need to be mounted where they won't interfere with suspension or wheel travel, and they need to have a 90-degree sweep from full extension to full compression of the suspension—no more. This is accomplished by measuring the amount of suspension travel and then using the chart supplied with the sensors to show which mounting arm hole to use. Then, using the bendable rods supplied, construct a mounting solution and assemble. I chose to make a bracket that mounted under the front inner U-bolt in the rear and mounted the sensor to the frame.

10 Up front is slightly more complex due to steering, but the front of the frame is a good, functional location. Double-check that your steering linkage and wheel travel won't interfere with the sensor from lock to lock and at all ride heights.

11 After that, all that's left is to grease all the front ball joints, double-check bolt torques, and give everything a once-over. Once the truck is completely reassembled, power up the system, set a few parameters using the RidePro software (or smartphone app), and your air suspension is complete.

12 *One of the nice things about the RideTech kit is that you don't need any body modifications to make it work, either at the bed or at the inner fenders in the front. If you're looking to continue to use the bed, that's important, and retaining the inner fenders is especially nice if you live in a rainy climate. This is about as low as you can go without body mods. Both the front and rear suspension can sit on the bumpstops, but there's still a tiny bit of clearance around the wheels and tires, depending on the tire size you've decided to run.*

13 *Ride height can be controlled by either the smartphone app or by this wireless controller. The wireless controller simply plugs into the cigarette lighter for a clean, hidden solution.*

There's a heavy cool factor with a frame that sits on the ground, but getting there means you'll be building a truck that has the ground clearance of a modern exotic car. A truck that lays frame when parked will typically have about a 5-inch ride height, as well as a modified bed floor.

Final Costs

At my build time, RideTech's kit was $5,950 for the 4-link, A-arms, shocks, spindles, bags, and hardware. The AirPod with RideProX was another $2,500, and the leveling sensors ran another $500.

While that may seem expensive, driving a truck with these modifications will quickly make you forget what it cost in terms of components. When stock, these rigs can be uncomfortable, especially when unloaded. With the air suspension and the 4-link, handling is completely transformed. The ride is smooth but firm, while speed bumps that would have previously resulted in a mule-kick rebound can now be taken at speeds that even a modern magnetic-ride GMC Denali can't handle.

Setting the Frame on the Ground

If you've decided your goal is to lay frame, you're going to need to make some significant frame and bed modifications to get there.

Typically, this requires installing a frame bridge at the rear axle, fabricating and installing a link-style rear suspension system, and cutting up the bed floor so it can move up to make room for the new suspension design. Up front, you'll need to remove the inner fender liners, fabricate new ones for tire clearance, and install custom upper and lower control arms.

Several companies, such as Porterbuilt Fab, make bolt-in front crossmembers and rear suspension systems that replace the factory units, relocate upper and lower control arms, add in link-style rear axle retention, and are available in several different versions that can allow the frame to sit on the ground when assembled with air springs.

Alternatively, swapping the complete frame from under the truck can achieve a lot of this same work. Squarebody Syndicate's SPEC-series frame, made by The Roadster Shop, is a great example, giving a 4½-inch ride height when aired up and placing the rockers on the ground when aired down.

BRAKES AND STEERING

Every one of your truck's components is important in different ways. But when it comes to driving in modern traffic, it's hard to overstate the importance of the brakes and steering. In both cases, this is where the rubber really meets the road.

Everyone likes big power, aftermarket wheels, and a nice-looking exterior finish on classic trucks. But if you have a hard time avoiding obstacles in front of you, none of that other stuff is of much use—or will last very long.

Of course, that's not to say that there's anything fundamentally wrong with the stock brake and steering setups on your rig. Fortunately for squarebody owners, GM learned a lot about braking technology by the time the first 1973 rolled off the assembly line. Front disc brakes had been standard in GM's 1/2-ton trucks since 1971, and the Saginaw steering box and related linkage had been worked out to give decent enough feedback for its time.

As a complete package, these trucks were and are very drivable, and their tech didn't change much over the years of production, which gets to the heart of how well it all worked for its intended purpose.

Then again, trucks were designed to haul loads and work for a living—not dodge cell phone–distracted drivers on today's crowded highways. The world is a very different place than it was in 1973—or even in 1987—and one of the first things you might notice about a stock square is light steering effort and just okay brakes, especially compared to something newer. Upgrades are worth the time and effort here.

Stock Steering

Every square C10 from 1973 to 1987 has the same basic steering setup: a frame-mounted steering box (either power or manual) is connected to a pitman arm, center link, and idler arm, and both inner and outer tie rods are adjusted for length with a pair of adjuster sleeves. The sleeves set the toe-in or toe-out for front-end alignment.

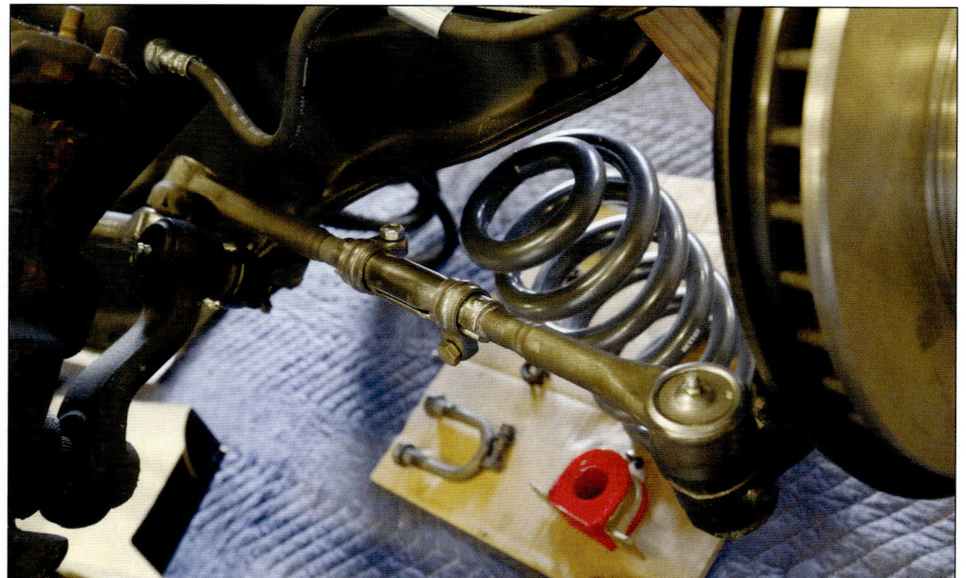

The factory steering linkage setup in a square C10 is similar to just about every GM product from the 1960s and 1970s. As such, service parts are relatively easy to come by, as are competent alignment shops that know how to work on them.

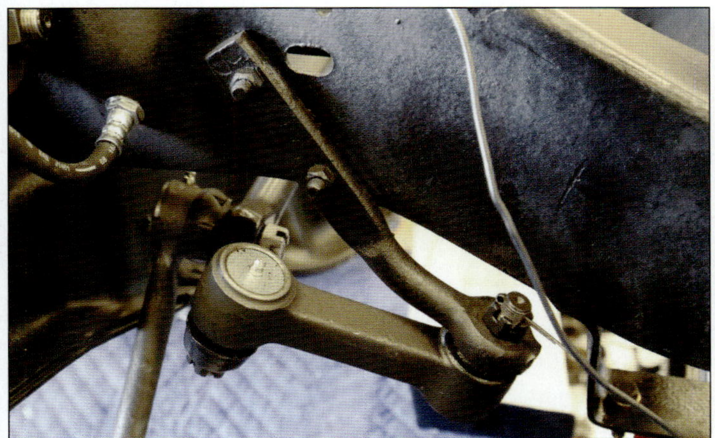

The idler arm supports the steering's center link on the passenger's side of the truck. This is a common wear spot, with worn units tending to flex up and down in addition to their normal arc of motion. Check for up-and-down play here while a friend turns the wheel back and forth. If you find any, replace the idler.

The stock Saginaw power steering box is a stout unit that rarely requires much in the way of service, but these do wear out over time, so it's a good idea to check yours for excessive play. If you can turn the steering wheel more than a few inches without the steering box reacting, you might consider upgrading it.

Each joint in this system requires regular greasing as part of a typical service, but that's often overlooked. Additionally, idler arms, tie rods, and center links wear out over time, which can easily make a truck wander on the road and add play in the steering wheel. All of that is relatively common, so at the very least, you should plan on inspecting your setup for any play and replace any parts that aren't tight and ready for service.

Note that wear here occurs gradually. An owner may not notice how bad a steering setup has become until he or she drives a rig with all-new parts as a comparison.

Also, steering boxes are known to wear out over time, so that should also be checked while you're looking at the system. Excessive play in the steering box—or leaks from the box itself—should be grounds for a steering box replacement.

Checking your steering components requires a friend to work the steering back and forth while you watch from below. Any up-and-down motion where there should only be left-and-right play—specifically at the pitman arm and idler arm—suggests worn components. Check the frame for flexing and cracking around the steering box mount as well. Slack in any of the joints is cause for replacement, but none of that is a big deal, as these trucks were built in high enough numbers that your local parts store should still stock all the linkage components you'll need.

Failing that, you can find it all at Classic Industries or Summit Racing. RideTech sells a complete front linkage kit for these trucks as well, using components much beefier than stock for better control over motion and longer life.

Steering Box Upgrades

Saginaw steering boxes were common in a lot of American cars and trucks into the late 1980s. As such, you might assume that you can just swap in any other similar box in your C10 and be on your way. But while the truck steering boxes are similar to what you might find in a car application, such as in a Chevelle, they don't interchange for one main reason: truck steering boxes mount on the outside of the frame rail, while car boxes are on the inside. So when it comes to swapping, find the proper truck steering box with the appropriate-style mount. What you need is a box known as a Saginaw 708.

Unfortunately, they aren't as common as they once were, and you'll need to make sure you get the correct box for the year of your truck because there were some fundamental differences among years and between four- and two-wheel-drive models.

Muscle car owners tend to like to swap out their factory 4-turn steering boxes for quicker-ratio units that speed up the steering's response time and make a car feel more responsive on the road. Truck owners have this same option, but it's important to note that squarebody trucks were given a variable-ratio quick 3½-turn lock-to-lock power steering box direct from the factory.

Mounting a Steering Box

GM steering boxes are heavy units that are bolted into place with four bolts that pass through the frame and hold the box in place. Alignment of something like this can be a chore, as these cast-iron boxes are heavy and a little awkward to hold in place.

The job is made easier if, when installing, you thread two shorter bolts through the steering box backward, with the head on the wheel side and the threads on the engine side and use them to align the box with the holes in the frame. This will help you get the other bolts installed and started, and then you can go back, remove your alignment bolts, and install the last two long bolts in their proper orientation. ■

If an upgraded, quicker ratio is part of your performance plan, CPP manufactures a 500 Series steering box for the C10 with a 14:1 ratio for improved handling characteristics. It's a bolt-in unit designed to take the slop out of the factory-style steering setup. (Photo Courtesy Classic Industries)

The variable ratio is a good compromise—it's slower reacting when on center and just off of it, but its ratio increases as the wheel is turned, giving a more performance feel in the turns while remaining mellow and not twitchy when cruising down the highway.

If you have a variable-rate box, there's no real reason to upgrade further for anything other than autocross use—unless you want Porsche-like steering input response. Generally, your upgrade money is probably better spent elsewhere, assuming your steering box and linkage are in good overall condition.

This steering box is quick enough to work well in most situations, but aftermarket boxes with even quicker ratios are available from Summit Racing, Classic Industries, CPP, and specialty companies such as Redhead Steering Gears.

Saginaw 708 steering boxes built prior to 1980 use inverted flare fittings for both the pressure and return power steering hoses. After 1980, GM swapped to metric fittings—16 and 18 mm—and used O-ring seals for the lines. As such, you can't easily swap between the two styles of steering box. Again, you need to make sure you get the right steering box for your application, but adapter fittings are available to allow you to use earlier power steering lines with a later box.

Rack and Pinion

Several aftermarket companies make bolt-in rack-and-pinion setups for 1973–1987 C10 pickups. It's a great upgrade if direct, crisp steering feel is something you crave in your C10.

Other than eliminating a bunch of potentially worn components in the original steering linkage, a power rack-and-pinion system offers a much more tight and direct feel for the driver. The only downside

There's a lot to like about a modern rack-and-pinion conversion in a C10. A steering rack is a simpler overall solution to steering than GM's factory box and linkage setup, offering reduced friction, lighter weight, smaller overall size, and reduced component wear thanks to fewer moving parts. This one is from Flaming River. (Photo courtesy Flaming River)

Understanding Ratios

If in doubt, a quicker ratio is the way to go for performance applications, but stock truck owners may find that faster ratio to be twitchy compared to a factory unit. However, if you want increased performance feel, that quicker ratio is the best bet.

If you're in the market for a new steering box for your C10, you've probably run into steering box ratios being used to describe replacement units. Typically, you'll see them advertised as 15:1, 14:1, or 12:1 in addition to or in place of the easier-to-understand four-turn, three-turn, and two-turn descriptors.

With regard to ratios, the first number corresponds to the number of degrees of steering wheel travel that the system needs to turn the truck's wheel one degree from center. So for a system advertised at 15:1, that's 15 degrees of steering wheel travel for every 1 degree of wheel travel. As such, a 14:1 will feel more responsive because it takes less effort to turn the truck the same amount as it did with a 15:1 box. A 12:1 is even quicker still.

The "turn" nomenclature is even easier. This is simply the number of complete turns from left-hand lock to right-hand lock. Obviously, the lower the number, the quicker the steering ratio and the more responsive the truck will feel. ■

here is cost and potential clearance issues, depending on any other modifications you intend to make; these include the oil pan, exhaust, clutch linkage, suspension modifications, etc.

If choosing a rack-and-pinion kit for your C10, be sure to verify that it will clear all the other components under the hood and suspension, and that it's installed using a solid, stout bracket; you don't want any motion in the mount because that will lead to a wandering truck out on the road.

Some custom work will need to be done to the factory steering column to use one of these rack-and-pinion setups, typically using a combination of small U-joints and rods with set screws to bring the steering column output shaft down to meet the steering rack. The input for the steering rack itself isn't in the same place as the input for the factory steering box, so some fabrication is often required.

Higher-end kits, such as the one offered by Flaming River, solve some of these issues for you by shipping with a new column and all the required parts for installation, and they're available in a variety of ratios and in both power and manual configurations.

Factory Brakes

Every 1973-and-newer C10 came from the factory with disc brakes up front and drum brakes in the rear. These systems are generally bulletproof, and a huge bonus is the sheer number of inexpensive parts available to service them.

Every parts house in America will have pads and shoes available for this era of C10, and those parts won't be expensive, so you have no excuse for not keeping up with your OEM brakes. After all, your brakes are the only things saving your front sheet metal from being rearranged into the shape of a Prius's butt. Treat them well.

Over the years, two different front brake options were available

GM's single-piston front disc brake assembly is a simple and effective stock setup. One huge pro is its durability and ease of maintenance, while the only real con is in lack of performance when pushed hard.

on C10s. From 1973 to 1979, the standard front brake rotor was 11 inches in diameter and 1¼ inches thick. In 1980, that was the "heavy duty" option, offered alongside a 1-inch-thick lighter-duty rotor. These parts can be swapped for the thicker versions, but you'll need everything to do the job from the calipers, brake lines, and wheel bearings all the way down to the spindles.

RPO codes on the build sheet or SPID label can shed some light (JB1 and JB3 are typically 1-inch rotors, while JB5 is the thicker HD version), but that's not to say your truck still wears those parts. The only real way to know which brakes are on your truck is to measure them.

In both cases, the stock front brake rotors are press-fit over the hubs. The only way to get a brake rotor off the truck is to remove the caliper, then the wheel bearing dust cap, the cotter pin, and the castle nut that holds the wheel bearing in place. Once all that is out of the way, the outer bearing slides out and the rotor can slide off the spindle with the attached hub.

Note that if you intend to have your rotors resurfaced, you'll need to get new seals for the inner wheel bearing, as both it and the seal will need to come out to chuck up the rotor on a brake lathe.

Yes, the factory disc brakes are plenty capable, but there are good options available to upgrade stop-ping ability without breaking the bank.

Brake Pads

Looking for the most bang for the buck in cheap stopping ability? An aggressive set of brake pads, such as what's offered by Power Stop, EBC Brakes, or Hawk Performance, can amp up a C10's whoa without cost-ing an arm and a leg. The only real trade-off is in noise and dust, both of which tend to increase as the pad material gets more aggressive. It's also important to note that rotor life tends to decrease with more aggres-sive friction materials. But in terms of ease of upgrade, there isn't a much simpler boost in stopping power than simply swapping over to a better set of brake pads from stock.

Whenever swapping brake pads, it's also smart to swap rotors—or resurface the ones you have. This allows the brake pad surface to bed into the metal of the brake rotor, which shortens stopping distances and also helps with pad life. You'll also want to be sure to always replace brake components in pairs: both fronts at the same time, and both rears at the same time. This helps to limit any imbalance in stopping power from side to side, which can make your rig pull to the left or right.

Brake Rotors

Upgraded brake rotors for stock spindles are also fairly easy to come by, and if you're serious about get-ting performance out of the braking system, it's wise to ditch your old stock rotors either for a pair of new stock units or for a set that's drilled and slotted.

While slotted rotors look racy, the voids are there for a reason: brake pads create quite a bit of heat, dust, and gas when they're pushed hard, such as on an autocross track, or in stop-and-go situations. The slots and

Remove Wheel Bear-ing Seals in One Shot

If you're going to resurface your OEM front rotors, you need to remove the inner wheel bearing and seal. But you can leave your seal removal tool in your toolbox. Once you have the outer wheel bearing out of the way, reinstall the spindle nut just a couple of turns. Then, with one fluid motion, firmly pull the rotor assembly toward you. The nut should catch the inner bearing, which will pop the seal free. Both the seal and the bearing will still be on the spindle, while the rotor will be in your hands. ■

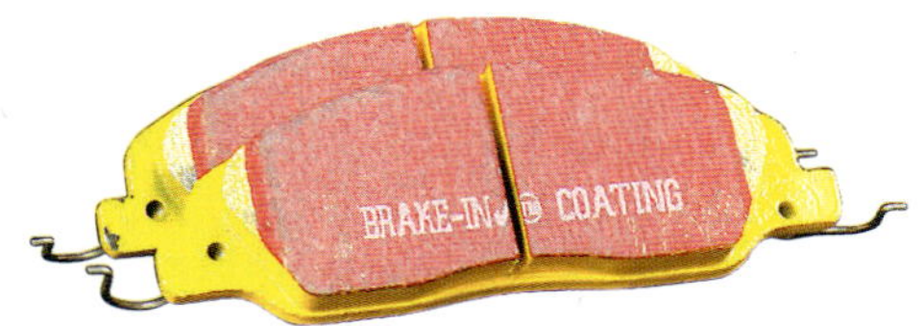

Chevy trucks use the common D52 brake pad, which was a GM standard for most disc brake applications for years. That makes them easy to find, and a number of aftermarket com-panies make higher-performance versions that fit in your stock calipers. These are EBC Brakes's Yellow Stuff pads, which bite like race brake pads but are flexible enough for street use. The part number for C10 use is DP41145R. (Photo Courtesy Summit Racing)

Slotted brake rotors are a great option for street-driven trucks because they do a better job of dissipating heat than stockers. Heat is what causes brakes to fade after hard or repeated use, so something like this—along with some good brake pads—can really help your C10 stop better than it did when it was new. (Photo Courtesy Classic Industries)

holes help to evacuate both dust and gas from the braking surface, thereby increasing the rotor and pad's efficiency. The translation? More consistent stopping under hard use—but not shorter stopping. These are about making the brakes work appropriately under hard use, typically past the point that other standard brakes would be heat soaked.

Several companies make drilled and slotted options for these trucks, and, like brake pads themselves, adding a set to your system can make a good bit of difference in your truck's ability to stop consistently.

Flexible Brake Lines

Though they're often overlooked, the factory rubber brake lines are likely a cause of some brake sponginess.

Why? Because they've probably been on the job since Reagan was in office. Even tough rubber brake lines can expand under pressure, and there are no greater pressures in your whole truck than inside the brake system.

From the factory, there are three rubber brake lines on an original C10: at the right and left front wheels, and one at the rear axle, connecting

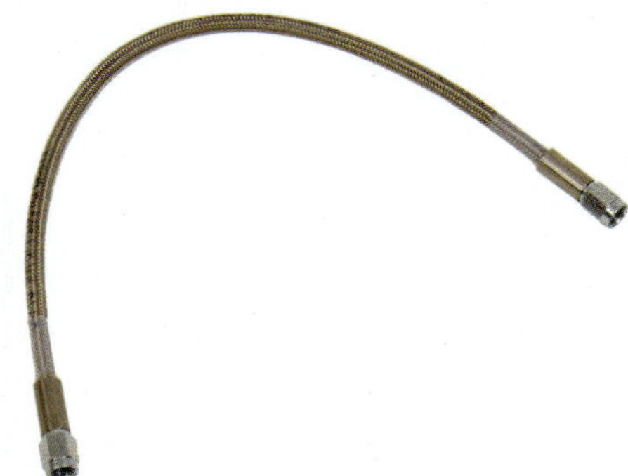

Braided steel lines are a great upgrade. This is a -3 AN brake line from Summit Racing with an 18-inch length (part number SUM-220305). (Photo Courtesy Summit Racing)

the axle-mounted brake lines to the frame. All of these should be checked for cracking related to age and weathering and replaced if needed.

Better options out there now include braided steel flexible lines that won't expand under pressure. They therefore transfer all the braking action through to the calipers, rather than losing some to expansion. This is a smart upgrade for any daily driver, especially one that's still running old rubber brake lines that are past their prime.

Power Versus Manual Brakes

Three brake options were available in C10s: manual, vacuum-operated power, and hydraulically operated power (known as hydroboost).

The simplest setup is the manual version, as it just uses simple pedal leverage to operate the brakes. Under the dash, these trucks have the brake

This dual-diaphragm power booster may look shot, but it actually works fine. If you're removing the pedal box from your truck, the booster will need to come off anyway, as it's part of what bolts the pedals to the firewall. If your booster still holds vacuum, there's no need to replace it. I washed and wire-brushed this unit and painted it semi-gloss black to match the frame.

If you intend to run a larger-duration camshaft in your engine, you'll likely end up with less engine vacuum at idle than stock. Think rock-hard pedal with no stopping assist. Budget for a vacuum canister or electric vacuum pump along with that cam. With a big cam and power brakes, you'll need both feet to stop your truck. ■

rod mounted higher on the brake pedal arm, which provides a more favorable leverage point.

Both power options work well, and both use a lower mount point on the pedal for the master cylinder pushrod assembly.

Vacuum-assisted brakes use a vacuum booster to add assist and reduce braking effort. It's mounted on the firewall between the brake master cylinder and the pedal assembly. Most of these were Delco 11-inch dual-diaphragm units.

There are several solutions, from a vacuum reserve canister to an electric vacuum pump. But you also might consider swapping over to GM's hydroboost setup. Parts are relatively easy to come by, as it was a common setup in heavier-duty and diesel squarebody trucks. You're almost guaranteed to find one on a square in your local parts yard.

As this type of system runs off the power steering pump, cam selection is a moot point for off-idle brake performance.

Rear Brakes

Just as the front brakes in C10s are all more or less the same across the model years, the rears are as well.

Before ordering any parts for your drum brakes, you need to know which drum brakes you have. The easiest way is to measure the width of the brake shoes. GM used two sizes—these are the wider, heavier-duty versions.

Here's a good example of just how dirty drum brakes can get. Note the buildup on the top of the shoes and on the wheel cylinder. These brakes are off of a low-mile truck too. Whenever working on brakes, wear gloves, as the dust is metallic and can be hard to remove from your skin.

Tools of the Brake Trade

Drum brakes can be daunting with all those springs and clips holding it all together. It's like a mechanical puzzle that has a 50-percent chance of making you bleed and a 90-percent chance of going back together incorrectly. But if you have the right tools in hand, drum brakes are just as easy to service as discs.

Snap-on makes a great brake tool, but you can also get one from Craftsman or Harbor Freight. Regardless of which tool you choose, source one before attempting to tear into a drum brake system. You'll end up hating yourself if you try working on a set of drum brakes with a screwdriver and a pair of Vise-Grips.

Something else to remember: disassemble one side at a time. The still-assembled side is a road map for reassembly after you've forgotten which spring goes where. ■

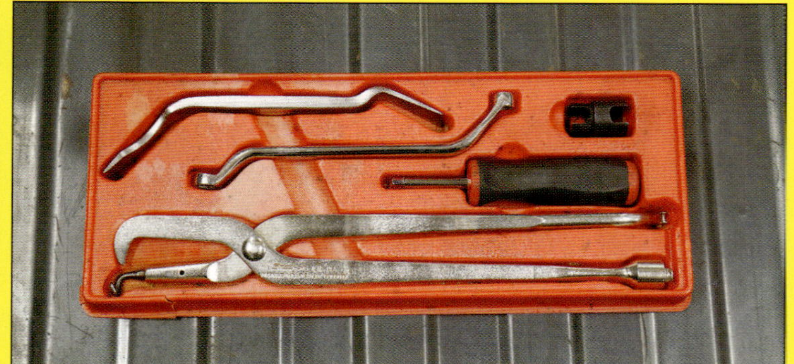

Snap-on's drum brake spring pliers (part number 131A) are some of the best in the business. The two long ends of the pliers are fantastic for drum-brake spring removal and reinstallation: no fuss, no swearing, and no bleeding required. If you plan to do any brake work at all—to your C10 or any other vehicle with drums—get a brake spring tool and learn how to use it.

Starting in 1973, GM used its reliable, standard drum brake on every C10, and the basic design stayed the same all the way through the end of squarebody production in 1987.

Heavier-duty models had some fundamental differences, such as brake drums press-fit to axles, but for the 1/2-ton models, other than size, there wasn't much variation.

Trucks came with two options: 11-inch-diameter drums with 2-inch-wide shoes and 11⁵⁄₃₂-inch-diameter drums with 2¾-inch-wide shoes. GM built these trucks with both versions throughout the production life of the model. Typically, the Big 10 models and anything with a towing package were equipped with the larger brakes, so that's a good place to start.

Drum Brake Upgrades

I won't argue that drum brakes are better—or even equal to—disc brakes, but they can be made to work well with the addition of more aggressive metallic shoe linings. That, along with a good adjustment, can really make a difference in how a drum-brake truck stops.

GM was smart in how these drums were designed, as they self-adjust whenever the truck is driven in reverse and the brakes are applied to stop. Therefore, once they're set up correctly, all you really need to do is use the truck normally. They'll adjust themselves as they wear in.

Beyond that, the only upgrade to a factory drum brake setup is to make sure that all the springs, clips, and adjusters are in good working order. Drum brakes tend to get pretty dusty internally, so periodically pulling the drum off and hosing the system down with brake parts cleaner is a good idea. When you do this, you'll want to be sure to have something under each wheel to catch the runoff, as that dirty brake cleaner will stain your garage floor. A drip pan works great, but so does a big piece of cardboard.

Beyond that, the only real wear items inside a drum brake are the shoes, wheel cylinders, and the drums themselves.

Those rear wheel cylinders are often overlooked as a wear item. Standard DOT 3 brake fluid, which is what most cars still use today, is hydroscopic, meaning it draws moisture to it. The wheel cylinders tend to collect that moisture, either from driving in the rain or through humidity in the air, and then they rust, which in turn causes them to start leaking fluid past their seals—not a good thing in a sealed brake system.

The best way to check wheel cylinder condition is to pull the drum out of the way and (with your finger) pull back the edge of the wheel cylinder's rubber boot. If it's wet underneath, or if fluid spills out, it's time for a wheel cylinder replacement. Fortunately, they're cheap, and the job is easy to do if you have the right tools—removing the upper shoe retainer springs is the only challenging part. The cylinders are held in with two bolts from the backing plate, and the brake line. Loosen all of that and they'll more or less fall out.

Disc Brake Upgrades

You're never going to be able to make a classic C10 as safe as a new one with regard to collisions, but you can make a classic rig stop better than everything else on the road—with nonexistent fade from heat—which goes a long way toward leveling the field. Upgrading the stock brakes with more-aggressive friction material is smart, but it can only take you so far. If you want your truck to stop like an exotic car, you have to up the size of the brake rotors and calipers in front and install rotors and calipers out back in place of the original drums.

C10 owners have many choices when it comes to brake kits from SSBC and CPP's factory-style disc conversion kits to Baer's monstrous 14-inch Pro+ and Extreme+ systems.

Baer Brakes, for example, has templates on its site that allow you to print out and check fitment of its brake systems with your wheels before you buy. This is invaluable, as brake systems and wheels are both typically very expensive components, so you want to be sure everything will work before you pull the trigger on a system.

Selecting a Brake System

Planning on hitting the road daily in your C10? Consider this: stopping power on even the most basic Toyota has long surpassed what your average C10 could do in 1987—never mind 1973.

If the daily grind is part of your truck's job, my suggestion for you is to get the biggest, baddest brakes you can for your C10 project. The aftermarket is here to help with a variety of complete systems to fit a number of budgets. The main things to consider are ease of service and the overall size of rim you intend on running. For service, being able to run off-the-shelf pads will help when it comes time for maintenance, and rim size is key—don't get 14-inch brakes if you like 15-inch wheels. They won't fit.

Baer Pro+ Front Brake System Installation

1 *Baer Brakes offers a huge 14-inch brake kit for C10s called the Pro+. It uses a six-piston caliper and D0731 brake pads (same as the C5 and C6 Corvette, for easy replacement), two-piece zinc-coated drilled and slotted directional rotors, billet aluminum hubs and brackets, all-new bearings, and all the installation hardware needed to do the job. These brakes require at least an 18-inch wheel, and they're engineered to work with CPP's popular 2-inch drop spindle, as supplied with RideTech's suspension kits.*

2 *Baer's hub comes preassembled with grease-packed bearings already in place, so installation is easy. A large washer holds the outer bearing in place and sits between the castle nut and the bearing. Tighten while turning the hub, as it will help to seat the bearings. Baer recommends 5–10 ft-lbs at first, then back it off, and then tighten again to remove all play, with another 1/16 turn to preload the bearing. Then install the cotter pin and dust cap.*

3 *The CPP spindle has two large threaded holes at the rear that serve as mounting points for Baer's brake caliper bracket. Two large 5/8 bolts fix it in place, but since they'll need to be removed for shims later, they should just be hand-tight here.*

4 *Next is Baer's massive brake rotor. Note that these are directional, with an R for right and an L for left. Installing three lug nuts keeps the rotor seated against the hub.*

5 With the brake pads removed from the caliper, it's the next piece of the puzzle. The caliper is fixed in place with two Allen-head bolts.

6 The trickiest part of Baer's brake install is shimming the caliper. These calipers don't have sliders, as factory calipers would. Instead, they're hard-mounted with any runout in the rotor absorbed by the caliper's pistons. To eliminate noise and wear, the caliper needs to be as close to centered over the brake rotor as possible. This is done by taking four measurements (one at each corner of the brake caliper from the caliper housing to the rotor) and doing a little math to sort out which spacers are needed.

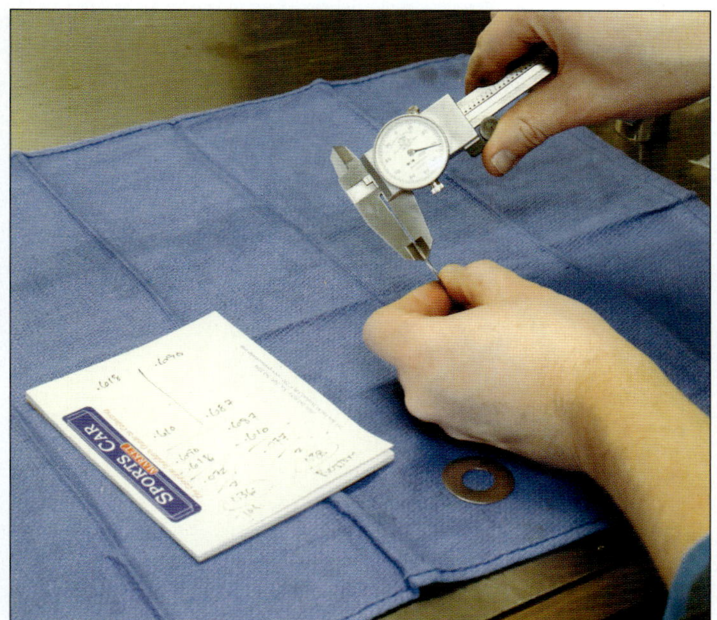

7 With the numbers in hand, subtract the top inside measurement from the top outside, and then divide that number by two. Here, that worked out to 0.690 inch minus 0.610, which was 0.072 inch. Half of that distance is what it takes to center the caliper: 0.036 inch. Baer sends a number of different-sized shims with its kit—all you need to do is to get as close as you can to that number using the shims provided. Repeat for the bottom and you have what you need to center the caliper.

8 The shims go between the brake caliper bracket and the spindle. Once installed, reinstall the caliper bracket bolts with threadlock compound, and torque them to 110 ft-lbs.

9 Next, reinstall the brake pads in the brake caliper, and reinstall the complete unit to the caliper bracket, again using threadlock and a torque wrench. Spec here is 75 ft-lbs.

10 Baer's calipers use banjo-style fittings that seal using copper washers. These fittings are leak-free when torqued properly—in this case, 15–20 ft-lbs. It's important to make sure that the hose end doesn't come in contact with any suspension or steering components.

11 The brake line that comes with the kit is a stout braided stainless steel unit with a -4 AN end. The kit ships with a conversion fitting that clamps in the original frame location using a spring clip and threads into a 3/16-inch brake line fitting.

12 The final product is a much larger than stock brake setup, which will provide superior clamping force thanks to its six-piston caliper and huge rotor. Fade will also be a thing of the past. From street driving to auto-cross, these brakes will be able to take whatever punishment you have in mind for your C10.

Baer SS4+ Rear Brake System Installation

1 The first step in upgrading the rear brakes is to remove all the factory drum brake components. A brake spring tool makes quick work of all the retainer springs.

2 Next is removal of the rear axles. To get them out, you first need to drain the rear axle by pulling the rear cover off. There is no drain plug, so be ready to catch the fluid in a drain pan. Then remove the center pin from the differential—it's held in place with a 1/2-inch bolt. With the center pin out, pushing in on each axle frees the C-clips. Then the axles can be slid out of the housing.

3 With the axles out, the backing plates are next to go, as they'll be in the way of any disc brake install. Four bolts per side hold these to the axle housing.

4 In place of the factory backing plate, Baer's SS4+ 13-inch brake kit uses a special machined plate that consists of both a mount for the rear caliper as well as an internal parking brake shoe. It installs in the same location as the factory plate using the same hardware. Torque spec is 45 ft-lbs.

6 *A lot of builders use a gasket to seal the rear cover to the differential, but I find it's best to use a bead of Right Stuff gasket maker. Run a bead, let it set up briefly, then install the cover and the bolts hand-tight. After the cover has set up for an hour or so, torque the bolts to spec. This will stop any leaks, and it will make the cover easier to clean the next time you have to take it apart. Don't forget to refill your axle with the proper gear oil.*

5 *With the park brake and caliper mount unit torqued, the factory axles can be reinstalled along with their C-clips, the differential's center pin, and the retaining bolt.*

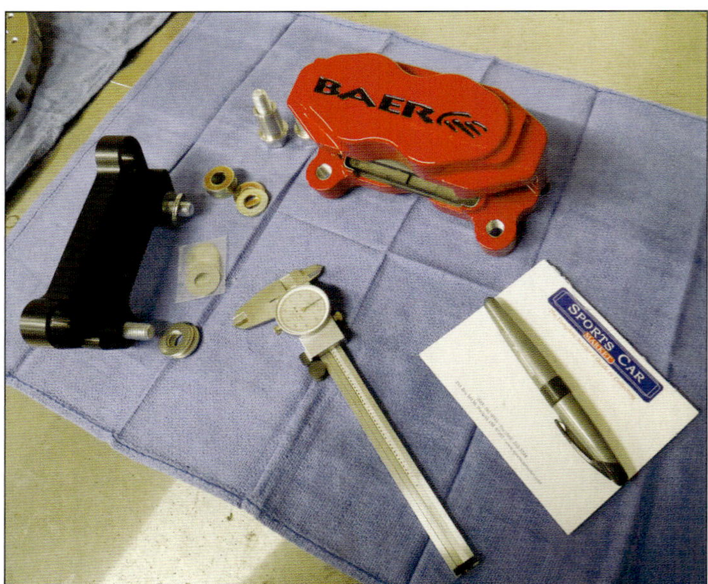

8 *The rear caliper mounting procedure is similar to the front, using shims to center the brake caliper over the rotor. Again, you'll need a precise way to measure the space between the rotor and caliper at the top and bottom inner and outer locations.*

7 *The Baer brake rotor installs next, with each again held in place using three lug nuts.*

9 The brake caliper mounting bracket affixes to the backing plate using two supplied bolts—but it needs to be left hand-tight, as it must be shimmed to achieve proper caliper-to-rotor alignment.

10 The caliper is next after its brake pads have been removed. It sits between the bracket and the rotor, with bolts that pass through sliders that mesh with machined reliefs in the mounting bracket. As with the front, take measurements at the four corners of the caliper, between it and the rotor, and write down each number. Subtract the inner from the outer and divide that by two to get your spacer measurement. The spacers install between the caliper bracket and the backing plate.

11 With threadlock compound applied and the spacers installed, torque the caliper mount bracket to 85 ft-lbs, and then the caliper bolts to 85 ft-lbs as well.

12 Baer's 13-inch SS4+ rear brake system will fit under a 17-inch wheel, and the fact that it has an internal park brake is also a big plus. However, you'll likely need to source some new park brake cables to make the system work, along with a Corvette-style clevis (Lokar part number EC-80CC).

Creating Brake Lines

Any brake upgrade will likely require brake line fabrication to support the new parts. This isn't a bad idea on any vehicle that has seen some miles or came from a rust-prone area, and it's not a challenging project if you have the right tools.

Something to note about C10s and GMs in general: the front-to-rear main brake line is a larger size than the brake lines that run to the wheels—typically 1/4-inch-diameter tube compared to the smaller 3/16 size. GM is one of the only companies of this era to use a larger-size front-to-rear line, and while it works fine with stock parts, a lot of aftermarket companies don't accommodate for that larger-size line with their modern performance brake parts.

If you're swapping from your stock setup, you have two options: make a new front-to-rear line using the same line and fitting size as your new aftermarket master cylinder (probably 3/8-inch by 24 for 3/16-inch line) or find an adapter to reduce the size of your bigger factory brake line to make it work with the new master. Be prepared to hunt, however—some GM fanatics refer to these as "ghost fittings," because of how rarely they're actually seen. Amazon is a good source, once you figure out exactly which fitting you need.

If you're going to make brake lines, do yourself a favor and buy some good brake line tools: a flare tool, a deburring tool, and a couple of hand-held benders are just the ticket.

When it comes to most tools, the cheap versions aren't worth the trouble—you'll spend more time trying to get the tool to work than you

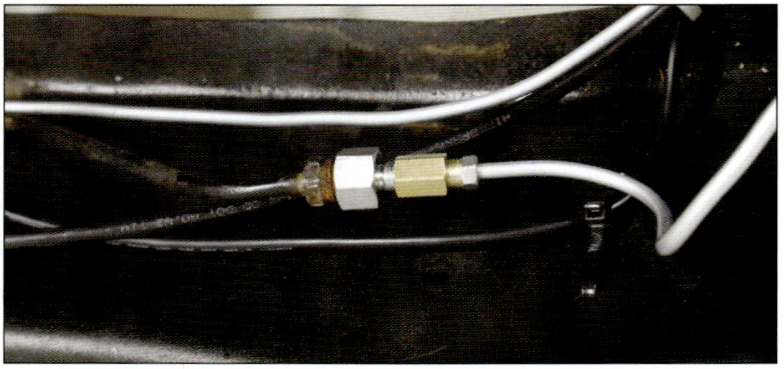

Brake lines aren't like fuel lines—flow isn't much of a concern compared to the transfer of pressure. I chose to adapt my OEM brake line, as it kept things simple at the back of the truck. I found a 9/16 x 18 female to 3/16 x 24 male inverted flare reducer on Amazon and used that to run a new 3/16 brake line from the original proportioning valve location on the front crossmember.

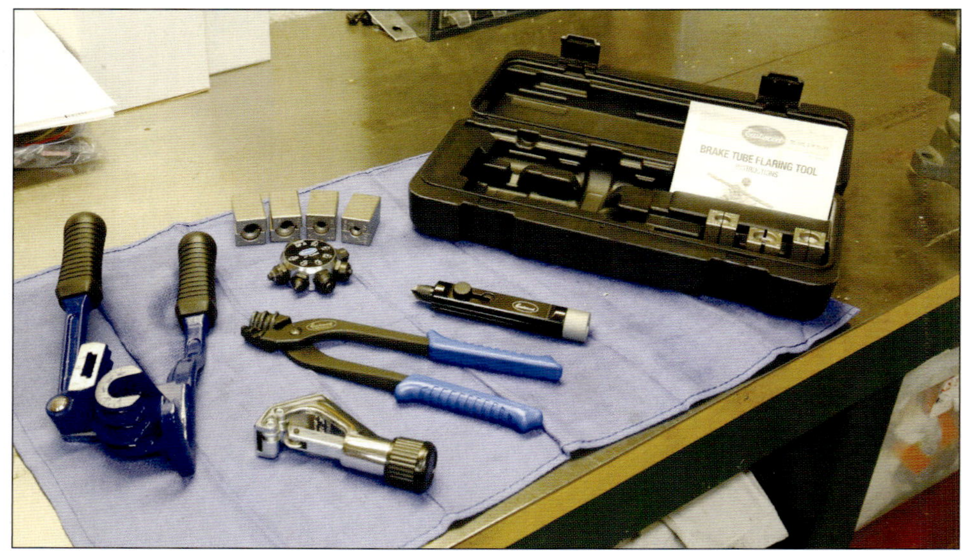

Eastwood has some of the best brake tools on the market today, specifically the brake line flaring tool (part number 25304-30005), which makes perfect 45-degree double flares in less than 30 seconds. With the proper dies, it will also make 37-degree AN-style flares as well.

will actually using it for its intended purpose. This is especially true with regard to brake flaring tools. To do this right, you'll need to spend some money, but the tools are worth it if you're going to be using them regularly. If you have room in your budget, spending here on high-quality tools will buy peace of mind later.

As for line size, 3/16 inch is plenty for your C10, and it's likely what your aftermarket master cylinder is set up to use, so that's a good place to start.

A 25-foot spool of steel brake line is perfect for a C10—especially so for a short-bed—and complete brake line fitting kits are available online. You can also piecemeal your system together if you know exactly what fittings you'll need.

One smart thing to do is to draw out your brake system on paper before you order any parts, just so you'll know for sure how many fittings of each size you'll need before you get started.

I used Eastwood's vise-mounted flare tool for the brakes and fuel lines on this truck. Here's how it works:

Brake Line Flaring

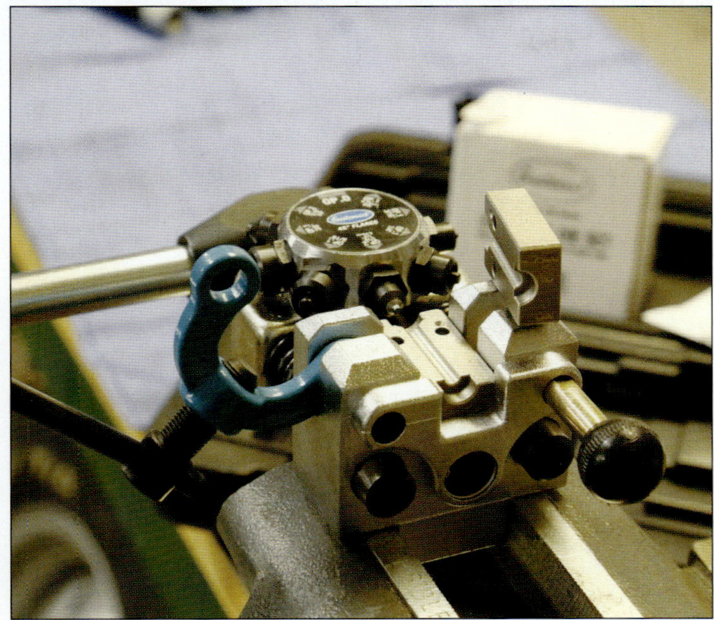

1 *Chuck the tool up in a bench vise and select the die you intend to use. Here I'm using the settings and dies for 3/16-inch brake line with a standard 45-degree flare.*

2 *Place your line in the die, snug it down slightly, and select "OP.0" on the dial. Then pull the lever to properly place the tubing in the die for flaring. Then tighten the line using the clamp handle.*

3 *Select "OP.1" for 3/16 line and pull the lever until it stops.*

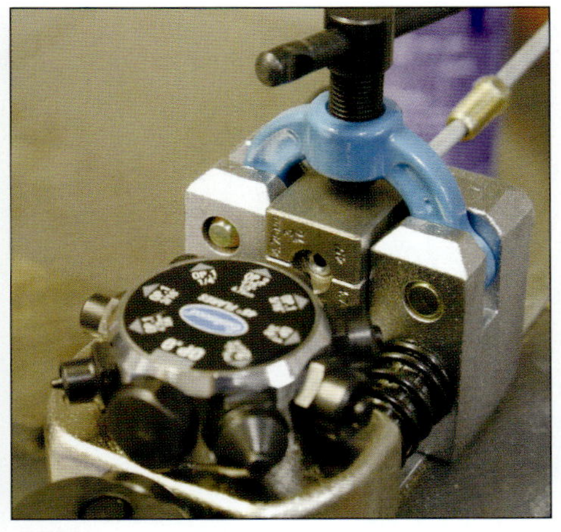

4 *Now select "OP.2" for 3/16 line and pull the lever again.*

5 *You should now have a perfect flare ready for use.*

Note that if the tubing isn't cut straight and deburred properly, your flares will suffer. Eastwood has you covered there too with high-quality tubing cutter and deburring tools (part numbers 30448 and 14502). If you're going to make brake lines more than once—or if steel fuel line construction is part of your build too—these tools are worth the price of entry.

Master Cylinder

If you're running factory-type components, such as calipers and drums in the rear, there's nothing wrong with also running a factory-style master cylinder—but it's smart to replace yours if you're unsure of its age. Any components that come in contact with brake fluid can and will rust from the inside out over time, and that will lead to brake failure. Be sure to get the proper unit for your truck, as several different sizes were used, depending on the truck's options and configuration.

Swapping to disc brakes in the rear requires at the very least a different brake proportioning valve. The original is set to provide more braking pressure to the rear, as the rear drums in a C10 were originally set to engage slightly before the front discs. That setup allowed the rear to settle and kept the nose from diving. Obviously, running that factory setup with rear discs won't work. Thanks to the design of drum brakes, which take more pressure to run, using the factory valve with discs will cause the rear brakes to lock up before the fronts do. In a truck with no weight in the bed, this will be even more pronounced.

An adjustable proportioning valve is ideal here, as the driver can use it to dial in the proper bias for the rear disc brakes to suit his or her driving style.

OEM stuff works fine in most situations, but if you're swapping to big brakes, you also need to factor in the cost of a new hydraulic setup to run the hardware, such as Baer's Remaster and matching custom proportioning valve.

These parts match the Pro+ and SS4+ front and rear kits detailed above, and installation is easy, as they simply bolt up to the factory location on the power booster. Run brake lines to them and you're done. Note, however, that you'll need to lose your original proportioning valve and plumb around where it was—the driver's side of the front crossmember, down below the power steering pump.

The Remaster, similar to stock options, is offered in three different bore sizes: 15/16, 1, and 1-1/8 inch. The smaller of the three is for manual brake applications, while the largest is for Hydroboost only.

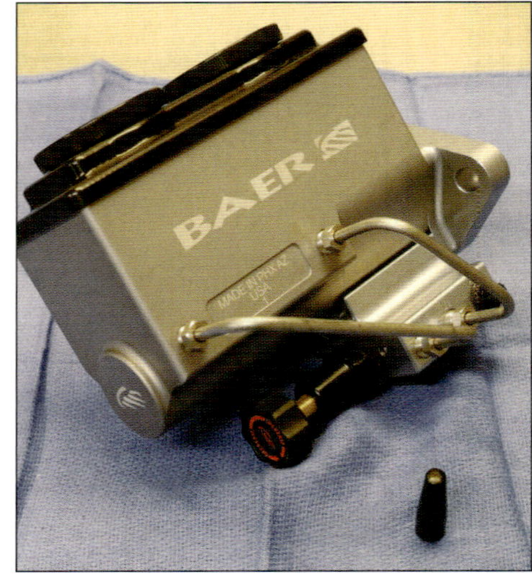

Baer's Remaster is a bolt-in replacement for factory master cylinders, and it's offered in versions to fit Ford, GM, and Mopar applications. It's machined out of billet aluminum and designed to work with the other Baer components. Something like this offers more control over what you get with factory units, but it also looks great under the hood of your rig.

A complete plumbing setup should be tucked out of the way as much as possible. The factory setup on C10s is obtrusive, but yours doesn't have to be. Also note the loops bent in both front and rear lines where they exit the master. Remember that the cab and frame move independently of each other, and that can stress brake lines that don't have loops to allow some motion.

All that's left is to bleed the system and bed in the pads and rotors per Baer's instructions: two light to medium stops from 65 mph to 10 mph, two heavy stops from 65 mph to 5 mph, and then a 10-minute cooling cruise to keep airflow passing over the brakes. Then perform three moderate stops and then eight heavy stops—again from 65 mph to 5 mph, finally driving another 10 minutes to let everything cool. This system works great with any new pad and rotor combination, and it should be done each time you swap out friction materials.

SELECTING AND BUILDING AN ENGINE

GM's squarebody pickups are reliable rigs. Apart from the sheer number of them built over 15 model years, these trucks were also fitted with a couple of tried-and-true powerplants. When things do go wrong, parts are cheap. That's all good news, especially for an end user who is new to classic cars.

Here's the rub: these trucks were built square in the middle of America's dark age of performance, where emissions regulations and a lack of technology meant low compression, retarded timing, small cams, poor-flowing cylinder heads with big chambers, exhaust gas recirculation (EGR), and restrictive catalyst exhaust systems. Performance was choked for all American cars in this era, right up through the 1980s, and GM's trucks were no exception to the rule. Never mind the fact that these were built with torque and economy in mind, not horsepower.

The Big Three learned a lot from the smogger era, and that, combined with breakthroughs in computerized engine controls, high-flow catalysts, and fuel injection components, brought us to where we are today: GM's basic 2018 Silverado with a 5.3 V-8 puts out over 350 hp. Step up to the 6.2 and you're over 400. Both can push 25 mpg on the highway using the new LT engine.

The aftermarket has brought a lot of modern technology to the hot rod world. Regardless of what original engine you have in your rig, you can now make it perform better, run cleaner, and be more economical if you choose the right modifications.

Available Engines

Squarebody trucks were built in many different configurations, depending on what the original owner needed. To suit just about anyone who marched through the local dealerships' front door, GM offered a variety of powerplants to suit a variety of needs. These included everything from small, thrifty inline-6s through Mark IV big-block V-8s.

Pop the hood on a square and this is what you can expect to see. In this case, my 1979 C10 came equipped with an LS9 350-ci small-block that put out a whopping 165 hp. Years and miles tend to cause 350s to lose horses as well, so this engine would be lucky to be putting out 150 hp. We can do better.

Sixes

Three sixes were available through these years: the 250 and the 292 inline engines and the 4.3 V-6. The inliners are known for fantastic torque production, but neither are much of a performance option for those of us looking to build a custom truck. Two 250s were available: the RPO LD4 at 105 hp, offered in K-series trucks from 1973 to 1978, and the RPO LE3, rated at 130 hp, offered from 1979 to 1984. The RPO L25 292 was rated at 120 hp, offered in K20s from 1973 to 1986.

The RPO LB1 and LB4 4.3 V-6s are similar in design to the 350 small-block. Each also makes respectable power and gets decent mileage, but neither is a good performance option in a full-size truck, as they just don't have the grunt needed to really move a C10—especially not since a 350 swap will be cheaper than building a 4.3 and will net more power. But a 4.3 is great for a driver if you're not interested in big power. Both were rated at 155 hp and were offered from 1985 to 1987.

350s

The vast majority of these trucks came equipped with a version of the 350-ci small-block Chevy V-8—typically the 165-hp LS9 (1969–1986) or the 160-hp LT9 (1981–1986) fitted with a 4-barrel Quadrajet carb. Fundamentally, the 350 can be a stout piece, especially if it's warmed up from stock with some carefully chosen aftermarket parts. There are hundreds of ways to do that, depending on your end goals. The 350 is a great starting point, and, fortunately, chances are you already have one under the hood.

Other Small-Block Chevys

Other small-blocks offered through these years included the 307 V-8, 400 V-8, and 305 V-8.

The RPO LG8 307 is a good, reliable driver's motor that won't be fussy if properly set up. It was only available in these trucks in 1973, so chances are that you won't be dealing with one. If you do find one under your hood, the best bet is to leave it there while you build something bigger. The factory rating on this engine was just 130 hp.

The RPO LF4 400 is known for being a good performer in general, especially when it comes to torque production—it had 185 hp and 300 ft-lbs of torque thanks to a longer 3.75-inch stroke over the 350's 3.48-inch unit. That said, it does have a few quirks that need to be understood, including Siamese bores that require special head gaskets and cylinder heads with steam holes to alleviate hot spots in the block. You'll find 400s in trucks from 1976 through 1980. Builders often use the longer-stroke crankshafts from 400s in 350 blocks, creating the legendary 383 stroker in the process. 400s were once the only source for these

The six was available in two versions and was popular for its good torque production. That said, unless you're really trying to be different with your custom build, there isn't much reason to keep a six around today. Even with injection, a trick head, and a bunch of boost, a six would still not make as much power as a similarly built V-8. Then again, for a driver, this can be a great choice, as they're smooth and build a lot of torque. (Photo Courtesy B. Mitchell Carlson)

The big dog of engines for square GMs is the LE8 454, which could be ordered in anything from a C10 through a K30. Yeah, it's a big-block, but no, it doesn't make that much power in stock trim. These were tuned for towing and had to cope with small heads, low compression, and super-conservative camshafts, all of which sapped power. But the good news is that all that can be remedied with the proper aftermarket components.

3.75-inch stroke cranks, but they're now available from places such as Summit Racing.

The RPO LE9, LF3, LG9, and L03 305s, much like the 307, are not performance options, but again, they're not exactly bad performers—especially if daily driving is in your plans. The LF3 is a California emissions engine rated at 155 hp, while the LG9 is a 2-barrel version with 130 hp. The LE9 had 160 hp, while the L03 with GM's TBI was the hottest performer of the bunch at a blistering 170 hp.

For modification, these engines are not ideal for a variety of reasons, from their small bore sizes to small cylinder heads that don't flow all that well. But these engines are great on economy and reliability. You'll find them in trucks from 1981 on.

Finally, the RPO LE8 454 big-block was also available throughout these trucks' production years. Like the 350, power output varied but with an architecture that was shared with muscle cars in the years prior to the 1973's launch, there's a lot that can be done to wake up a sleepy, wheezy, 230-hp 454. They were optional through 1987. A TBI version—RPO L19—was available starting in 1987.

Small-Block Upgrades

Squarebody truck engines weren't hot even when new, and decades later, an engine with a bunch of miles isn't going to be much of a performer, even if it still seems to run fine. Chances are that it has lost a bunch of its horses over the years, and getting them back will require a rebuild. While you're at it, you might as well add some modern technology into the mix and make some better power out of that old powerplant too. Sub-200-hp from a 350? Not good enough.

For the sake of argument here, I'll stick with the LS9 350 as the basis for an upgrade. That said, most all of the products and modifications mentioned here will apply to just about every engine GM made for these pickups, minus the diesels.

What's a Vortec Head and Why Should You Care?

If you intend to run a traditional 350 or 400 small-block in your C10, you need to be schooled on Vortec heads.

Launched in 1996 on GM trucks, the Vortec head was a complete redesign of the small-block Chevy cylinder head, based on the LT1 heads used on the 1996 Impala SS. GM added more flow via changes to the intake and exhaust runners and integrated tumble instead of swirl into the port's design, which boosted flow—and power—further.

So they flow well—typically better in stock form than warmed-over earlier designs, including the legendary double-hump head from the muscle car era. But what you should really note is their effective combustion chamber size: 64 cc. For a smogger-era squarebody LS9 350 that had 76-cc heads from new, that's a big boost in static compression—on an 8.3:1 LS9, with everything else being equal, the smaller-chamber Vortecs push compression to approximately 9.5:1.

Some things to consider: Vortecs require a different intake manifold, as they use an 8-bolt-style intake compared to the original small-block's 12-bolt intake. They also don't work well with cams that feature over 0.500 inch of lift. And big valve spring pressures are a no-no, as stock versions have press-in rocker studs that can come out under heavy load.

All that said, they're cheap, and you don't need to scour wrecking yards to find a set. Both Classic Industries

The small-block world changed for the better in 1996, when GM introduced the Vortec head. A set of these can wake up a smogger 350, especially when paired with a hotter-than-stock cam and a matching intake manifold. Some tests have shown gains up to 100 hp on an LS9 350. The aftermarket has stepped up, which means that you can buy a brand-new set for the same or less than it would cost you to get a core set from a wrecking yard and have them set up by a machine shop. (Photo Courtesy Classic Industries)

and Summit Racing sell complete, ready-to-run heads for around $400 each as of this writing.

For the money, this is a great upgrade to an otherwise-stock C10 engine. Add in a decent cam with a modern profile, new lifters, and new rocker arms and you have a pretty good boost in power over stock while keeping the stock block intact. ■

Cylinder Heads

The number-one enemy of smogger-era pickups is low compression ratios, followed by choked airflow both on the intake and exhaust sides of the engine.

Remember that trucks weren't designed to make a lot of horsepower. Torque is the name of the game when it comes down to towing and hauling, which is why smaller-valve "truck" heads were used in the first place. It doesn't take a lot of airflow to make low-RPM torque, and it doesn't require loads of compression, either. But for fun-level horsepower, like the kind you likely want in your C10 project, those are both vital areas for improvement.

Vortec heads are a great option, as are any of the aluminum heads on the market today. Aluminum offers better heat dissipation than cast iron, which helps to both build power and limit detonation when running lower-octane pump gas and higher compression ratios.

There is also a much wider array of aluminum head performance profiles on the market today than you'll find in cast-iron designs, specifically from companies such as AFR, Edelbrock, Trick Flow, Dart, GM Performance, etc. If you're looking for big runners, big valves, and larger exhaust ports for higher-RPM power, aluminum heads will be easier to source for your specific needs.

Carburetors

A carburetor has a tough job. It needs to properly meter fuel to your engine in a variety of conditions, from idle to full throttle and everywhere in between. What type of carburetor you run—and the condition it's in—can really make a difference in how your truck behaves out on the road, and so in that sense, there's probably no more important component under your hood.

Quadrajet

If you're running an original 350 or 454 in your C10, it's a good bet that the carburetor feeding it is a Rochester Quadrajet.

In stock, operable, low-mile condition, a Q-jet is arguably the closest you can get to modern fuel-injection drivability in a carburetor. When they work right, they offer easy starting, great off-idle response, good fuel economy due to their small primaries, and a punch of power thanks to their huge secondaries. They're tunable and tend to stay just how you set them, meaning you shouldn't need to fuss with one once you get it set up.

These carbs use metering rods that can be swapped for different fuel delivery characteristics, like an AFB Carter or Edelbrock. Tuning one isn't quite as easy as one of those aftermarket AFBs, but if you can source the right components for your carburetor—and know what part numbers to look for in the first place—setting one up to run well isn't too tough.

They sound great, right? Not so fast.

These carburetors aren't the simplest things to disassemble and assemble, and they're known to warp at the base plate due to overtightening at installation, which can cause vacuum leaks and make tuning a nightmare. Chances are that your original Q-jet has been rebuilt at least once, and it may be suffering from that work at this point.

When set up right, those huge secondaries give crisp response. After 100,000 miles of abuse and poor adjustment, you may just get a big bog when snapping the throttle open—hence the nickname "Quadrabog."

They're also known for developing leaks around the throttle blade shafts because from the factory the shafts ride right on the carburetor's aluminum baseplate housing. High-mile carbs tend to have this issue, and extreme cases can lead to throttle blades that don't completely shut within their venturi bores. If you have a hard time getting your truck to return to idle and you've ruled out an external vacuum leak, this may be your issue.

All of the above issues can have you chasing your tail on an old Q-jet, especially if you're trying to get your rig to pass an emissions test.

If you have a stock-ish engine, it's hard to go wrong with a Q-jet—but try to find a low-mile example or rebuild

Aluminum offers a number of benefits over cast iron when it comes to cylinder heads, the most obvious being weight. But they also dissipate heat better than iron, and they tend to hold off detonation slightly better, which means you can run slightly higher compression on pump gas. The downside is cost. This set from Edelbrock (part number 6101) is designed to make power on smaller SBCs, such as 305s and 307s. (Photo Courtesy Edelbrock)

Tiny primaries and huge secondaries are a Rochester Quadrajet staple, and thanks to that, they can offer fantastic throttle response and great mileage for a daily driver—which is a big reason GM used them so extensively in the 1970s and 1980s. That said, they have some quirks, and they don't always age and wear well. Do your homework on these carbs if you intend to run one.

If your truck's been swapped over to an aftermarket carburetor, it's a good bet that it's one of these: an Edelbrock AFB. This is basically a Weber-built version of the Carter AFB used in the 1960s, and it offers good street reliability as well as easy tuning—no gaskets below the fuel level is a big plus. This tends to be a set-and-forget kind of carb, and they're really easy to adjust and repair. Edelbrock's user manual and carb tuning rod and jet kits are must-have items if you own one of these carbs.

yours with quality parts. There are still NOS versions out there—but be prepared to pay a pretty penny if you can find one. You could probably get close to converting to a fuel injection setup with the money you'll spend on an NOS Q-jet in the factory box.

If you intend to keep your Q-jet around, I recommend picking up a copy of Cliff Ruggles's *How to Rebuild and Modify Rochester Quadrajet Carburetors*. This applies to both mild street builds and hairy drag machines—the Q-jet can be set up to excel at both tasks.

Edelbrock AFB

The Edelbrock AFB is a fantastic all-around carburetor with great adjustability, and a main plus here is a lack of gaskets below the fuel level. That means less engine intake

fuel staining. They offer a lot of the same benefits of the Q-jet in a simpler, easier-to-tune package. The only downside here, at least on a C10 that had a Q-jet, is the need for an adapter to run one, as these are square-bore carbs versus the Q-jet's spread-bore design. If you don't mind having an adapter plate on top of your engine, swapping over is easy, although it's not especially attractive. Swapping the intake manifold to a square-bore aluminum unit is a good solution to that problem. Both Holley and Edelbrock are the market leaders when it comes to intake manifolds.

Holley

Holley is the gold standard for carburetor performance and has been for decades. In fact, most of the specialized carburetor tuning shops

that build high-end race carburetors still use the Holley 4150 and 4500 designs as a basis for their creations.

Holley offers a number of great carbs for everything from street vehicles through 8-second drag machines. The Avenger series is a good choice for a street truck—easy to tune, great power delivery, and a wider range of tuning options than the Edelbrock.

For racing engines, a 4150-style Holley HP is the way to go, as they offer tunable air bleeds and much more adjustability than you'll get with a street carburetor. They do, however, tend to run rich on the street, and they don't have provisions for chokes, which can be a deal-breaker if you're planning to do mostly street driving.

Along those lines, it's important to remember that smaller carbs can deliver more bang for the buck in most situations. Being conservative on CFM size will make for a better experience, especially if street driving is the primary concern. The smaller venturi size speeds up flow through the carb, making it more responsive to tuning, and therefore a better, more-usable unit for your average end-user.

A 600 or 650 is just right for a stock or mildly modified street-driven 350. Anything bigger is just going to waste fuel and make tuning more challenging—unless you're running some large cylinder heads, a lot of compression, and a large camshaft.

Fuel Injection

The next step for an old-school 350 is a fuel injection system. Many aftermarket companies now have bolt-on self-learning systems that take all the guesswork out of adding fuel injection to an older engine—and they work very, very well. Yes,

---

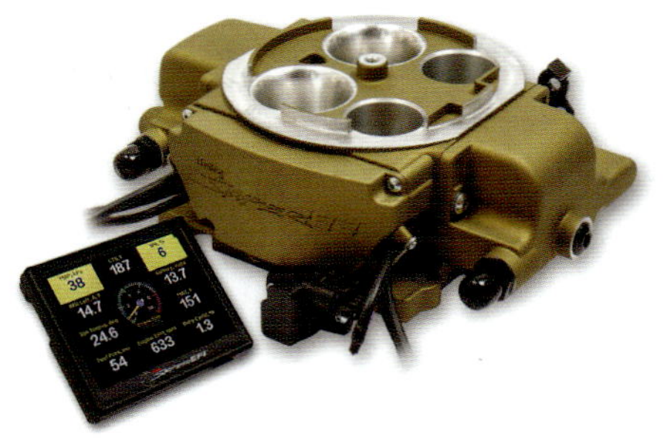

Holley's Sniper Q-jet electric fuel injection (EFI) is perfect for C10 builders who want the stock look. As a spread-bore design, it will bolt right up to your factory C10 intake manifold without spacers or adapters. Plumb in the fuel system, add a few sensors, connect a few wires, and your C10 will run much more like a modern Silverado. Plus, it's self-tuning, so you don't have to know how to adjust fuel maps to make it run. This system supports up to 500 hp. (Photo Courtesy Holley)

There are thousands of cam designs available for a small-block Chevrolet, each of which can really change how your engine behaves. But note that a cam with a lot of lift and duration won't help if you're running a low static compression and restrictive heads, as most of the square GM trucks did. This is Summit's part number 1103, which has 288/298 degrees of duration and a 0.444/0.466 lift. This cam has a smooth idle and creates enough vacuum for power brakes, but it would be best in an engine making more than 9.0:1 compression. (Photo Courtesy Summit Racing)

they're more expensive than a carburetor, as they require an electric control unit (ECU), wiring, and a new fuel system, but they're really worth every penny of their purchase price, as well as all the time it takes to properly install one.

Benefits include easier use when cold (no more choke, no warm-up time needed), better economy, more power, and no flooding at startup. Installation of all of these systems is simple if time-intensive, and they really do transform the drivability of a classic pickup. If a full engine build or swap isn't in the budget, this is a really smart thing to look into. It will transform the drivability of your LS9 350 and give you better economy with it as well.

Camshafts

The heart of your engine is its cam, and if you still have an original in your engine, it probably has a flat lobe or two.

GM ran through a batch of soft cams in the 1970s, and modern oils with limited zinc content have caused a lot of flat-tappet engines to start chewing themselves up. So, swapping a cam is a good idea in your C10—there are some fantastic cam profiles out there today that won't impact emissions while making better power than your stocker would have had on its first day of operation.

Custom cam grinds are available if you really want to get technical, but off-the-shelf grinds are also well suited to C10 owners who want a little more power from their engines. The key here, again following the model of streetable performance, is to keep duration relatively mild for good traffic manners—and to keep in mind that huge lift will also require valvetrain modifications so the parts will live a long life.

But, as there are so many factors that come into play when selecting a cam, all the way from transmission type to rear gear ratio, the best bet is to contact Comp Cams, Crane, Lunati, Edelbrock, or Crower with your specific needs and let them suggest a profile that will work best for your rig. They can also source all the related components, including new lifters, a new timing set, new pushrods, and any valvetrain com-

ponents such as valve springs that are required to match the new cam profile.

Electronic Ignition

This really only applies to trucks from 1973 and 1974, as by 1975, GM's High Energy Ignition (HEI) system became standard in pickups.

The HEI is a direct swap into any 350, and it offers quicker starts, better fuel burn, and less required maintenance than the earlier breaker points style distributors.

Later HEIs suffered from limited advance curves due to those strangling emissions regulations of the late 1970s, but that can be cured with a spring kit and different advance weights to bring on more ignition advance a little quicker. The benefit of that is more seat-of-the-pants power delivery.

The idea is to get all your centrifugal advance in by 3,000 rpm; big- and small-block Chevrolets with performance cams typically like around 36 degrees total as a starting point. The larger your cam, the more advance you'll likely need to run at idle to make it behave. Some builders run as much as 22 degrees or more, which helps with vacuum signal (and therefore carburetor tuning) at idle with a large-duration cam. That can be tough to achieve with a stock

Your square truck almost certainly has an HEI ignition, which controls your engine's advance curve with a set of centrifugal weights and springs—but stockers aren't set up for performance. This is MSD's Pro-Billet version, which offers increased spark energy and the ability to fine-tune advance timing thanks to positive stops for the advance weights. If you run a large-duration cam that needs more advance at idle, say up to 21 or 22 degrees while keeping total at 36, this is what you need to achieve that idle without overshooting your total advance. (Image Courtesy MSD)

HEI, but units from companies such as MSD offer advance stop bushings that can help dial in a high initial advance and a total of 36 degrees.

LS Swaps

The 350 and 454 are great engines, but the LS family of engines is better. You simply can't beat the drivability, power, and economy the LS brings to the table, which is why LS swaps are now so common in squarebody C10s—or really anything these days.

GM has built millions of LS-series engines since the first 1997 Corvette, and as such, LS engines are common, and they respond extremely well to aftermarket modification, tuning, and power adders. If you're looking to build a great-driving C10, an LS swap should be your goal.

Selecting an LS

When hunting for an LS, you'll find three common versions: the 4.8, 5.3, and 6.0. All three of these engines were used in Chevrolet and GMC trucks starting in 1999, and as such, there are a lot of them out there in wrecking yards and on Craigslist. All of them can be built to make good power, and as iron-block truck engines, they're the most inexpensive of the bunch. But there were a number of versions of each, and they are by no means the only LS options available to you.

Junkyard LS Engine Spotter's Guide								
Displacement	Name	Years	Vehicles	VIN Code	Block	Heads	Horsepower	Additional Information
4.8L	LR4	1999–2007	Chevrolet/GMC vans, 1500 trucks, Chevrolet Tahoe, GMC Yukon	V	cast iron	aluminum	255 (1999), 270–285 (after 1999)	—
4.8L	LY2	2007–2009	Chevrolet/GMC vans, Chevrolet Suburban, GMC Yukon	C	cast iron	aluminum	260–295	This is the only Gen IV truck engine without variable valve timing
4.8L	L20	2010–2017	Chevrolet/GMC trucks and vans	A	cast iron	aluminum	260–302	—
5.3L	LM7/L59	1999–2007	Chevrolet/GMC 1500 trucks; Chevrolet Avalanche, Suburban, and Tahoe; GMC Yukon	T	cast iron	aluminum	270–295	—
5.3L	LM4	2003–2005	Chevrolet TrailBlazer and SSR; Isuzu Ascender, Buick Envoy XL and Rainier	P	aluminum	aluminum	290	—
5.3L	L33	2005–2007	Chevrolet/GMC trucks	B	aluminum	aluminum	310	—
5.3L	LMF	2010–2014	Chevrolet/GMC trucks and vans with AWD and 4-speed transmission	4	cast iron	aluminum	301	No active fuel management
5.3L	LH6	2005–2009	Chevrolet/GMC trucks, Chevrolet TrailBlazer and TrailBlazer EXT, GMC Envoy XL and Envoy Denali, Buick Rainier, Isuzu Ascender; Saab 9-7X 5.3i	M	aluminum	aluminum	302–315	—
5.3L	LY5	2007–2009	Chevrolet/GMC trucks, Chevrolet Avalanche and Suburban, GMC Tahoe	J	cast iron	aluminum	315–320	LMG is a Flex Fuel–capable version (VIN code "0")

Junkyard LS Engine Spotter's Guide								
Displace-ment	Name	Years	Vehicles	VIN Code	Block	Heads	Horsepower	Additional Information
5.3L	LC9	2007–2014	Chevrolet/GMC trucks, Chevrolet Avalanche and Suburban, GMC Yukon	3 (2007–2011), 7 (2012–2014)	aluminum	aluminum	302–315	—
5.3L	LH8	2008–2010	Chevrolet Colorado, GMC Canyon, Hummer H3 Alpha	L	aluminum	aluminum	300	LH9 is a variant with variable valve timing (VIN code "P")
5.7L	LS1	1997–2005	Chevrolet Corvette and Camaro, Pontiac Firebird and GTO	G	aluminum	aluminum	305–325	—
5.7L	LS6	1999–2004	Chevrolet Corvette Z06	S	aluminum	aluminum	385–405	—
6.0L	LQ4	1999–2007	Chevrolet/GMC 2500 and 3500 trucks, Chevrolet Express van and Suburban, GMC Yukon, Hummer H2	U	cast iron (1999–2000), long-style crank (2001+)	cast iron (1999–2000), aluminum (2001+)	300–330	—
6.0L	LQ9	2002–2007	Chevrolet Silverado SS, HO, and VotecMAX trucks; Cadillac Escalade	N	cast iron	aluminum	345	—
6.0L	LS2	2005–2009	Chevrolet Corvette and TrailBlazer SS, Pontiac GTO, Saab 9-7X Aero	U	aluminum	aluminum	400	—
6.0L	L76	2006–2009	Chevrolet/GMC trucks, Pontiac G8 GXP	Y	aluminum	aluminum	355/367	L77 is a Flex Fuel version offered in Holden-sourced Chevrolet Caprice police cars (VIN code "2")
6.0L	LY6	2007–2013	Chevrolet/GMC HD trucks, Chevrolet Suburban and GMC Yukon 3/4-ton trucks	K	cast iron	aluminum	361	Similar to LQ4 specs with variable valve timing and rectangle-port heads; L96 is identical other than Flex Fuel capability
6.0L	LFA	2008–2009	Chevrolet/GMC pickups, Chevrolet Suburban hybrid	5	aluminum	aluminum	332	LZ1 is an upgraded version with Active Fuel Management and variable valve timing (VIN code "J")
6.2L	L92	2007–2008	Chevrolet Tahoe LTZ, GMC 1500 Sierra Denali and Yukon Denali, Cadillac Escalade	8	aluminum	aluminum (rectangle port)	403	L9H is Flex Fuel capable (VIN code "2")
6.2L	LS3	2008–2017	Chevrolet Corvette, SS, and Camaro SS (manual); Pontiac G8 GXP	W	aluminum	aluminum (rectangle port)	426–436	—
6.2L	L99	2010–2015	Chevrolet Camaro SS (automatic)	J	aluminum	aluminum (rectangle port)	400	—
6.2L	LS9	2009–2013	Chevrolet Corvette ZR1	T	aluminum	aluminum (rectangle port)	638	supercharged
6.2L	LSA	2009–2015	Chevrolet Camaro ZL1, Cadillac CTS-V	P	aluminum	aluminum (rectangle port)	556–580	supercharged
7.0L	LS7	2006–2015	Chevrolet Corvette Z06	E	aluminum	aluminum	505	dry-sump oiling

If you shop around long enough, you can find a great deal on an LS engine. GM built millions of trucks, vans and SUVs with LS V-8s. This 6.0 LQ4 had some needs, but it was complete and only cost me $400 as a core engine. That's cheap, but it's what you can expect to find if you hunt around. Be sure to watch Craigslist, and check your local wrecking yards too.

The most common LS in today's wrecking yards is the 5.3, as there were a bunch of variants of it. One of the most popular engines for performance build-ups is the 6.0 found in trucks, again made in a few versions with different parts over the years.

Any of these LS engines are good candidates to swap into a squarebody C10, as they share the same basic external dimensions and all make good power relative to their size and weight.

Obviously, the bigger the bore and stroke, the more power potential you'll have, but you'd probably find that a stock 4.8 with the right gearing will be more drivable (and even offer more usable power) than a stock smogger-era LE8 454 in a 1973–1987 C10. Seems like blasphemy, doesn't it? But it's true.

Look for low-miles versions out of wrecked rigs, and plan to budget anywhere from $500 to $2,000 for a sub-100,000-mile truck unit, depending on which engine it is and where you're located. All the normal checks apply here: look for oil consumption on the plugs that suggests worn rings or valve seals, and avoid any engine that doesn't come with some sort of guarantee unless you intend to do a full rebuild yourself. If so, pay less: you're buying a core engine.

Prepping an LS for Installation

So you have a C10 and a bone-stock, likely high-mileage LS motor that needs to go in it. Before you get excited and slam that engine in the truck, now's the time to make a few changes.

LS engines are fantastic performers from the factory, but they really react well to camshaft upgrades, cylinder head swaps, and other performance tricks. Now's the time to do these things, before your fenders get in the way.

Building a 6.0L LQ4 Street Terror

The plan for the truck I built was to give it a high cool factor while also making it the best street driver possible. Sufficient power is a big key to both fun and safety—somewhere between 400 and 450 hp is perfect for a truck like this. To keep things simple, this engine is to be naturally aspirated and will be fed pump-sourced premium fuel.

To that end, I bought a 6.0 LQ4 out of a 2003 GMC truck. It had, at some point, lost oil pressure due to a bad oil pump, which took out the bottom end and the cam bearings at a reported 80,000 miles. This kind of thing wasn't uncommon, and it isn't that hard to fix. Here's what I did:

Building an LS Engine

1 This LQ4 was complete when I acquired it, and a quick teardown showed good cylinder bores and not too much grime. The reported 80,000 miles is believable. This is what you might expect to find in a junkyard LS—they'll typically come complete with an intake and all the proper front drive components, such as an alternator and water pump.

3 I took the engine to Wilson's Cylinder Head in Beaverton, Oregon, and had the block tanked, cleaned, and honed, with new cam bearings installed. The shop also resurfaced the crank and hung new Summit Racing–sourced flat-top LQ9-spec pistons on the factory rods in place of the factory dished LQ4 units. These are Speed-Pro hypereutectic pistons (part number H1129CPA) for stock 4-inch bore.

5 The LQ4 came with 317 truck heads, which are said to flow as well as the 243 heads used on Corvette LS6 engines. But 317s have a bigger 72-cc combustion chamber that works with the factory LQ4 dished piston to build a truck-friendly 9.4:1 compression ratio. I chose to swap my 317s for a set of 799 heads, which were used on some later 5.3s and many performance LS2 6.0s. 799s have a smaller 64-cc chamber and are functionally identical to the 243 castings. They boost compression in conjunction with those flat-top pistons—somewhere close to 11:1 in my case. The cleaned-up 799 is on the left, compared to the 317 on the right.

2 That said, looks can be deceiving. This engine ran for some time with no oil pressure, so I needed to tear it apart—hence the core price. Note the scoring in the crank. The main, rod, and cam bearings are all toast, as is the crankshaft surface.

4 For LS engine assembly, you'll need to have a good torque wrench that will read in degrees as well as ft-lbs. LS engines use a number of torque-to-yield fasteners that need to be turned a set number of degrees in addition to a ft-lb rating. Here I'm torquing the rod bolts: 15 ft-lbs on the first pass, then another 75 degrees, as per factory spec.

6 *I originally reassembled this engine with a 2002–2004 LS6 cam. With a duration of 204/218 at 0.050 and 0.551/0.547 lift on a 117.5-degree lobe separation angle, the LS6 cam is a good performance option that also offers a smooth idle. It's a good choice for a street-driven truck that's aiming for LS6 (405 hp) power levels and off-idle drivability with a 6-speed manual. LS truck cams are ground on a large base circle, while the car cams are on a smaller circle, which means you'll need longer pushrods with the car cam. How much longer depends on the components you use.*

7 *The cam retainer plate goes on after the cam, and that, along with the upper timing chain sprocket, keeps the cam from walking back and forth in the engine. Torque spec on the plate bolts is 18 ft-lbs.*

8 *A steel roller timing chain is next, again sourced from Summit Racing. Even with just 80,000 miles on the original unit, it's smart to replace this with an upgraded unit while the engine is apart. Here's a quick tip: mark the gear either with a scribe or a dab of paint above where the oil pump mounts because you can't see the lower gear timing mark with the oil pump installed. This is useful for cam swaps later on.*

9 *Next is the component that killed this 6.0: the oil pump. This is a new Summit Racing pump, which actually has a Melling part number cast into it. I've removed the cover here and am using six shims to center the pump on the crankshaft, an important step for the longevity of the pump. Six 0.002 shims center the gears relative to the crankshaft. Then you can tighten the mount bolts to 18 ft-lbs and remove the shims.*

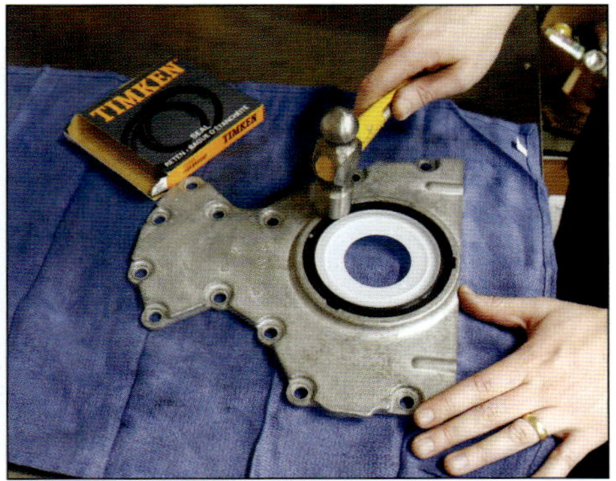

10 *It's also wise to replace both the rear main seal and the front cover seals while the engine is apart— this is the rear main, which taps into place in the rear cover. If you look closely, there's a marking in the rubber seal that shows which way it goes. The plastic center piece is the installation tool, which keeps the seal surface from being damaged as you push it over the crank. The front cover needs to index off the harmonic balancer, so don't tighten its mounting bolts until the balancer is pressed on the crank snout.*

11 *In an LS engine, the lifters install under the cylinder heads—which is reason enough to install a new set, as any problems later mean pulling the heads. Summit Racing sells new LS7 lifters in a set for under $200 (part number NAL-12499225), which is cheap insurance. Then the heads can be installed and torqued to spec using new head bolts. Specs are 22 ft-lbs first in sequence, then 90 degrees, and then another 90 degrees (excluding the shorter bolts at the front and back of each head, which need 50 degrees). The smaller, upper head bolts get torqued to 22 ft-lbs.*

13 *If you're looking to paint your engine, now's a good time to do it. I chose GM blue—the same color the 350 in this C10 was originally, as it'll look at home under the 1979's hood. Now the basic long-block is complete and ready for installation.*

12 *With the new gasket behind the cover and two bolts loosely installed to line everything up, the rear cover just slides on with a careful push. Then install and torque the cover bolts to 22 ft-lbs.*

Performance Upgrade Selection

The sky is the limit on power production with an LS. It really just comes down to your budget and your plan for the pickup. A truck that's going to tow is going to need vastly different parts than a drag strip rig. This is why that plan you made when you started is so important—it will direct you to the right parts to suit your goals.

LS Power Modifications

LS engines took pushrod engines to a new level, and the stout LS bottom end design means they tend to live even when taken to silly power levels.

LS engines can be turbocharged and supercharged into four-figure horsepower levels with some bottom-end modifications, such as forged pistons, H-beam rods and quality rod bolts, and upgraded cranks. Some racers have run big boost on stock internals with no problems: 700-hp levels are common on boosted but otherwise-stock engines. The key to that is all in the tuning of the system and control over detonation.

Swapping a cam in an LS is much easier than in a traditional small-block. The hardest part is selecting which cam to use; for that, it's best to consult with a professional and cover all the details of your build, as it all factors into cam selection. But if you're working over a stock LS that's otherwise complete, and a total teardown isn't in the cards, you can do just a cam swap easily.

Here, I practiced what I preach and called Lingenfelter Performance Engineering (LPE) in Brighton, Michigan.

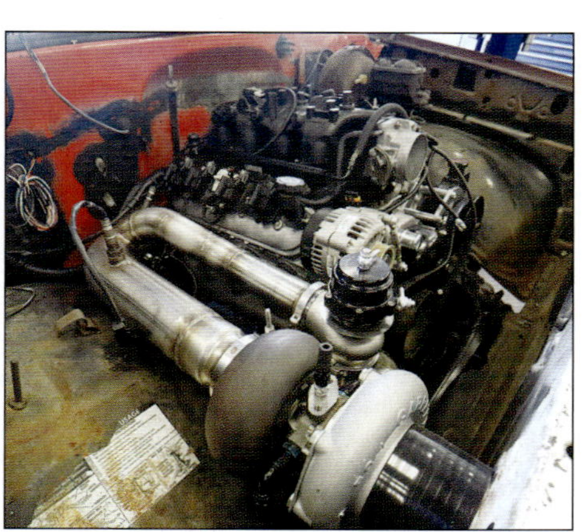

If you're looking to make use of the LS engine's massive power potential, forced induction is the way to do it. This is a 5.3 LS mated to a Garrett turbo via a set of Hooker cast-iron turbo manifolds and a custom wastegate. The engine is basically stock, but it will live under boost if run with the proper fuel injectors and a custom tune. There's plenty of room under a squarebody hood for this type of setup.

LPE has been building hot LS engines since GM introduced them in 1997. It has come up with a number of hot cams for LS applications, ranging from mild to wild, and as such, LPE is a great source of information for builders looking for something both powerful and usable in a street application. Many of Lingenfelter's builds are modern, computer-controlled emissions-compliant vehicles, which is just the ticket for a truck that is going to see street use on a regular basis.

Taking into account the cubic-inch rating, cylinder heads, induction and exhaust systems planned, and the 6-speed manual drivetrain with a 4.11:1 rear gear ratio, the Lingenfelter team recommended its GT11 cam for my build.

The GT11 is a Lingenfelter-designed hydraulic roller cam ground by Comp Cams. It has 0.631/0.644 inch of lift and is ground on a 118-degree centerline for low overlap and a smooth idle. It has 215/231 degrees of duration at 0.050. While it seems like a huge cam based on lift alone, the wide centerline and relatively tame duration give it a good, nearly stock idle with fantastic power production—just the thing for extended stoplight idling as well as freeway ramp light fun.

The only downside to a cam like this is in valvetrain control, as GM's best OEM beehive valve springs won't hold up to that kind of lift for long. Fortunately, LPE has that covered as well with its dual valve spring kit (part number L230075897).

Five LS Tips from Mark Rapson, COO and VP of Operations for Lingenfelter Performance Engineering

Q: What LS modifications offer the most bang for the buck over stock, and in what order should they be done?

MR: The LS platform is ideal for any type of aftermarket upgrade. Our approach has always been to understand what the owner has in mind and how they will use the car to determine the package for their investment. Generally, the best power gain for the money is with forced induction. Superchargers, for example, integrate seamlessly within car and truck platforms, typically adding from 100 to 200 or more horsepower over stock numbers while retaining original equipment drivability.

For those who prefer traditional hot-rodding upgrades, replacing the camshaft, cylinder head porting, aftermarket intake manifold, and exhaust system is the recommended package.

Q: What should buyers look for in cam and head selection for a street car/truck?

MR: When looking into cam and head packages, it's important to match components with the overall motor and drivetrain configuration along with drivability requirements. The biggest mistake people make is believing the marketing hype that bigger is better.

Camshaft lift/duration, lobe center, and timing are determined based on the engine displacement, compression ratio, type of transmission, weight of the vehicle, and final-drive ratio. This also directly translates into the type of cylinder head modifications. The stock LS GM head castings are generally good up to about 500–550 hp. To make additional power with more aggressive cams will then require CNC porting or aftermarket castings.

Q: When should forged internals be considered?

MR: This is very usage dependent, but the general rule is that anything over 550 hp should consider upgrading, particularly if the vehicle is road-raced or autocrossed. There are stock bottom-end drag racing classes with people making big Horsepower numbers, but the engines are very short lived. The rods and pistons are the weakest link.

Q: Are there any factory LS weak links that should be corrected before installation?

MR: There are no major design issues. The cast pistons and powdered metal rods are a weak link when boosting horsepower along with cranks. Change to stronger units for bigger power outputs. The rocker arm trunnion bearings should be upgraded with a bigger cam and heavier valve springs. LS7 heads have had some valve guide–related issues, but those can be corrected by having the valve seats properly aligned with the valve seats.

Q: What benefits do the newer LT engines have over the LS in terms of power production? Is it a better idea, from a power standpoint, to look for an LT instead of an LS?

MR: The LS/LT platforms are very similar in architecture—particularly in the short-block. Although they continue to use cast pistons and powdered metal rods in the LT1, they are stronger than LS. LT4 has a steel crank, forged pistons, and heavier rods.

The biggest difference is in the heads and fuel system. The LT motors are direct injected (fuel is sprayed directly into the cylinder under very high pressure) versus port injection (fuel sprayed into the intake runner at low pressure) in the LS, which gives the LT improved combustion efficiency, allowing more power with fewer emissions and better fuel economy.

Because of the complexity related to the fuel system and calibration requirements, the LT is not as flexible of a platform for hot rodders. Our experience to date is that when the LT fuel system is properly configured, it is the preferred platform for power. ∎

Swapping a Performance Camshaft in an LS Engine

1 The GT11 and dual valve spring kit is well built with all the springs, spring seats, keepers, seals, and titanium retainers you need to handle the conversion.

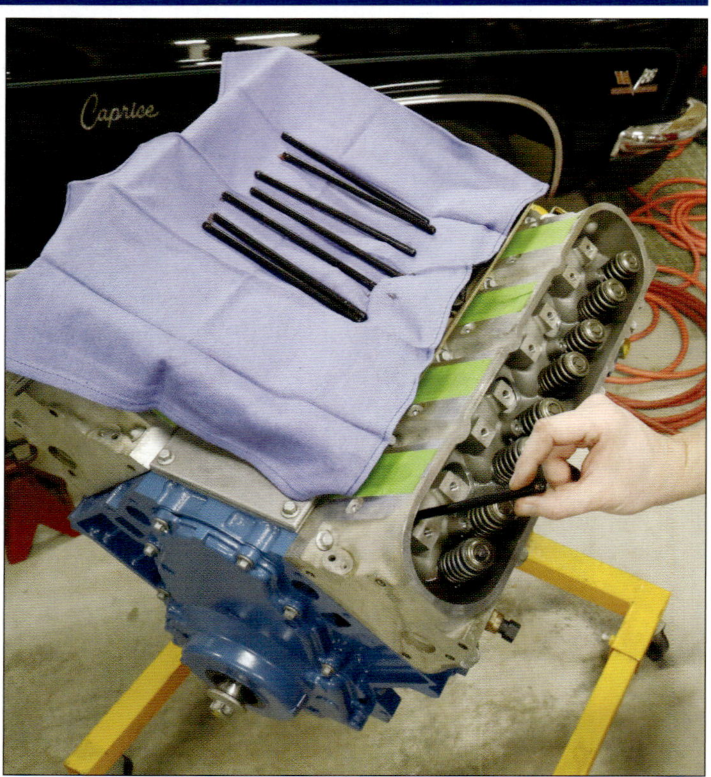

2 With the balancer, water pump, and rocker arms removed, pull the pushrods out of the way to prep for spring replacement.

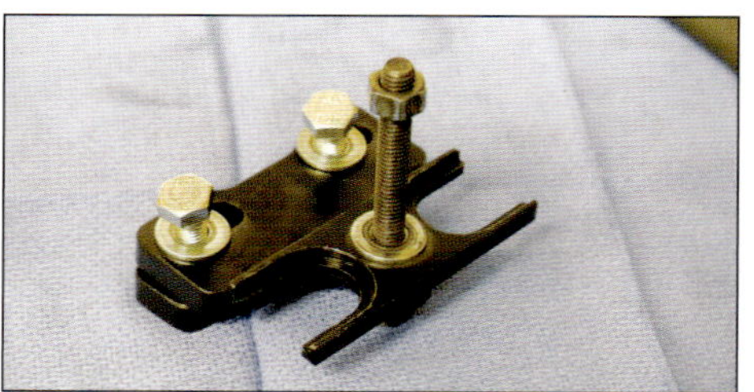

3 You don't need to pull the heads to replace the springs. Several companies offer slick tools like this one that allow you to replace both springs on a cylinder at once. This tool is from www.bluegrassperformance.com. It bolts to the cylinder head and compresses two springs at a time using a plate on a threaded rod.

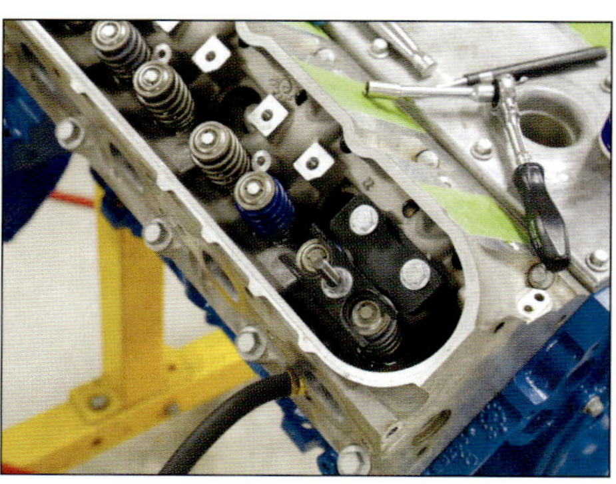

4 If installing new valve springs with the cylinder head installed, you need to use compressed air to hold the valves in their seats while you disassemble the springs. But you don't need a fancy special tool for this—it just so happens that LS spark plugs are the same size and thread pitch as most air compressor fittings, so it's likely that your air lines will thread right into the cylinder. I used a short section of air line with a disconnect at the end and Teflon tape to seal the threads. 90 psi ensures the valves won't move. Then you can install the tool and begin removing springs.

5 With the tool tightened to the head and the springs compressed, you can use a magnet to remove the locks. Then loosening the spring tool frees the springs.

6 *The new spring kit comes with new valve seals for an important reason: the factory-style seals interfere with the new inner spring, keeping it from seating fully. A light twist with a pair of pliers frees the OEM seals.*

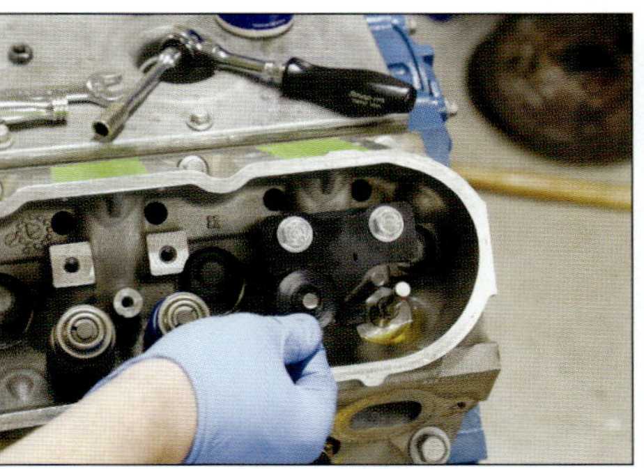

7 *With the seals out of the way, the new seats can be dropped into place over each valve, followed by the new valve seals. A special installation tool works best on seals, but in a pinch you can use a deep-set 12-mm 12-point socket set over the seal and tap them into place with a rubber mallet.*

8 *After that, the new springs are next, including the new retainers. Tighten the tool, install the new keepers, and then loosen the tool. That's all there is to it—but there are seven more cylinders to do.*

9 *After reinstalling the pushrods, the front cover can come off, exposing the timing gear. Rotate the engine until it's at top dead center with the timing marks pointing at each other. Then remove the three bolts holding the upper cam gear.*

10 *With the gear out of the way and the chain set aside where it won't fall into the pan, the cam retaining plate can be removed to get to the cam itself.*

11 *The LS cam is hollow, so a long 3/8-inch ratchet extension or long screwdriver can be inserted into it, giving you something to use to help guide the cam out. But before you pull the cam out, it needs to be rotated 360 degrees while you watch the pushrods. By design, the LS lifters are retained by plastic keepers, and with the rocker arms removed, rotating the cam will cause them all to move up and stay up out of the way of the cam so you can remove it. The pushrods tell you if any lifters are still in the down position. If they're all up, the cam can slide out.*

12 *The new cam goes in just as easy with assembly lube on the cam bearing surfaces applied as you go. It's also smart to cover the lobes with a thin application of assembly lube as well. Again, a long extension inserted inside the cam can help you avoid nicking the bearings with the newer, beefier lobes as you slide in the cam.*

13 *With the cam retainer plate in place, the chain and sprocket can be reinstalled, being careful to align the two timing marks on the gears. The cam bolts should get a quick dab of threadlocker with a torque of 26 ft-lbs. Before reinstalling the cover, it's best to check the cam's installed specs against the cam card with a degree wheel, piston stop, and dial indicator.*

14 *Longer pushrods are required when swapping from a truck cam. A pushrod length checker is key here, as it will allow you to adjust pushrod length to find zero lash, and then you can do some math to figure out how much lifter preload you wish to run. Since LS engines are "net lash," adjustments are made in pushrod length only, as opposed to a traditional small-block, which features adjustable rockers.*

15 *Roll the engine over to ensure the lifter is on the base circle of the cam. When the exhaust valve starts to open, the intake of that cylinder is on the base circle. As the intake starts to close, the exhaust is on the base circle. Then simply install the adjustable pushrod and the rocker arm on that valve. Tighten the bolt until it bottoms and adjust the pushrod length to zero lash (no play up and down). Remove the pushrod, measure it, and add in the amount of preload you'd like to run. Recommendations vary from 0.050 to 0.100 of preload for best results with LS7 lifters. These pushrods ended up at 7.425 inches to achieve 0.100 preload at the lifter.*

16 *The final step, once you're satisfied with the degree readings, is to torque the rocker arms to 22 ft-lbs, then reinstall all the remaining removed components.*

INSTALLING AN *LS* ENGINE IN A *C10*

Now you have a C10 and a prepped later-model LS engine. How do you put them together and make it all work?

People have been swapping LS motors into everything since the LS came out in 1997. Over those 22 years, the aftermarket has woken up to the need for easy swaps, and fortunately for C10 owners, we have a lot of room under our hoods, which makes this whole process that much easier.

Many aftermarket companies make all the mounts you'll need to make an LS at home under that wide, flat C10 hood, but this is one area where it does pay to plan ahead and buy the all the parts you'll need from one source. Why? Because a system that's designed to work together— motor mounts, transmission mount, etc.—will get your LS situated where the transmission, exhaust system, and front drive components all play nice with the C10's body. Swapping LS engines into C10s isn't a new science, and it pays to make use of some of the well-engineered kits out there because they'll make your swap cleaner and your conversion less complicated.

You can piecemeal your way into a successful swap, or you can source parts that are known to work together already. Either way, getting that LS into your C10's engine bay has never been easier.

Oil Pans

Before you get busy with your engine hoist, there are a few fundamentals to tackle. To start, you'll need a different oil pan, as the LS pans— especially the truck pans—are deep units that tend to hang down too low in two-wheel-drive C10 applications. F-Body pans, such as what you'll find in an LS Camaro or Firebird, interfere with the C10's crossmember location. Junkyard truck parts won't work in a two-wheel-drive application, unless you're at a stock height—even then, the factory 4.8, 5.3, or 6.0 pan will probably hang down too low for comfort. Smacking that pan on a speedbump will ruin more than just your day.

GM's standard LS truck oil pan is a tall unit, which is fine in a stock late-model rig but isn't so great in your two-wheel-drive C10—especially if it's lowered. LS engine pans are cast aluminum, which doesn't respond well to impact. You may or may not have clearance issues with a pan like this in you rig, but it's smart to consider your options before attempting to mount this in your truck. Trying to swap this out later with the engine in the truck will be a challenge. The time to swap it is before you install an LS in your C10.

Holley's part number VK090000 is a complete oil pan conversion kit. It includes Holley's 302-1 oil pan, which is much shorter than the stock truck pan, as well as the proper oil pump pickup, internal baffle, pan gasket, mounting hardware, and gasket maker to seal the corners of the pan to the front and rear corners of the engine block. This pan fits the C10 chassis well, but if you're concerned about clearance, part number VK090001 has increased front clearance at the crossmember under the front of the engine. When installed, the crossmember becomes the lowest point in the front of the truck—perfect for running coilovers or air suspension.

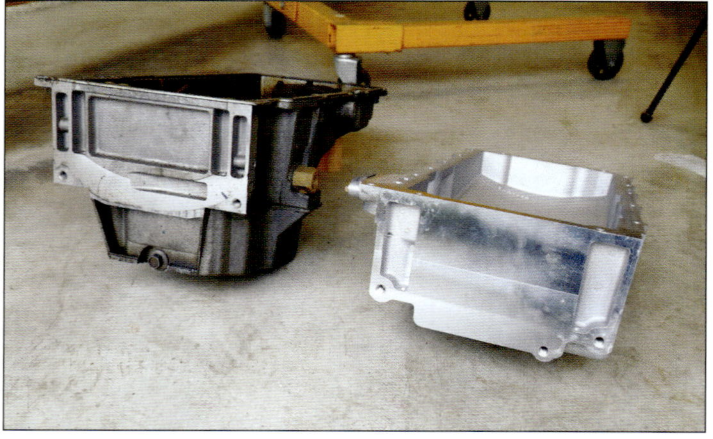

How much of a difference is there between the OEM pan and the Holley unit? About 4 inches of clearance, which is huge. Both pans are cast aluminum and are very thick—they're structural on LS engines, as you can see with the threaded holes at the rear of each pan, used by certain transmission applications.

With that, the oil pan bolts into place using the supplied hardware from the Holley kit. On this LS, one bolt hole was blind, so I ended up with one extra bolt leftover. This view also gives a good look at the stock LS engine mount location, which isn't the same as a Gen I or II small-block.

The factory windage tray installs first, followed by the new oil pump pickup tube and O-ring. In some applications, you may need to trim the steel windage tray to make clearance for the oil pump pickup tube. On this 6.0L, that wasn't required—but I did need to notch the tray at the mounting stud of the pickup so it would sit flat when torqued down. The gasket that comes with the kit is a nice metal-core Mr. Gasket unit. Be sure to place a dab of gasket maker at each of the four corners of the block's sealing surface before setting the gasket in place. This is to fill in any irregularities and stop potential oil leaks where the front and rear covers bolt to the engine.

There are several solutions to this problem, but unfortunately they all require you to buy a different oil pan.

One option is to source a pan from a Cadillac CTS-V (GM part number 12631828), which is only about 5½ inches tall compared to a stock truck pan's 8½-inch height. If your truck is lowered, like my subject truck, this is an especially important consideration because you don't want the oil pan anywhere near the ground. The chances of finding one used are pretty slim, but it's possible. Otherwise you'll need to source one from GM, and you'll need to also be sure to get the proper dipstick tube and stick to go with the pan—not to mention the proper oil pump pickup tube, as that is unique to the CTS-V pan.

A better option is Holley's part number 302-1 or 302-2 oil pan. These are complete units that tuck up nicely to the engine while retaining a good 5.5- and 5.7-quart oil capacity. They're thick aluminum castings just like the original LS pans but with a much cleaner look and way more clearance for dropped vehicles. Either pan will work in a C10 application, but 302-2 has increased front clearance at the crossmember. Both are available as complete kits with an OEM-style pan gasket, the proper oil pickup tube, the required bolts for installation, and a tube of RTV to seal the corners of the oil pan where the engine's front and rear covers contact the engine block.

Engine Mounts

On an LS engine, the engine mount location is pushed farther back than it is on a Gen 1 small-block, like what would have come from the

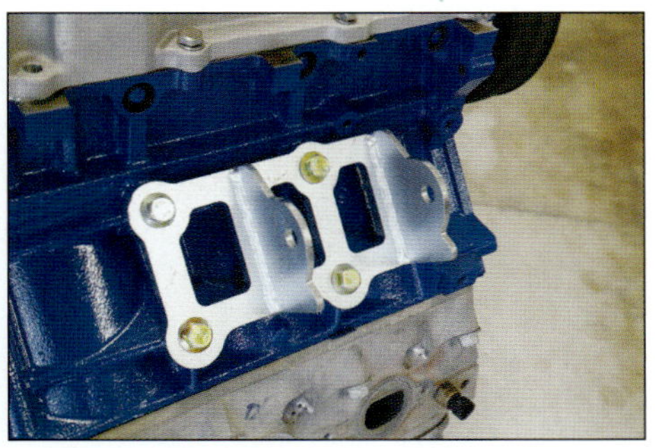

Hooker's Blackheart LS engine mounts (part number 12621HKR) work great in a 1973–1987 C10. They're made of thick 3/8-inch welded steel plate and bolt up to both the factory LS block and the original clamshell mounts on your C10's frame. They work well with the 302-1 Holley oil pan as well and were developed as part of a kit that makes LS swapping into two-wheel-drive C10 pickups simple.

factory in your C10. As such, you can't just use the SBC mounts with your LS—but there are a bunch of conversion mounts on the market today that can put your engine right where you need it to be. Holley, Summit Racing, Trans-Dapt, ICT Billet, Speedway, and Dirty Dingo all offer various engine and transmission mount solutions for LS swaps.

The LS engine shares most of its basic dimensions with the small-block that came before. The small-block is 26 inches wide, 28 inches long, and 27 inches tall. The only difference between those measurements and those of the LS is that the LS is 2 inches shorter at 25 inches tall.

Dirty Dingo is one of the more popular LS engine mount companies out there, and it offers slider mounts that allow you to move the engine forward, gaining up to 2 inches of clearance at the back of the block if needed.

Your mounts are the foundation of your swap, and it pays to know exactly what other parts you're going to be running when you choose which mounts to run. Where the engine is placed can affect a lot of other things, from exhaust system plumbing through firewall clearance. Additionally, if your truck is lowered, that also factors into where the engine and transmission need to go—and what kind of clearance you'll need around parts such as the oil pan.

Complete, engineered engine mount sets, such as the ones from Hooker's Blackheart line, have taken most of the guesswork out of locating the engine and transmission, and they work with the OEM-style clamshell engine mounts that GM used in

The benefit to using a complete, engineered kit for an engine swap is the turn-key nature of it. Hooker's Blackheart transmission crossmember works with the Hooker engine mounts as well as the Hooker headers for LS swaps in C10s. The crossmember uses high cutouts to allow for the exhaust to tuck up inside it, keeping it above the frame rail level for lowered trucks.

C10s of this era. They also work with Hooker's LS exhaust manifolds and long-tube headers, which removes a bunch of headaches down the road for builders who want a direct, bolt-in solution for their rig and are intending on running those parts as well.

If you're swapping from a 350/700R4 to an LS/4L60E, the Hooker mounts will allow you to use your factory shift linkage and driveline.

Fitting the Engine in the Truck

You'll need a couple of things for a successful engine swap, the most important one being an extra set of eyes and hands that you trust. Yes, you can install an engine alone, but it's a lot easier when someone else is there to help watch as things go together, and to help jostle things around if something's not fitting right.

Beyond that, you'll need a good

Once the engine is bolted in place, check for clearance issues, specifically at the oil pan and at the rear of the cylinder heads. You'll want to be sure there's clearance for the LS around everything, as that makes later work easier—say, if you need to pull the heads at a later date. You won't need to remove the engine from the truck to do so.

engine hoist, and some way to get your truck's frame high enough for the legs of the hoist to slide underneath it. Jack stands work well, but I'm a bigger fan of wide wood blocks or ramps under the truck's wheels because they won't be in the way of the engine hoist as it slides under the truck.

If you're installing your engine and transmission as one unit (as I did), having the truck up higher will help make this process easier because you'll need to come in at an extreme angle to allow the transmission and engine assembly to slide fairly far back into the truck before you can drop the assembly down and bolt the motor mounts in place.

A floor jack works great as a temporary (and adjustable) transmission mount to help get the proper angle for the engine-mount bolts to slide into place. Beyond that, all that's required here is to be careful, watch what you're doing to save your paint and your hands, and stop to address and fix any issues that pop up along the way.

Engine Accessories

Getting your engine installed in the truck is one hurdle, but it's certainly not the only one. You also need to figure out everything from your starter through your water pump, alternator, power steering, and A/C compressor.

The LS family came in a variety of vehicles, and assuming you've

There's really no quick and dirty method for engine installation, other than to have as much help available as possible, tools to gently pry and wiggle, and at least one floor jack to help with transmission alignment prior to installing the transmission crossmember. An adjustable engine plate really helps to get the angle of attack correct.

Holley's high-mount front drive kit (part number 20-138) is another option, which uses GM-style parts along with Holley's proprietary brackets to bring the alternator and A/C compressor up and away from the frame rails. This kit comes with a Sanden SD7 A/C compressor, Corvette Type II power steering pump, and CS130D alternator. When it's mounted in a C10, the Holley kit leaves plenty of room around each of the drive components and other items inside the engine compartment.

The stock GM truck drive kit is a good fit in a square C10, and it's probably the cheapest option because in many cases it will come with the donor engine you source. These were the same on trucks running the 4.8, 5.3, and 6.0 engines. The nice thing here is knowing exactly which replacement parts you'll need later on down the road—but this solution doesn't give you much clearance around the A/C compressor and frame in your classic C10. You'll likely need to notch the frame rail if you intend to run A/C.

sourced a complete engine with a complete drive kit, you may or may not be able to use it in the C10. While there is a lot of room under that truck hood, you may run into clearance issues on either side of the engine depending on which engine mounts you've decided to run.

That said, GM offered three different lengths of front drive kits on the LS engines based on harmonic balancer depth. Corvettes had the shortest, measuring in at 1½ inches from the face of the pulley to the crank bolt surface. Camaros and Fire-

TECH TIP

Making Power Steering Lines

The GM-style Saginaw Type II power steering pump is standard LS engine equipment, but you won't find an off-the-shelf pressure line that will fit both it and your factory Saginaw 708 steering box. To make these parts work together, you'll either have to use something custom made or get creative.

The pressure fitting on the Type II box is M16 x 1.5 with an O-ring seal, while the fitting on the factory 1973–1979 C10 power steering box is an 11/16-inch inverted flare.

If you'd like to save some cash, the best method is to source two power steering pressure lines: one from a 2001 Corvette and one from the year of truck you're building. Neither should be very expensive—I found each of them locally for under $10 each. You can then take both lines to a hydraulic hose shop and have something custom made using the two ends—a Corvette metric O-ring end at the pump and a C10 inverted flare end at the steering box with a swivel in the middle that will help with aligning each fitting.

A factory replacement return line for C10s is a cut-to-fit item, fixed to the reservoir hose barb with a clamp, so that will work on the Type II pump as well. ■

birds used one that was slightly longer at 2¼ inches, and trucks had the longest at 3 inches. If you intend to run a stock drive system, you'll need to be sure you have the right parts here, otherwise your belt alignment will be off—if you have an F-Body balancer, you'll need an F-Body water pump, and so on. Don't swap-meet source this unless you get the entire

kit and you know it will fit.

Adding to that complexity is the fact that some low-mount accessories, such as what came on Corvettes, can interfere with the C10's frame rail location—specifically the A/C compressor. Therefore, you might need to either notch the frame for clearance or change up that stock assembly to something aftermarket.

Again, that's dependent on what drive system you're using and which engine mounts you've selected.

GM's long truck drive kit, such as what came on most 4.8s, 5.3s, and 6.0s will work in a squarebody C10 without much fuss. But if you're running A/C, you'll need to do some clearance work to make the compressor fit. Considering how many trucks are in junkyards today, that's great. You should be able to find an LS truck drive setup easily, assuming your LS didn't already come with one.

If you'd rather go with a bolt-in aftermarket solution that solves any clearance issues, Holley has several designs that will work well with the C10, including both a mid-mount kit with a special water pump and a high-mount kit that's a lot more affordable and makes better use of the C10s ample underhood space.

Exhaust

Just as there are a bunch of engine-mount options out there for C10 owners, there are also a lot of exhaust manifold and header options as well, ranging from cast-iron stockers all the way through high-dollar

For those of you who don't want to make your own exhaust system, the final piece of the Hooker Blackheart line is the complete cat-back exhaust for a C10. This is a great setup for a static-drop truck that's running an axle flip out back, but a 4-link conversion may interfere with the over-axle pipes. This system utilizes an X-pipe for increased torque and tucks up nicely underneath the frame. It's also available in stainless. (Photo Courtesy Blane Burnett/Holley)

stainless long-tube headers. What you end up using here depends on your engine's intended power level and what you intend to do with the truck.

The factory LQ truck exhaust manifolds flow relatively well for cast-iron units, but fitting them in 1973–1987 C10s can be a challenge, depending on your exact engine placement. However, if you ask any 1998–2002 F-Body owner about long-tube headers and the gains they provide, you'll end up taking those factory manifolds right off your workbench and directly to the scrapyard. LS engines love long-tubes, especially when they've

been tuned for them—significant power gains aren't unheard of from the addition of headers and a tune to support them.

From the headers back, you have a lot of options for your C10 in terms of sound and flow—the best idea is to listen to as many systems as you can before you pick something for your truck. Every exhaust system sounds and performs differently depending on your engine's power output, manifold/header design, pipe size, crossover pipe style, muffler design and size, and type of tailpipe, so hearing what others have done is pretty important.

It's also important to remember that the shorter the system, typically the louder it will be. Nothing can make you hate a long-distance cruise more than a brain-rattling drone from a poorly chosen exhaust system. If you have an air suspension system and a 4-link, as I do in my project truck, clearance over the axle can be an issue when the truck is aired down, so that's something to take into consideration before choosing a system or designing something custom.

If you live in an emissions-testing county and have a truck built after

A good set of factory exhaust manifolds will do the job, but they have been known to crack after many heat cycles, and they're relatively restrictive. That said, it's hard to go wrong with the longevity of cast iron, especially in a daily driver. However, LS engines really perform when allowed to breathe, in terms of both intake and exhaust. There's plenty of room for a set of long-tube headers in a C10 chassis—and they'll last as long as cast iron if you source a set with a ceramic coating. Even a painted set of headers will last a long time if they're finished with a ceramic header paint before installation. This set is Hooker's part number 70101504-1HKR.

There's really nothing that should stop you from making your own custom exhaust system—or having one made at your local exhaust shop. C10s have a lot of room underneath them, so there's a lot you can do with regard to exhaust routing. It really just comes down to personal preference for noise level and tone, all of which can be tuned by the components selected. I used two universal 2½-inch U bends and three 4-foot-long sections of 2½-inch pipe from Summit Racing—along with a set of universal cats from Flowmaster and a couple of Summit-brand chambered mufflers. Installation is as simple as cutting the bends where needed and tacking them together with a welder, then following up with a complete weld to finish each joint. This system is 2½ inches in diameter.

1974, you'll likely need high-flow catalytic converters. While cats are never cheap, they don't impede flow the way they once did. Power loss is negligible with a modern set, so the only real downside here is in cost— but it's worth it if that's what it takes

to get a trouble-free DMV registration for your truck.

In some states, cat removal can be punished with steep fines, so be sure you know the rules where you live before you make a call on whether or not to include them in your own build. If your truck had them and you're in doubt about whether you should run them, buy a set and install them.

Intake Manifold Selection

The intake manifold is one of the more important aspects of an engine build, right up there with the camshaft and cylinder heads.

For the Gen 1 small-block Chevrolet, Mark IV big-block Chevrolet, or anything with a carburetor, there are really two fundamental designs: single plane and dual-plane. The rule of thumb is this: for lower-RPM torque and good off-idle response, a dual-plane is the ticket. It effectively splits the carburetor's feed into two different plenums with long runners, each feeding half the engine. There's less turbulence inside one of these intakes at lower RPM, so the carburetor simply works better at delivering atomized fuel evenly from idle up to about 5,500 rpm. Your factory C10 Q-jet intake is a dual-plane.

The single-plane isn't as responsive just off idle, but it makes more power at higher RPM because the turbulence created inside its single plenum helps to keep the fuel suspended in the incoming air as it enters each combustion chamber. If you're running at high RPM, say with a drag truck, you should consider a single-plane for more power output.

All of that applies only to carbureted engines—fuel injection is a completely different story because

The stock 6.0 truck intake features a long-runner design intended to build a bunch of torque for towing and hauling. In reality, its performance isn't far off what can be achieved with an LS6 Corvette intake—it's just not very attractive, and for some, hood clearance is an issue. That isn't the case for a C10, so if you're looking to make good power on a budget, this is a great choice. Note that the factory fuel injectors on these intakes were only 25-pound units in 2001–2007 GM trucks, so an injector swap should be in the cards for performance use. I chose 42-pound EV1-style injectors (Holley part number 522-428).

the injectors are typically mounted downstream of the majority of the intake manifold, except in the case of a throttle body injection (TBI) system, such as what was offered by GM in the 1990s, or Holley's Terminator system. These systems have fewer, larger injectors than a multi-point fuel injection (MPFI) system, each of which operates on top of the intake, like a carburetor.

When it comes to an MPFI system, such as what's used in most LS conversions, there's less of a trade-off in intake design. A lot of builders use the car-style LS6 intake with good results, while the truck intake, offered on the 4.8, 5.3 and 6.0, flows just as well and is actually capable of making the same power thanks to its

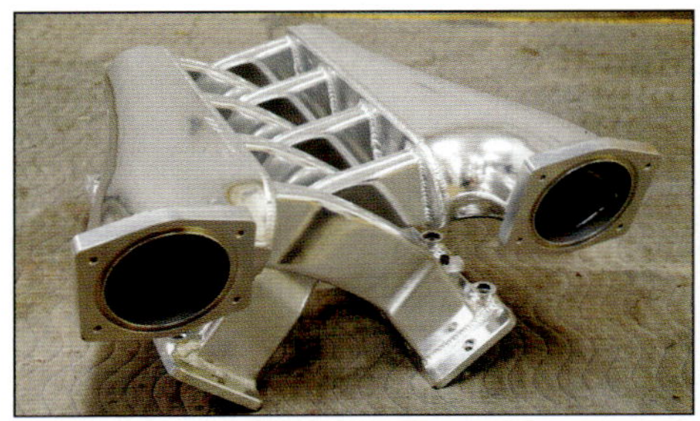

For my project pickup, I chose Holley's Sniper Dual-Plenum intake (part number 820201) for cathedral-port cylinder heads. This intake is unique in the world of LS power because it's really two intakes in one with a right and a left plenum divorced from one another. By design, it flows a lot of air, does a good job of evening out flow to each cylinder, and makes power off idle all the way to 7,500 rpm. This is a best-of-both-worlds solution for a daily driven rig that needs to wow people when the hood is popped. This, paired with Lingenfelter's GT11 cam, will make a freight train of torque starting just off idle. The intake comes with fuel rails and mounting hardware.

The nice thing about the C10's engine compartment is the vast amount of space available under the hood. The Holley Dual-Plenum intake is 11 inches tall, 19 inches long, and 19½ inches wide—and it fits great under the hood of the C10. The throttle bodies are GM part number 12605109 for an LS3 Camaro, while air intakes are twin 120-degree polished aluminum 4-inch-diameter tubes from Spectre. All of this fits with space to spare—superchargers, turbos, or even that tall OEM intake will fit fine here.

long runner design. Its one downside? Its ugly.

Whatever you choose for your own project, be sure it's designed to give you the power and the look you want.

Charging System

GM's 10SI alternators are what you'll find under the hood of pretty much all C10s from the square era. Launched in the Corvette in 1969, these were the first of GM's internally regulated alternators. The SI stands for "System Integrated," meaning no external components were required to make one of these charge, other than a 12-volt signal wire.

The majority of these put out 63 amps max—although some put out

The internally regulated SI-series alternator was standard in C10s throughout squarebody production, and they're great units when properly matched to the needs of the truck. That said, if you intend on adding power-hungry accessories, such as cooling fans or electric fuel pumps, you'll likely need to consider an upgrade over a stock unit—most of these stockers put out about 60 amps at best.

as little as 37 amps, which was more than enough for a bare-bones truck with just a heater, wipers, lights, and an AM radio. The alternator that came stock in your truck really depended on the options it came with from the factory.

Starting in 1983, an upgraded 12SI alternator became the standard, sharing the same basic dimensions as the 10SI but with a larger cooling

If you're running a factory-style engine, the easiest way to upgrade is to use another SI-style alternator with higher output. This is a 140-amp unit from Summit Racing, and it will bolt up to the factory brackets. You'll need to upgrade the charging wire to support the output capabilities of this unit. (Photo Courtesy Summit Racing)

fan mounted to the nose, just behind the V-belt drive. These units put out more power at idle—up to 94 amps to power all those new computerized systems of the Big '80s.

Both of these alternators are known for decent power output and longevity in stock form—but once you start adding electric fuel pumps, air suspension systems, electric cooling fans, and power-hungry ECUs into the mix—and most owners are doing that—these OEM units won't be able to keep up with demand. Neither will the factory 10-gauge charging wires in your truck.

As mentioned above, the biggest, baddest factory 12SI alternator only put out 94 amps max, which isn't a lot when you consider the power demands of a modern rig—especially one that may see extended time sitting still in traffic with its cooling fans running on a hot day.

Even a stock rig can benefit from a boosted charging system from a more modern car or truck, and swapping is a straightforward job.

GM switched to a larger, more powerful design called the CS130 in 1986 and used it through 1999. These units produced much more amperage at idle and are a fantastic upgrade for C10s regardless of the engine

The CS-style alternator replaced the SI series in GM vehicles starting in the mid-1980s. If you can find a 1986 or newer small-block or big-block truck unit, it will have mounting ears that are 180 degrees apart, just like the earlier SI-series you're looking to replace. You will need to modify your brackets slightly to make this alternator work, as well as source a couple of 8- x 1.25-mm-pitch metric bolts. LS engines, like the one pictured, use a different mount.

used. An upgraded version called the CS130D was introduced in 1994 and is also a good choice if you're dealing with increased load on your electrical system. They're available in wrecking yards with typical outputs of 100 and 105 amps, while the aftermarket offers up to 250-amp versions.

Yes, you can get upgraded alternators based on the 10SI/12SI architecture. They will work, but they don't cool themselves as well as the CS-series, which is important for long alternator life. The CS is inherently more reliable than an SI at idle and at lower revs, which is where most of its major load is going to be in your C10—loping along in traffic, keeping cooling fans running, and, potentially, an ECU humming.

As these units came out in 1986, that means there are two model years of square C10 that used them. Look for 1986 or 1987 units with mounting tabs located 180 degrees apart. The only downside in converting is in the mount, which will need slight modification to work with the new, larger alternator. If you're running an LS, you'll be running a CS-series already, as those were OEM throughout LS production.

With a bigger amp comes the need for a larger charging cable. The factory setup won't work with anything over the original rating of the alternator your truck had from new. A new CS130D could very easily offer double the output of the original alternator, and assuming your system calls for that much juice, funneling all that through your truck's original 10-gauge charge wire is a recipe for smoke, if not fire.

The rule of thumb is to run 8-gauge wire for alternators up to 60 amps and 6-gauge wire for 100+ amp units, with 4-gauge reserved

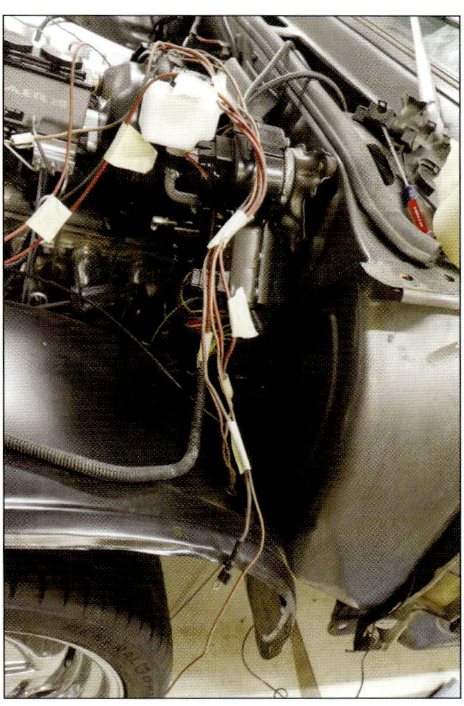

If you want to run a higher-capacity alternator, regardless of its design, you'll need to modify the C10's wiring harness to keep from overloading the original wires. A stock C10 runs its charge wire from the alternator, to a junction at the rear of the block, and then down to the starter lug. Pictured are all the wires that run to the starter: one of these feeds power from the alternator to the system, while the others feed power from the system to other parts of the truck.

for greater-output units. This wire should be run from the alternator charging post directly to the battery in the shortest distance possible, with at least a 6-inch-long section of fusible link between it and the battery—and that fusible link should be four sizes smaller than the wire. So, in the case of a 6-gauge wire, the fusible link should be 10-gauge, and it should be as close to the battery as possible.

You'll need to make some modifications to the original harness to handle the increased load of the big-

How Much Alternator Is Too Much?

Your truck's alternator will only produce as much power as is called for by the vehicle—therefore, if you add a 200-amp alternator to a stock rig that only needs 10 amps at idle, it'll only produce 10 amps. In that sense, there's no such thing as too much alternator. The trouble occurs when adding on power-sucking items through factory wiring that wasn't designed to support them—such as cooling fans, big stereo systems, etc. Use heavy-gauge wire for items that will require greater amperage. ■

ger alternator, but it doesn't need to be a complex job, depending on how you intend to wire your rig.

The factory fuse panel under the dash does a good job for the major-

Depending on your truck and the condition of its wiring, you may decide to use either the factory wiring or swap it all out for a Painless or American Autowire replacement harness and fuse panel with more flexibility. My factory wiring was completely intact, so I used it to run the truck's stock components and to trigger relays for added-on circuits. Terminals labeled "BAT" are hot all the time, while terminals labeled "IGN" are hot in crank and key-on situations, and "ACC" are hot key-on.

ity of the truck, but for most of your bigger-ticket add-ons, it shouldn't be your source of power.

Higher-amperage add-on items, from an ECU to cooling fans, or an air suspension compressor, are going to need a rather large fuse and heavy-gauge wire pulling power directly from the battery. Your factory fuse panel can't handle that kind of load without also upgrading all the wiring that feeds it—but it can serve as a trigger point for relays that pull power direct from the battery. Since relay triggers don't pull much current to work, additional load on the factory wiring is minimal, and you don't need to go hacking up a factory harness to make it all work.

Generally, this is a plug-and-play solution: your factory fuse panel will have several key-on hot and constant-hot terminals that you can use as triggers to power all kinds of things, and unless your wiring has been hacked up by a previous owner, there's nothing wrong with going this route.

If you don't mind getting involved with wiring work, replacing a complete harness isn't a bad idea, either. Wires tend to get brittle after years of heat cycling, and you can source either an aftermarket or factory-style replacement harness and fuse panel from several sources.

Aftermarket kits offer greater flexibility in customization, offering things like power window wiring, large-gauge charging wires, modern blade fuses, and more, all right out of the box. That makes adding on components all that much easier, and it also removes any sketchy wiring work done by previous, ham-fisted owners.

Modifying a Factory Harness for a New Alternator

The factory setup for most C10s from this era had an SI-series alternator feeding power to the starter lug, which then charged the battery through the main power cable from the starter to the positive battery post. Another wire also sent power from the alternator directly through to the fuse panel—all through 10-gauge wires and a handful of fusible links.

Upgrading the alternator requires running a larger cable, which you can route directly to the battery either through a big fuse or a section of fusible link.

After that, you can set up all your additional power needs directly from the battery—fans, ECU, stereo amps, etc. Your original fuse box wiring will now connect to the battery in the same way, via the main power cable to the starter and then from the starter to the fuse panel.

This effectively creates a new wiring harness in your rig, parallel to the factory underdash unit. That preserves the integrity of your factory setup—no meltdowns from channeling big amperage through the OEM wiring.

The net result is that your factory wiring works just like it did before but with more power supply when it needs it—and no overloaded wires from too much power being run through them.

Why Fusible Link Over a Simple Fuse?

A fusible link exists to protect your truck's wiring in the event of an unexpected short or overload—think of it as a fuse that is hard to blow but will blow if something drastic happens. It will save your truck from burning to the ground over a short-circuit.

The wire itself is a special design, encased in fire-resistant coating that will burn up before the rest of the circuit. When it goes, it breaks the connection. This typically happens with some smoke and sometimes a few sparks, so it's not smart to use fusible link inside the passenger compartment. That's where your best bet is using a traditional blade fuse.

Why not use fuses everywhere? You can, and they do work. But fuses are much more susceptible to voltage spikes, whereas a fusible link can take more punishment before tripping. In underhood main-power wire situations, which can be subject to power spikes from jump-starts and the like, a fusible link is the best option when it's used correctly. It needs to be sized properly: 6 inches in length, four sizes down from the wire it feeds.

Look for sections of the factory fusible link at the starter positive post where it feeds the main power distribution block and at the junction from the alternator to the main power distribution block. If your truck loses power to the fuse panel for some unknown reason, these are the first places you should check. ■

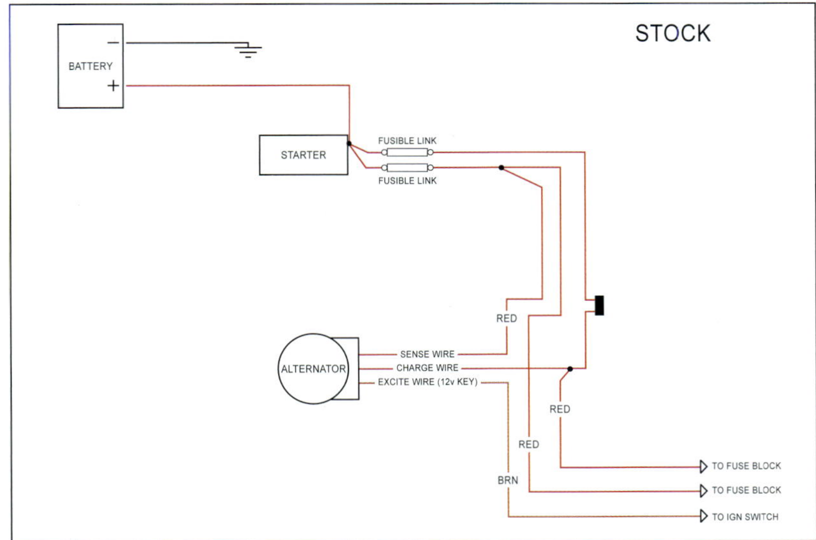

SI-equipped C10s use a three-wire charging system from the factory—a charge wire to feed the battery, a signal wire to tell the regulator how much to charge, and an exciter wire with key-on 12-volt power.

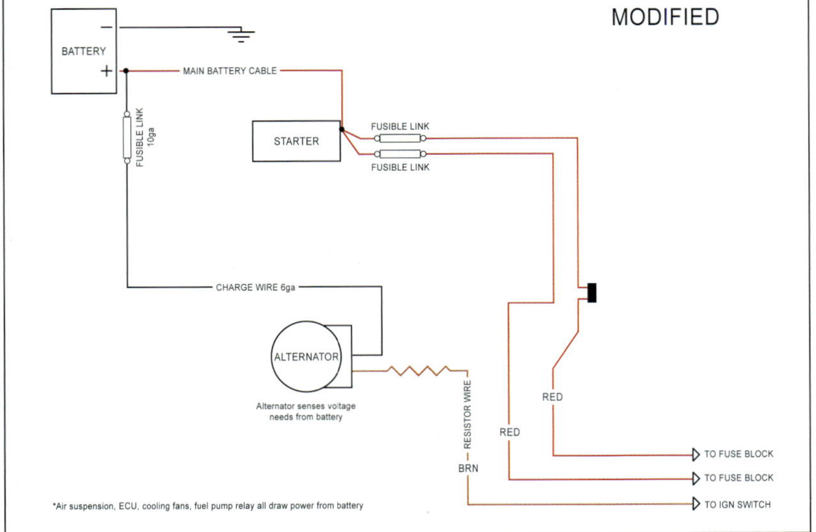

Here's how to modify a factory harness to work with a higher-output CS-series alternator: I simply removed the 10-gauge wire that fed the starter and added a 6-gauge wire direct to the battery. The fuse panel still gets its power from the starter lug. If header heat and wire crowding isn't a concern for you, there's no reason you couldn't run the 6-gauge charge wire down to the starter as well for a cleaner look.

FUELING, ECU, AND COOLING

Bringing an LS—or any other engine—to life in a C10 requires a good fuel system, a brain to run it (assuming it's fuel injected), and some way to keep it all cool.

In many cases, you can get away with using some, if not all, of what the factory offered on these trucks, regardless of what engine you're running. Of course, there are exceptions to every rule: Don't think that a factory two-row brass radiator will cool a 1,000-hp turbocharged LS engine, for example. There are plenty of smart upgrades out there to make a C10 work with whatever powertrain you've installed.

Fueling

The fuel system on a C10 is basic and fundamentally the same as just about every other truck or muscle car from the 1960s and 1970s era: There's a feed line from the tank that runs along the frame rail and up to the carburetor, typically 3/8 inch and mostly steel. There are a few sections of rubber line that connect everything together, and dual-tank trucks have a switching valve that allows the main fuel line to be connected to both tanks, using a solenoid to change between left and right via a switch on the dash. That same switch also controls which tank sending unit is feeding signal to the dash fuel gauge.

Additionally, depending on the year and the configuration of the truck in question, there may also be steel fuel vent lines that run to charcoal canisters mounted under the hood. These filter fumes from the tanks and keep them from releasing into the atmosphere—and they're part of your truck's emissions system, so don't toss them on the junk pile until you've read your state's rules on that sort of thing.

The above applies to trucks that ran a carburetor from new. Trucks built in 1987 use a different fuel supply system than the earlier rigs, set up for the higher pressures and return-to-tank features that a fuel-injection system requires.

Fuel Injection

If you intend on swapping over to fuel injection in a rig that didn't have it from new, there are a number of things you'll need to consider, with the largest one being your fuel system. Most modern aftermarket systems are basic bolt-on-and-go self-learning units, which is great—

Every carbureted C10 from the square era featured a mechanical pump like this one. It's great at delivering enough fuel to run a stock Q-jet on a stock 350 or 454, but add in performance options and it will become inadequate quickly.

but there is more to a swap than just throwing the throttle body in place of your old carburetor.

Fuel Lines

A lot of builders simply use the factory fuel line in their builds, and there's nothing wrong with that—assuming the line is in good condition and, for pre-1987 rigs, that the truck is still fitted with a low-pressure carbureted system.

The factory SBC block-mounted mechanical fuel pump only builds a small amount of pressure inside its fuel lines—somewhere between 8 and 12 psi for aftermarket pumps and carburetors and only about 5 psi for factory pumps and Q-jets—and note that all the pressure is really only on the outlet side of the fuel pump, between the pump housing and the carburetor. The pump creates a vacuum on the other section of line, drawing fuel from the tank.

As such, the original line didn't need to be too stout, as it never saw higher pressure than what was required to feed that Q-jet. But that's a problem, especially when you're looking at an LS engine, which from the factory required 58 psi and a return line.

Considering that, if you have any questions about your fuel line's condition, you're going to swap over to fuel injection on your SBC, or you will be running an LS, you'll need to replace your factory fuel line with something better suited to the task of delivering fuel at injection pressures and returning it to the tank.

If you intend on cutting and flaring your original steel fuel line for use with AN-style fittings, you may run into issues with its straight, welded seam. This is particularly troublesome if you're using 37-degree single

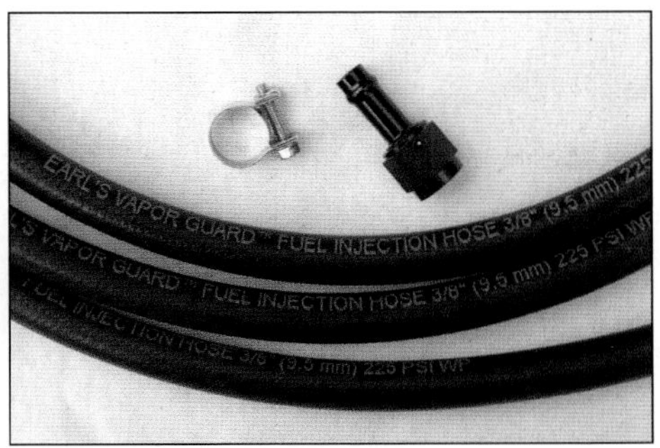

Earl's Performance offers a number of flexible fuel line options that are reasonably priced and engineered to work with their lines of aftermarket AN-style fittings. This is a good way to go, as these hoses can stand up to EFI pressures and are available with special fume-blocking liners and ethanol-resistant formulas.

flares and AN fittings—that original line seam will transfer into the sealing face of your flare and leak if you try to mate it with an AN fitting.

It's smarter, and not that much more work, to make all new fuel supply and return lines using spiral-wound brake-rated steel 3/8-inch line. I prefer Edelmann 3600ST, which is a 25-foot spool of -6 (3/8-inch) steel line. Or you can swap to a high-quality flexible line, such as Earl's Vapor Guard, which is available in a variety of lengths and diameters.

Routing new, flexible hoses is much easier than making new steel lines from scratch, so if you're working on a truck that's still completely assembled, using new, flexible line will make your life a lot easier.

That said, modern steel line is stronger than most flexible options, and there's no worry over eventual leaks like you'll get with hose. All rubber-based lines will break down over time, but that's less of a concern with steel line—especially with regard to caustic fuel additives that change by the season and by the year.

The downside here is that steel fuel line can be hard to work with, and it's easy to put a critical bend in the wrong place or heading in the wrong direction, which will force you to start over from scratch. The best time to tackle this project is when the truck is torn apart, preferably with the bed removed and the engine and transmission out of the way.

Tanks

Factory short-bed tanks are 16-gallon units, while long-bed tanks, with their longer length, hold 20 gallons. For obvious reasons, you can't switch from one style of tank to the other, as the long-bed tanks won't fit in short applications.

If you intend to run a carburetor, there's nothing wrong with running a stock tank and a stock fuel pickup. But if you're going to an electric pump, the job isn't as simple as hooking up an external pump to your original fuel line.

An electric pump is a much better pusher than it is a puller. What that means is that it needs to be mounted as close to the tank as possible, and down below the fuel level, so it can gravity feed rather than be forced to suck fuel from the tank. However, a bigger problem lies in the design of a factory carbureted tank, which had no internal baffling from new—and an electric pump won't live long without some way to keep fuel fed to it.

Fuel slosh is a real concern with an electric pump, as every time you stop, turn, or accelerate, your fuel will slosh around inside the tank, the factory pickup will suck air, and the pump will run dry for a second—bad for performance, terrible for pump life. That isn't as much of a concern with a carburetor and a factory fuel

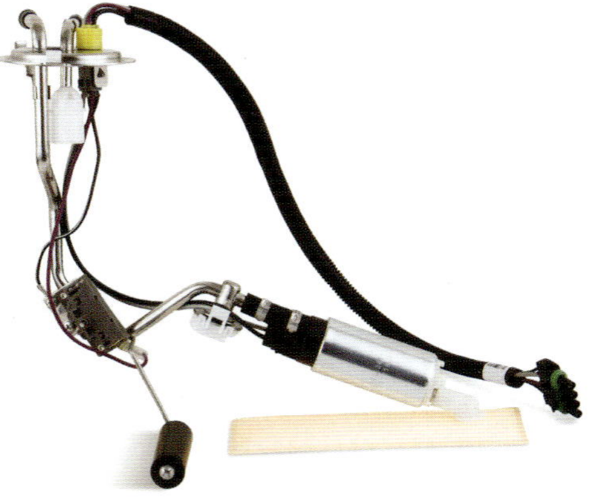

Holley's drop-in Muscle Truck EFI fuel pump module is a good option for builders looking to run an electric pump while maintaining the stock fuel tank in a C10. It mounts just as a factory sending unit would, but with a 255 LPH fuel pump and Holley HydraMat fuel system reservoir. This system is pre-regulated at 58 psi for LS applications and can support up to 550 hp. No special tank required. (Photo Courtesy Holley)

Is That Sidesaddle Tank Safe?

The fuel system in the 1973 C10 was initially seen as a marked improvement over the trucks that came before. The 1967–1972 GM trucks featured an in-cab fuel tank, which wasn't ideal for a number of reasons, from the perceived safety issues of having 20 gallons of gasoline riding right behind the driver to fumes in the cab. So for 1973, GM came up with another idea.

That year, the GM engineering team moved the fuel tank out of the cab and relocated it to the frame rails of the truck, mounted sidesaddle on the exterior of the frame, tucked up underneath the floor and the bed of the truck. Dual tanks became an option, with single-tank trucks using the passenger's side for the tank mount until 1981, when it moved to the driver's side.

Doing it that way seemed smart, as it eliminated the fuel slosh sound from the cab and made use of otherwise unused space under the body of the truck. It did, however, create a problem, as the tanks were exposed to damage in a T-bone situation—damage that could cause leaks and a subsequent fire, Ford Pinto style.

You probably remember hearing about this issue, either on the internet or from the *Dateline NBC* segment "Waiting to Explode," which aired on November 17, 1992.

In that segment, NBC producers rigged a truck to explode in a controlled crash but didn't disclose their pyrotechnics—which earned them a defamation lawsuit from GM.

GM, however, at the time had just lost a $105 million lawsuit over a fatal fire in one of these sidesaddle trucks in Atlanta—one of a number of such lawsuits stemming from the dangers of sidesaddle tanks and accidents. In 1993, the NHTSA requested GM recall all of the 1973–1987 trucks to solve the issue. In response, GM submitted evidence that its trucks were safe. The push for a recall died with a judgment from the Transportation Secretary who dismissed the poten-

The Blazer mounted a square tank behind the rear axle and ahead of the rear bumper, nestled inside the frame rails. Mounting a tank here is a simple solution, but it does limit what you can do with your exhaust system, and it also eliminates the factory spare tire mount. Also, depending on your rear suspension system, there may be other interference issues to work out. Factor in all of this before making the decision to convert your tank. (Photo Courtesy Classic Industries)

tial recall but required GM to pay $51 million for other safety programs. Some say that deal was politically motivated.

Ultimately, as a truck builder, you have to choose: retain the factory tank in the factory location or convert your truck to something different. Several companies, such as LMC Truck, Brothers, and Classic Industries, offer conversion fuel tanks designed for Blazers, which in a C10 moves the tank back behind the rear axle. This is a fine solution, but it will require some custom work to install a fuel filler either in the bed floor, rear bedside, or rear stake pocket, as well as longer fuel lines and wiring for the gauge. But considering that more collisions, on average, are rear-end collisions, this isn't exactly a magic bullet either.

Whichever tank design you choose to run, be sure that the tank itself is in good condition, as are the mounting straps, fuel lines, and all associated rubber parts, including at the filler neck. Remember that these trucks simply don't have the safety features of something newer, so drive accordingly. ■

The sidesaddle tank may not be the best design in the world, but it's also not the bomb that some news stories tried to sell to the public. There are options out there for relocating the tank, so if you're concerned about the safety of the OEM tank, move it.

sock on the end of the pickup tube—but the stock setup isn't adequate for electric pump use.

The solution is in one of two products: either a new fuel tank that has baffling inside it to eliminate fuel slosh, or a fuel mat that replaces the OEM fuel sock, designed to function as a fuel sponge, keeping liquid fuel at the pickup regardless of cornering or acceleration. Holley's HydraMat does just that, and it's a good solution to fuel control if you intend on running a factory tank without internal structure to limit fuel slosh.

Conversion fuel tanks are also available from places such as Tanks Inc., Aeromotive, or Holley, which also mount a pump inside but use traditional baffling to keep the fuel where it needs to be. The style you use depends on your fuel system goals and the condition of your factory fuel tank. Rust, scale, and rocks have a way of accumulating inside old, used fuel tanks, so be sure yours is clean before going any further. A good radiator shop should be able to clean out and fix any factory tank issues.

Building a Fuel System

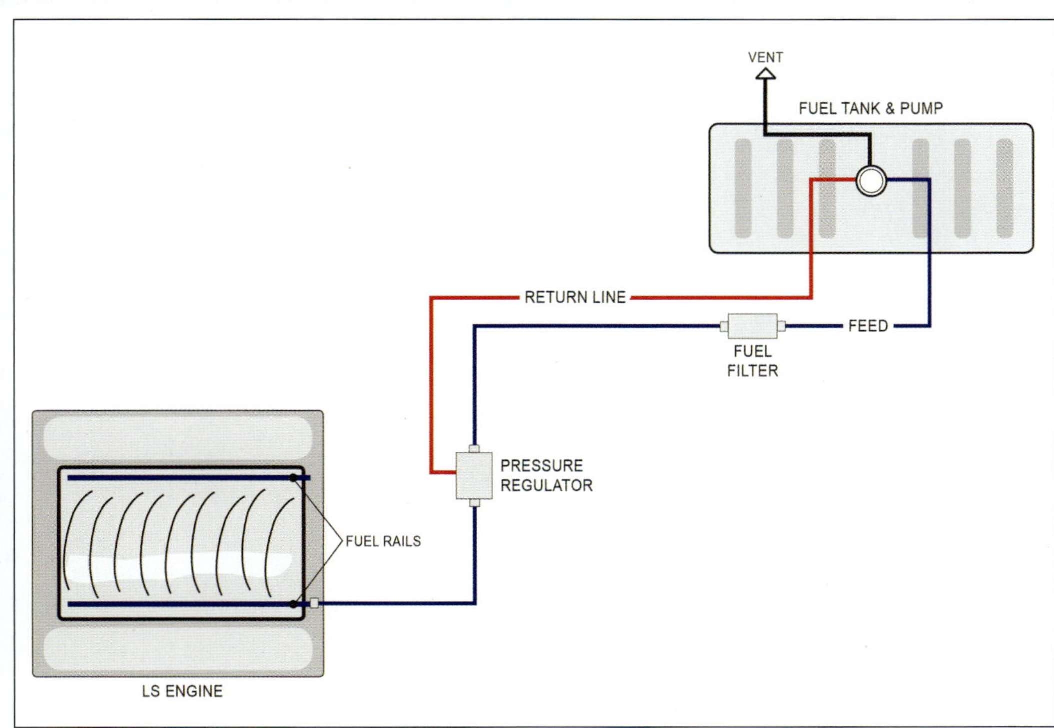

1 *This is a deadhead-style fuel system—it includes both a feed and a return line, a high-flow fuel filter, an adjustable fuel pressure regulator, and a section of rubber line that feeds the fuel rails (or carburetor) to allow for engine motion. This is a basic layout designed to use an in-tank pump, but an external pump system is plumbed much the same way. This isn't the only way to fuel an LS, but this layout is reliable in high-demand situations and helps keep the fuel cool, as all the fuel that ends up at the warm fuel rails is burned by the engine.*

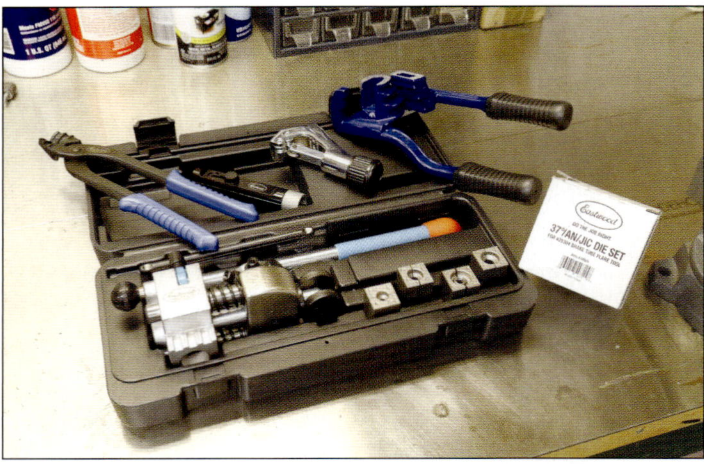

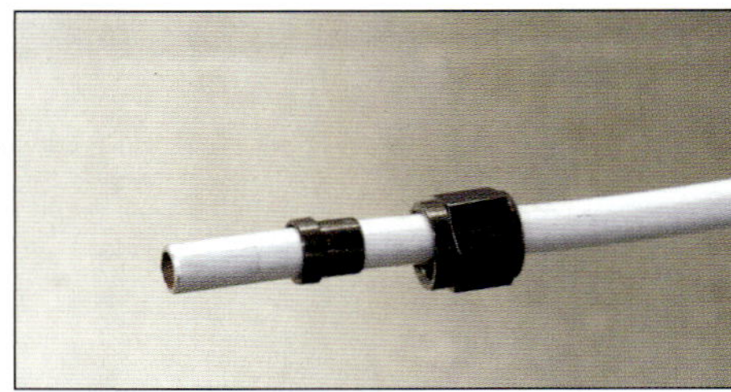

3 *Edelmann part number 3600ST is a 25-foot-long spool of 3/8-inch (or -6) steel line. It's classified as brake line and is spiral-wrapped, so it's great for high-pressure applications, higher than what your fuel system will build. It's easy to bend and flare, and it can be used with -6 fittings. Also, being steel, it won't degrade regardless of the fuel run through it. The fittings are from Summit Racing part number 220633-2B tube nut and part number 220634-2B tube sleeve, designed to slide up behind a 37-degree AN flare and support it from behind.*

2 *The proper tools, fittings, and hose/line are a must when it comes to making a good fuel system. Fortunately, if you already bought tools to work on your brake system, the same tools will also help you build your fuel system. These are from Eastwood.*

4 *The first step is to map out your fuel system on paper, as that will help you visualize what fittings you'll need and where they'll go. All of these fittings went into my feed and return fuel lines, and all came from Summit Racing.*

5 *C10 fuel lines weather heavily at the top of the fuel tank, so to combat that, you can simply make that part of the system out of steel. However, that presents a problem for tank removal, as the steel line isn't reachable to remove from the top of the tank once the tank or the bed is installed. To solve this, I created a -6 junction above the frame rail for both the feed and return that are easy to reach—and shouldn't be hard to disconnect if the tank ever needs to come back out of the truck.*

6 *Steel line is unforgiving—once you bend it more than slightly, it's not going to straighten back out. Therefore, a wire coat hanger is a good thing to use to help map bends and lengths before you go cutting and bending up line.*

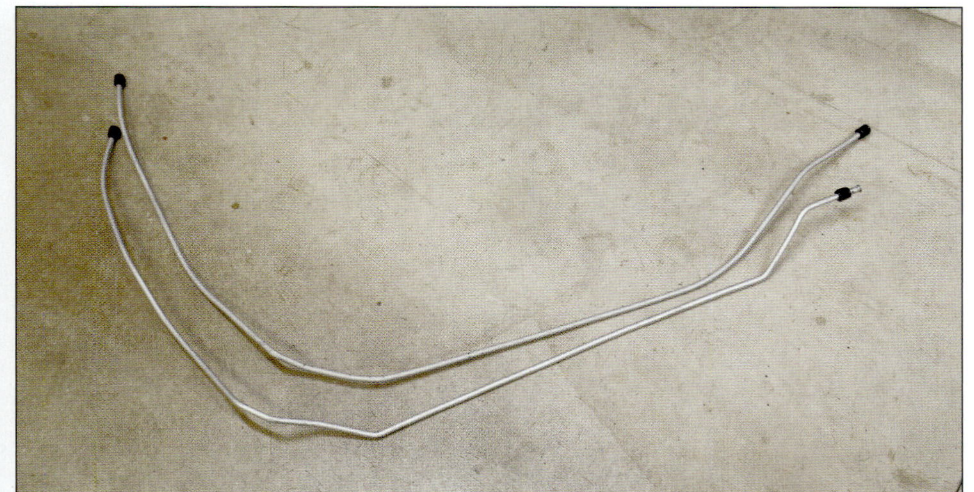

7 Injection systems will need a feed and return fuel line. Here, both are -6 steel with double 37-degree flares on either end, to mate up with AN-style -6 fittings. The hardest part here is making two lines that match—and that run close together along the frame rail. Plan on making several sets because you won't likely get it right the first time. These should tuck up close to the frame (away from heat and moving parts) and should be fixed in place with rubber-lined metal clamps.

8 This is Holley's conversion fuel tank (part number 19-154), manufactured by Tanks, Inc. It has internal baffling and an internally mounted fuel pump that can support up to 550 hp. This, along with an adjustable fuel pressure regulator, can supply plenty of pressure and volume for a high-output LS engine—or any fuel-injected application—and it bolts right into the factory sidesaddle location. It also comes with a fuel-gauge sending unit with a range of 0–90 ohms, which works with the factory GM gauge.

10 The final component is a fuel pressure regulator—preferably a bypass style like the one pictured. This allows any excess fuel to return to the tank through the return line. The only rubber line in this setup is from the outlet to the fuel rail. For that I used Earl's Vapor Guard and the matching fittings, as standard injection hose will emit fuel fumes and stink up your garage.

9 It's important to run a good fuel filter, especially in fuel-injected applications. This is a 10-micron filter with a -8 inlet and outlet, which mounts on the feed side of the fuel system, after the pump. If running an external pump, you'll also need a pre-filter as well, with at least a 100-micron rating.

Edelbrock's Pro Flo 4 kit is a good choice for builders running a generally stock LS engine—especially if the stock ECU and wiring is missing. This kit works well with factory injectors and sensors and is easy to use, with a touch-screen interface and self-learning capabilities. (Photo Courtesy Edelbrock)

Holley has a great reputation when it comes to EFI, and its Terminator LS EFI system is what I chose for both simplicity and in-depth tuning options. When fitted with the Dominator ECU, it can control twin drive-by-wire throttle bodies, electronic overdrive transmissions, boost, nitrous, traction control, and more. The system is self-learning, but Holley also offers a great laptop-based tuning program to modify the tune beyond what the self-tuning tables and the handheld touchscreen can do. This system is for the 6.0L LQ4 (part number 550-615), which comes with all the proper wiring to make it a plug-and-play installation.

LS Computer Controls

Any modern injection system needs a brain to make it all work. If you've swapped to LS power, you have a lot of options for your C10, from a factory GM powertrain control module (PCM) to an aftermarket ECU. What you use depends on what kind of flexibility you want in terms of tunability versus ease of use right out of the box, as well as what future upgrades you might have in store, such as nitrous or turbos.

To be clear, a factory ECU can handle most aftermarket modifications without much trouble, but the self-tuning systems on the market today work quite well, which is a huge benefit for the end-user. Plus, they offer more general tunability, thanks to most of them having an in-the-cab touchscreen interface. Stock units don't allow for that. This really is a situation where you get what you pay for. The bigger, badder aftermarket ECUs tend to be quite modular and adaptable to a wide range of speed parts—a big bonus if you intend on running different parts in your engine during your time owning your truck. An aftermarket ECU, such as Holley's Dominator or FAST's XFI, can be configured and adapted to a number of different parts combinations without building a sweat. That isn't always the case with stock ECUs.

As of this writing, there are a handful of great aftermarket options available to run an LS engine, and undoubtedly more are on the way. Some systems come with everything you'll need to make your engine run, from a fuel system through a handheld tuner, while others rely on you to source your own fuel system and offer greater flexibility by being sold as components rather than as kits.

What to use really depends on the specifics of your project—but it's hard to go wrong with any of today's aftermarket LS engine control kits.

A stock PCM is a good, robust choice for an LS swap. However, tuning one of these ECUs will require either expert help or a laptop running a program such as EFI Live, which gives you control over all the engine's running parameters. You'll also need a factory-style wiring harness, which may need to be modified for your application.

Holley EFI Installation

1 It's smart to mount the ECU in a place where you can reach it easily, but it needs to be out of the way as well. It's also a good idea to keep it isolated from heat and moisture, although it is sealed and can be used inside the engine compartment. You're really only limited by the length of your wiring harness—this spot tucks it up under the carpet inside the cab and gives good firewall access for the 2-inch hole needed for the wiring harness to pass through.

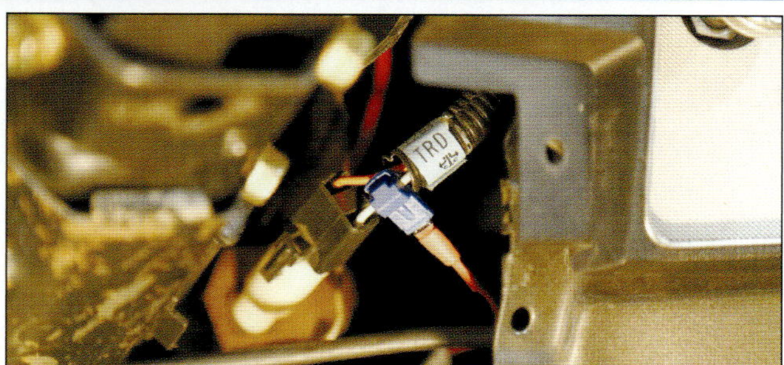

2 The Terminator LS system for drive-by-wire applications is set up with a wire to sense 12-volt power from the brake light circuit. When you hit the brakes, the system will automatically limit throttle position to 10 percent. Two wires run to the brake switch in a C10—the white one leads from the switch to the rear lights and is hot only when the brakes are depressed. Making this system work simply requires tapping into the white wire.

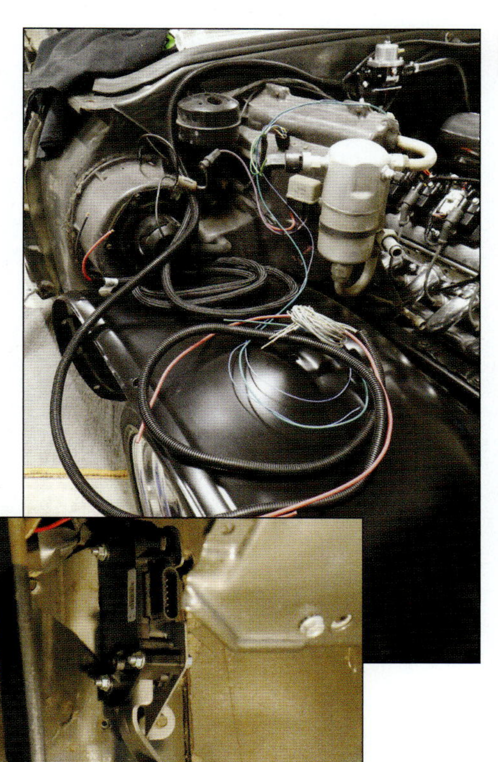

3 The majority of Holley's wiring harness is fitted with OEM-style plugs for things such as the injectors, coil packs, cam and crank sensors, and more. There are several loose wires that will need to be connected, including a green wire to trigger a fuel pump relay, a blue wire for the tach signal, and several gray wires to trigger cooling fan relays. The main power and ground must be connected directly to the battery to ensure a clean power supply to the system.

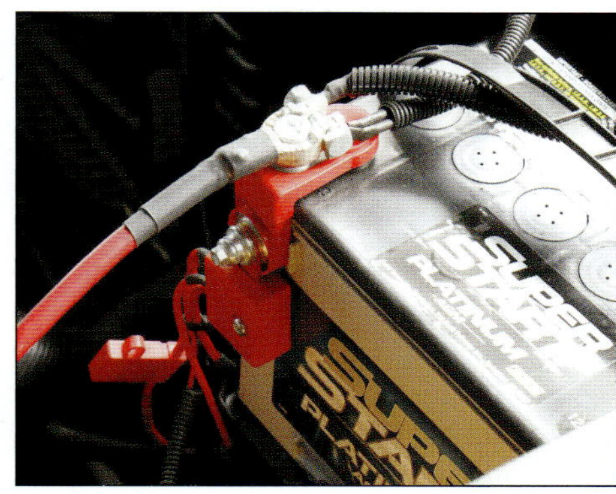

4 Consider installing a dual-terminal battery if you're running a bunch of modern electrical components in your C10. Here, the top terminals feed the main power supply and ground to the starter and fuse panel, while the side terminals handle the ECU power and ground, as well as several other components. I sourced the side-mount terminals at a local auto parts store for a cleaner install.

5 If installing a drive-by-wire system, you'll also need an appropriate pedal. GM's part number 10379038 is for the Cadillac CTS, but it works great with its bracket bent slightly and indexing off the original upper passenger-side mounting hole for the old cable setup. I also used the original pedal's mounting screws and three 3/8-inch plastic spacers between the bracket and the firewall to make it all work.

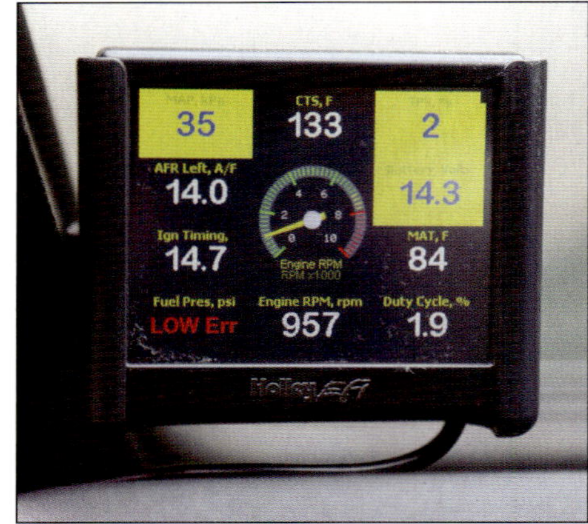

6 *Every EFI system will need an oxygen sensor to run properly. Some systems use one; others use two. Either way, the sensor should be mounted in the header pipe collector (or in the down-pipe from a cast-iron manifold) and positioned in such a way to keep moisture from pooling up on the sensor. A slight upward angle achieves this. Most kits come with a bung to weld into your exhaust system.*

7 *Once the fuel system is plumbed and all the ECU's wiring is hooked up, the next step is to power up the system. Holley's handheld tuner contains a GCF Wizard, which asks several questions about your engine and then picks a basic tune to get you up and running. After calibrating the throttle position via a TPS Autoset procedure, the next step is to start the engine.*

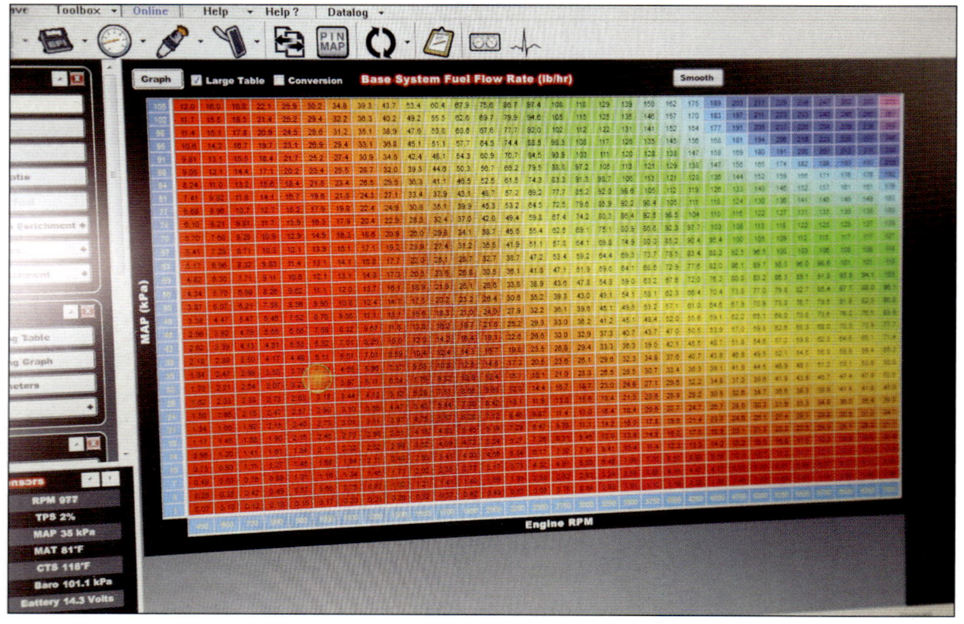

8 *Where Holley's system really shines is here, inside the V5 laptop software, which is free to download from the Holley site. This is where you go to add things like dual throttle bodies, which I'm running on my project truck, and to fine-tune the fuel map, timing curves, cold-start settings, acceleration enrichment, and more. You can tune your engine manually as it's running using this program.*

Cooling

Keeping your C10 cool is especially important. Chances are that you'll end up using this truck when the weather is nice, and that usually means you'll be out in the hot ambient temperatures of summer. The stock cooling system in a C10 is up to the task of cooling a stock motor, but if you've added any power to that old V-8 (or swapped in an LS) it's time to upgrade your cooling system too.

Radiators

Every C10 built from 1973 to 1987 came from the factory with a cross-flow radiator as standard equipment. They were copper/brass construction, and they came in two different heights (17 and 19 inches) and several different core thick-nesses. The larger four-row units offer the best cooling of the stock options. Those tended to be available only on the higher-spec trucks, typically those with towing packages, big-blocks, or diesels. But over the years, as parts wore out, many trucks gained aftermarket replacements that may or may not have matched what was originally equipped. The largest versions also require special mount-

This two-row radiator came with my project 1979, and while it's in great shape both inside and out, I don't foresee it cooling a hot LS well in the heat of summer. The more rows of cooling fins, the better a radiator can work—and you should plan for the worst-case scenario to avoid any potential cooling issues before they happen.

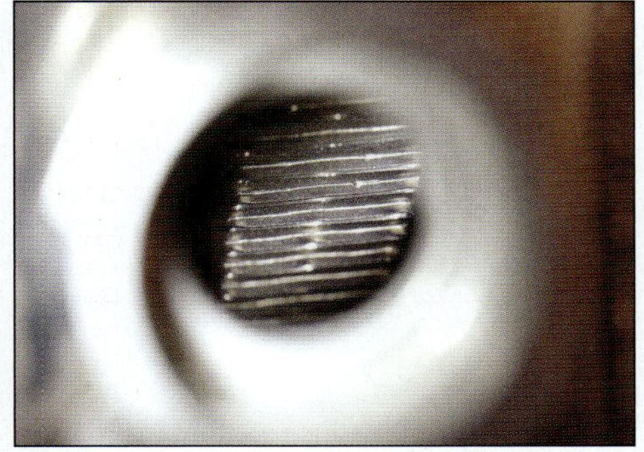

The main difference between a modern aluminum radiator and an original brass/copper unit is in the size of the internal cooling fins. This unit from Griffin features massive 1-inch-wide cooling fins, which is what makes it capable of cooling big power engines while only having two rows of cooling fins.

If you want the best cooling available, either because of big power under your hood or because you live in a hot part of the country, you can't go wrong with an aluminum radiator, as they feature larger cooling fins than the old brass/copper designs. This is a Griffin unit made in the USA and complete with fans. This bolts in place of a stocker and will cool four-figure horsepower effectively.

ing brackets to accommodate their extra height, so if you're looking to swap over to a bigger unit, you'll need the upper bracket and the lower rubber mounts to match the larger radiator.

Even the three-core units did a good job cooling most small- and big-block engine options, and in most cases (provided there aren't any leaks or buildup inside the radiator that impedes flow or cooling surface area), a stock version should suffice for a not-too-crazy V-8 engine in a C10. But, as is the case with most car-related things, bigger is usually better when it comes to radiators.

If you're looking to make some power with a hot V-8, or if you simply don't want to have to think about overheating in traffic, today's aluminum radiators are the best choice for your C10. Sourcing one isn't a problem. The aftermarket offers a number of good solutions, either in terms of stock fit or in terms of extreme cooling ability. Most of them are priced at around the same money as a

Holley's Frostbite series is another good option for C10 builders, as they're engineered to bolt right in—this is a dual-pass unit, meaning the coolant passes through the core twice before returning to the engine. It also has its inlet and outlet on the same side, and they're available in three different diameters to aid in hose selection. They also have a steam line built in for LS engine use. (Photo Courtesy Holley)

Radiator Substitutes

If you can't find a C10 radiator, look for a unit from a 1968–1972 Chevelle or a later C/K truck, as they are generally the same in terms of overall measurements. The radiator I ended up running in my C10 came from a 1969 Chevelle, and it quite literally bolted right in place. Just be sure to measure twice so you only have to buy once. ■

Cooling fans need to draw power directly from the battery or alternator via a relay that's protected either with a fuse or a section of fusible link. They'll also need a trigger for that relay, either via an ECU that connects a wire to ground at a certain temperature or via a thermostatic switch that plumbs into the cooling system, such as this 185-degree unit.

stock-style replacement in brass/copper, and a lot of them are engineered specifically to fit without any fuss.

The older brass/copper construction is actually better at transferring heat than aluminum—the trick with modern radiators is the size of their cores. A classic brass/copper radiator may have three or four rows of cooling fins inside its core, while a modern unit may only have two. The difference is in the size of those tubes: the new aluminum unit's fins are up to 1 inch wide compared to the 7/16- or 1/2-inch tubes seen in a classic radiator. That translates to way more surface area for the aluminum unit, and therefore better cooling across the board, from freeway cruising to long-standing idles. This is a fundamental upgrade. Look to Griffin, Be Cool, Holley's Frostbite, Champion, and others for a wide range of prices and options—but you do get what you pay for, and you don't want to skimp on something as important as engine cooling, especially when sunny summer weather is when you'll want to be driving your truck.

Fans

C10s also came from the factory with belt-driven steel cooling fans, operated by viscous fan clutches. These units are effective, especially when paired with a factory fan shroud. However, they are known horsepower hogs, they don't work well at slow engine speeds, and they're noisy.

For a driver C10, either with or without fuel injection, electric fans are a better choice—especially mounted to the relatively wide cross-flow C10 radiator. An ECU such as Holley's Terminator can control two separate fans with unique, customizable on/off temperatures sourced from the factory coolant temperature sensor in an LS engine, or you can source a fan controller with a thermostatic switch, which connects to ground at a set temperature and

triggers a fan relay. You can also wire up a manual switch in-line from the thermostatic switch that connects to ground, which will trigger your fans whenever you want them to run.

The C10's stock radiator width

Bigger is better when it comes to cooling fans, and there's a lot of room between an LS engine and a factory radiator in a C10. Cross-flow radiators tend to be wide enough for a pair of 12-inch fans. A setup like this will cool much more efficiently than a factory belt-driven fan, and it won't rob horsepower.

is 28¼ inches, which is plenty wide enough to mount two 12-inch fans to it. If you're going this route, use puller fans mounted on the engine side of the radiator rather than pushers mounted on the grille side; pullers tend to be more efficient at moving air across the radiator's fins. Also, use a proper relay setup for your fans, along with either a fuse or fusible link and power sourced direct from the battery or starter lug. Summit Racing offers simple fan relay kits from a number of manufacturers that will have the proper-gauge wire and fuse size for a pair of high-performance fans.

Radiator Hoses

If you've swapped in an LS engine, one of the more challenging aspects can be sourcing proper radiator hoses. This is mainly due to the bevy of options in radiators and water pumps—what you'll need in terms of hoses is completely dependent on the parts that you're running.

LS water pumps have three main differences in hose routing: Truck pumps have an outlet on the passenger-side top, while LS1 Camaro-style and Corvette-style pumps have their outlet on the passenger-side front. LS3 Camaros move the outlet to the front of the driver's side, which can be helpful in certain situations. All three will require a unique hose solution.

Adding to the complexity are LS radiators versus stock C10 radiators, which have their upper hose locations reversed from each other. LS radiators are a dual-pass design with the inlet and the outlet both on the passenger's side of the vehicle. These are more efficient, as the coolant must pass through the radiator's fins twice before returning to the engine block. The stock C10 units are

The best method for hunting radiator hoses is to steal a coat hanger from inside your closet, cut it apart, and use the wire to mock up what the perfect angles for your upper and lower hoses would be. Then, take your template to your local parts store, as most have a wide selection of hoses for a variety of makes and models. You're bound to find something that will work with your setup.

single-pass with the upper and lower radiator hoses on opposing sides.

LS engines also require a coolant steam line to be run from the block to a remote location within the cooling system—either to the radiator, as would have been factory in most stock GM vehicles, or to another place where the steam pocket that forms in the upper sections of the engine block can be eliminated. This is critical for long-term engine health.

Some aftermarket radiators will have the proper fitting already installed as a routing location for this steam line, or you can purchase a special fitting that ties in to the upper radiator hose. Some builders swear by drilling and tapping the top of the water pump to keep the line short, while others tie into the return line from the heater core, as GM did in the TrailBlazer SS. Regardless, if you've gone with an LS, don't ignore this line.

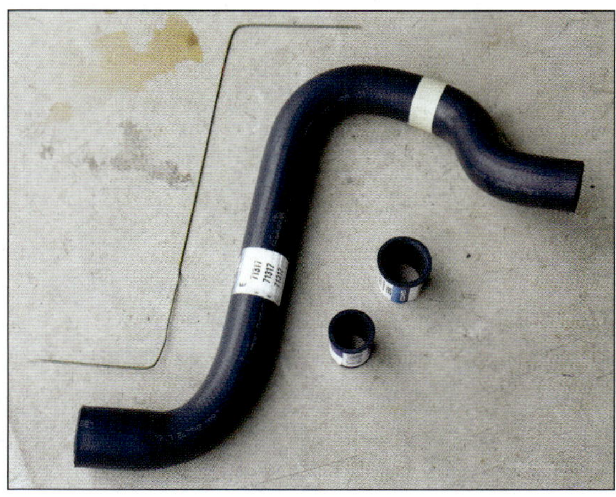

For my setup, which includes an LS3 water pump and a stock C10-style radiator, I ran Dayco part number 71317 for the upper hose, which I cut to fit, and then a factory 2003 Silverado 6.0 LS lower hose, which matched up well. I used two hose reducers with the upper hose: 1¾ to 1½ inches (radiator side), and 1½ to 1¼ inches (water pump).

TRANSMISSIONS

GM built squarebody trucks with a range of manual and automatic transmission options throughout the production run. But while most of them are stout gearboxes that still work well today (likely even after 100,000 miles), there are improvements you can make (or swaps you can undertake) to bring your truck into the modern era while also improving its shifting performance.

As a custom truck builder, what you're likely planning to do with your rig is very different from what the designers could have envisioned at the time your truck was new. In short, you should plan on some transmission work (either upgrades to the factory unit in your rig or a complete swap to something newer)if you intend to get the most out of your truck.

The production run of these trucks coincided with the introduction of factory overdrive automatic transmissions, which have become the industry standard in modern rigs. While the Turbo-Hydramatic 350 had three gears and the 700R4 had four, today's Silverado transmissions have a full 10 forward gears, all tuned to keep the engine in its power band for the best performance and mileage it can achieve. The 1982 and

newer squarebody trucks are where that trend started.

The best engine in the world isn't worth much without a built transmission behind it, and even the lamest, low-compression small-block can be helped out with a tight, modern overdrive unit geared to provide a more favorable starting ratio as well as lower engine revs on the highway.

But before getting to the nuts and bolts of swaps, let's take a look at what was available from GM over the square years.

Automatic

GM's automatics have a great reputation overall, earned through millions of trouble-free miles even

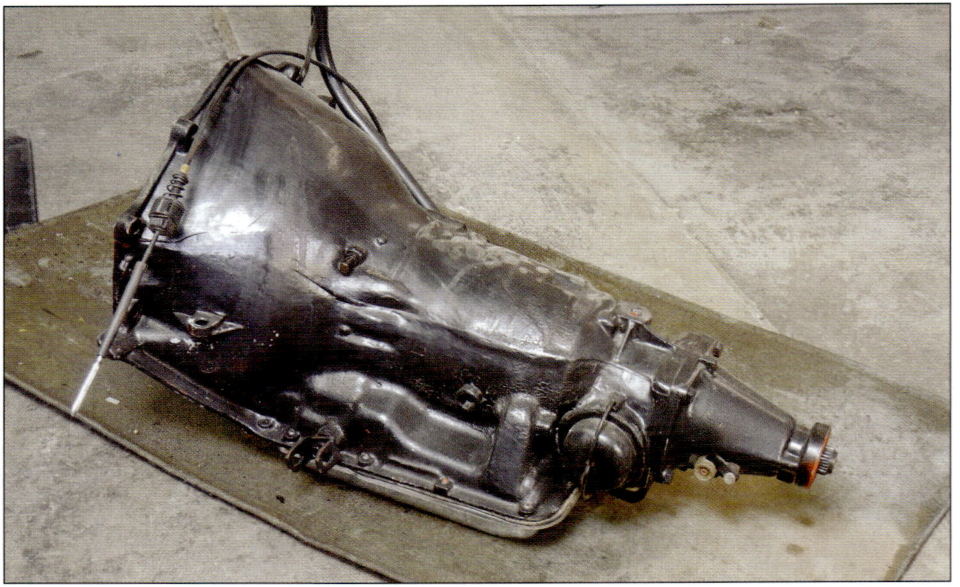

The TH350 is a robust, simple unit that saw use in nearly every year of the squarebody era. Unless you're looking for an extra gear for better cruising mileage, there's nothing wrong with running a TH350 in your custom rig. These units can be built to do just about anything, from street driving and towing to drag race performance. Also, thanks to huge production over the years, both parts and service on a TH350 are easy to come by. (Photo Courtesy Todd Ryden)

under some pretty severe use. Just about any GM automatic offered in GM's square trucks will be capable of performance use if properly set up—but not all of them were created equal.

Turbo-Hydramatic 350

Just as you'll find a 350 under most of these trucks' hoods, you'll also likely find a TH350 3-speed automatic underneath the hump in most of these trucks' cab floors. Introduced in 1969, it was the go-to automatic for most 1/2-ton and 3/4-ton trucks throughout the squarebody's production run. These units are typically trouble-free, minus about 10 trans fluid leaks that you'll chase around, plugging them like holes in a boat. These can be identified by their rectangular oil pan with one angled corner.

The TH350 was designed to be the replacement for GM's widely used Powerglide 2-speed automatic, and as such, it was used in many applications throughout the 1970s and early 1980s. Parts—and complete cores—are widely available, even today. But be sure you're sourcing the correct transmission for your application because a 4x4 TH350 is not the same as the two-wheel-drive unit, and different applications used different tailshafts as well.

Turbo-Hyrdramatic 400

Compared to the TH350, the TH400 is a much stronger 3-speed piece used in heavier-duty applications. They're great for performance too, as they can hold up to more power than a comparable TH350. The only downside here is that they require slightly more power to operate compared to a 350, which may or may not be a big deal to you. They're spotted by a unique-shaped pan, which for the purposes of quick identification looks similar to the shape of the state of Texas. These also use an electronic kickdown solenoid mounted on the side of the transmission.

The TH400 is known for its torque capacity—450 ft-lbs in stock form—and was put in everything from heavy-duty trucks through L88 Corvettes. If you're building a big-inch big-block and don't want to row your own gears, it's really hard to go wrong with a simple, stout TH400 to back up the cubes.

Both the TH350 and TH400 are known for long life and an ability to take a good deal of punishment, at least up to a point. Anything in stock form with a lot of miles is going to need to be freshened at minimum; otherwise, figure that you're living on borrowed time with it.

Transmission work is a science unto itself, and if you plan to take one of these units apart, you need to make sure you have the right tools in hand, as well as a large, clean place to work while staying organized. There are a lot of small pieces inside a GM automatic, and they're all important. If you're going to attempt a rebuild at home, be sure you get and read a complete overhaul manual first.

The TH350 is spotted by its rectangular oil pan with one angled corner. Watch for transmission fluid leaks at the shifter shaft, tailshaft seal, input shaft seal, speedometer gear, and accumulator O-ring. Fixing one leak will often make another worse, so be ready to fix them all.

The TH400 is quick and easy to identify, thanks to this oddly shaped pan. There's no beefier, simpler 3-speed auto than a TH400—these units can live behind big power when properly set up. This is a fantastic factory-style upgrade over a TH350, but it may not be worth the trouble of a swap when you could install an overdrive transmission, such as a 700R4 or 4L60E, without too much more trouble.

700R4

Finally, the 700R4 is an automatic overdrive with four forward gears, introduced in 1982. These transmissions offer better cruising mileage than a TH350 or TH400 thanks to that fourth gear, as well as a lockup torque converter that eliminates torque converter slippage in top gear.

These transmissions were intended to be the replacement for the TH350, and they were widely implemented at their introduction. As such, you'll likely find one in your 1982 or later C10.

However, early examples of these transmissions (which covers all the years of squarebody production) were known to be weak in a variety of areas, such as its relatively small 27-spline input shaft and a number of internal components. Unless a swap with a later, stouter piece is planned, an original 700R4 isn't exactly a plus. All 700R4s can be identified by their square oil pan and overdrive selector on the column, as well as the throttle valve (TV) cable that connects to the throttle arm on the intake, used by the transmission to sense throttle input and alter shift timing and firmness.

Manual

Several different manual transmissions were available in two basic configurations: the column-shift 3-speed and the floor-shift 4-speed.

3-Speed Saginaw

The 3-speed Saginaw was found in the most basic trucks from 1973 to 1980, fully synchronized for ease of use, but it's mostly overlooked today. These are great if you want to make sure your truck never gets stolen, as the (presumably young) thief won't know how to drive something that has what looks like an automatic column shifter and a clutch pedal.

Another 3-speed was available from 1981 to 1984, this one with slightly revised gearing for better low-end grunt. It's known as the M15.

Muncie SM465

More common is the Muncie SM465 4-speed, which has a very steep first gear used to get big loads moving. These are typically driven like 3-speeds, with first rarely used as it's just too steep for stoplight duty. These transmissions can take a beating because they were designed to be used in heavy-duty applications, such as in school buses and dump trucks.

That said, they don't shift quickly, and the shifter throw is about a mile long, so they're not a great choice if performance is on your mind. An SM465 will remind you every time you shift that you're driving a truck—even a short-wheelbase two-wheel-drive rig. But this was the manual transmission of choice for many buyers throughout the square years, so they're easy to find today.

Trans-mission	First	Second	Third	Fourth	Overall Length	Bellhousing to Transmission Mount	Output Splines
TH350	2.52:1	1.52:1	1.00:1	—	27⅝ inches (short), 30⅝ inches (long)	20⅜ inches (short and long)	27
TH400	2.48:1	1.48:1	1.00:1	—	28¼ inches (short), 34 inches (long)	26¾ inches (short), 28 inches (long)	32
700R4	3.06:1	1.63:1	1.00:1	0.70:1	27¾ inches	22⅜ inches	27

GM Automatic Gear Ratios and Measurements

If you're looking for a simple overdrive automatic to swap into your C10, look for a later 700R4—preferably one built after 1988, as the design was improved that year with the addition of stronger parts. These use a TV cable, which is mounted to the throttle arm of the carburetor and tells the transmission how much throttle input is applied at any given time, which will firm up shifts when necessary.

The SM465 is a truck transmission through and through. It has a long-throw shifter and an extremely low first gear ratio for getting big loads moving. It's also short in length, but it's extremely heavy, being a cast-iron unit. GM used these throughout the square years as its go-to 4-speed. They're great for 4x4 use, but beware that you can't easily swap a two-wheel-drive and 4x4 unit due to differences in the output shaft. This is a two-wheel-drive unit.

There was also an available truck 4-speed manual that offered an overdrive gear as well. Only available from 1982–1987, it's known as the MY6 or MM7. These are derived from the Mopar-famous A833 and offered by GM in both cast iron and aluminum for either two-wheel-drive or 4x4 applications. These are easy to spot, with a shift knob that has overdrive denoted, as well as reverse located in the same spot as car-spec Muncies.

Make no mistake about it: any of the factory GM automatic or manual transmissions offered in these trucks will be a solid worker in your rig. However, chances are that you have things other than towing and hauling on your mind, and both GM and the aftermarket have come a long way in the years since the last square GM truck rolled off the assembly line.

Automatic Upgrades

Assuming your TH350, TH400, or 700R4 is in good overall shape and functions as it should, there are a couple of ways to boost its firmness and output to match a hotter engine under the hood.

Shift Kits

GM's automatics were sloppy, mushy shifters from new—a product of GM needing transmissions to suit, a public who would complain about a too-firm shift, regardless of that sloppy, slipping OEM shift, creating heat and wear that was detrimental to the transmission.

A shift kit is the first thing you should consider for your TH350, 400, or 700R4. These kits install inside the OEM transmission valve body, helping to firm up those sloppy factory shifts for a more performance-oriented feel and less heat from slippage inside the transmission.

The key to these kits is their reconfiguring of the transmission line pressure and increasing flow to the clutches. The end result is a firmer feel through the shifts, which is better suited to a truck that's going to be pressed into performance duty.

Summit Racing offers kits for all three transmissions that offer a quicker, firmer shift over what the stock units can provide—installation requires digging into the transmission's internals, at least as far as the valve body, to install. That means draining all the fluid from the transmission and removing the oil pan. In some cases, the transmission crossmember may be in the way, so you may have to remove it to get the pan off.

Strictly speaking, if you're planning on an automatic transmission rebuild in the future—one with new clutch packs, seals, and bands, or with upgrades to later, stronger parts

Manual Gear Ratios and Measurements						
Transmission	First	Second	Third	Fourth	Case to Tailshaft	Output Splines
Saginaw 3-speed (1973–1980)	2.85:1	1.68:1	1.00:1	—	16¼ inches	27
Saginaw 3-speed (1981–1984)	3.50:1 (2.85 and 3.11 available)	1.68:1	1.00:1	—	10⅝ inches	27
SM465 Muncie 4-speed	6.55:1	3.58:1	1.70:1	1.00:1	12 inches	35 (early 2WD), 32 (1982+ 2WD and 1984+ 4WD), 10 (early 4WD)
NP833 4-speed Overdrive	3.09:1	1.67:1	1.00:1	0.73:1	12 inches	32

A shift kit is a great upgrade for any GM automatic transmission. It includes a number of springs and related hardware to effectively reprogram your transmission's shift quality and firmness by altering fluid flow through the transmission's valve body. Some kits convert automatics to manual control, but all will greatly improve drivability. (Photo Courtesy Classic Industries)

in the case of a 700R4—the best time to install a shift kit is at this time. The transmission will already be apart, so it makes sense to do it all at once.

Torque Converters

An automatic transmission functions with a fluid coupling between the engine and the transmission. That fluid coupling is the torque converter, and your truck's transmission performance can be tuned through the configuration of that converter.

A converter utilizes fluid between an impeller, a stator, and a turbine, all mounted inside its housing—the impeller is connected mechanically to the engine's crank, while the turbine is meshed to the transmission's input shaft. By design, a torque converter also multiplies torque during periods of high slippage via that sta-

tor—say, when you're rolling away from a stop.

700R4s use a lockup converter, which locks the impeller and turbine together at high-speed low-load conditions, such as when on the freeway, offering no slippage and better economy.

Torque converters are measured in stall speed—as in, how much you can rev the engine with the brakes applied before the transmission overpowers those brakes and the truck moves.

From the factory, most C10 transmissions will have a stall speed that's relatively low—say about 1,200 rpm. That's great for a stock engine that's designed for regular commuting, but any performance modifications under the hood will tend to want more stall to really make the truck move off the line. This is especially true of long-duration camshafts—more stall speed is a requirement to get the most out of a cam with greater-than-stock specs.

Just as there are endless camshaft options for small-block, big-block, and LS Chevy engines, there are many torque converters that offer higher-than-stock stall speeds for better off-the-line performance. As a rule of thumb, you won't want more than a 3,000-rpm converter for a street-driven truck—any more than that is drag race territory, offering great full-throttle launches but mushy, loose response around town, similar to a manual transmission with a slipping clutch. For a mild-cammed small-block, about 2,500 rpm is a great street stall speed, offering a little more slippage for the engine to rev a little higher to make power before the transmission applies it to the drivetrain.

Upgrading a converter requires pulling the transmission out of the

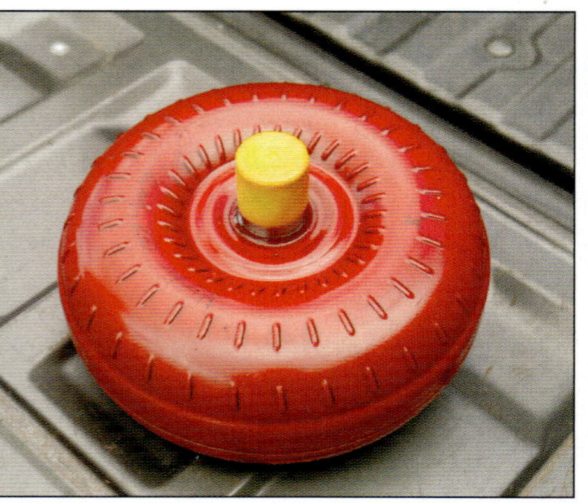

A quality torque converter is key for a well-performing automatic, but it needs to be properly matched to the truck. Everything from curb weight to camshaft profile can factor in here, but for a street-driven truck with a mild cam and few other performance mods, something in the 2,000–2,500 rpm stall range is about right. This unit is a 2,500 stall from Hughes, and it fits either TH350 or TH400.

truck, which isn't a small job—but it is worth it, depending on the other modifications you've already done to your rig. Spec'ing out a performance converter is an important step in making your truck drive the way you want it to, so it makes sense to consult with a transmission specialist—or with any of the major performance transmission companies, such as Hughes, B&M, TCI, ATI, etc.—before you buy. Everything from camshaft specs to tire size can come into play when selecting a converter for your rig—not to mention intended use—so do your homework, ask for help, and be prepared to answer a lot of questions about your project truck before you select a converter.

Swaps

Any of the available transmission options from these trucks will interchange with small-block and big-block engines, as well as with the LS series, as they all share a similar-design bellhousing interface at the rear of the block. However, you'll need a special crankshaft adapter or spacer for LS conversions, as most LS cranks are 0.400 inch shorter than SBC/BBC cranks. The only exceptions to this rule are early iron-headed 6.0 truck engines, which shared the SBC/BBC crankshaft spacing. You may also need a different flexplate or flywheel, depending on the engine and transmission you chose to run.

For any swap, be sure to collect all the required parts to do the job. That includes the transmission itself, any cooler lines, the shift assembly, the crossmember, and the slip yokes and driveline. In the case of a manual swap, you'll need the pedal assembly for the clutch, as well as the factory Z-bar or hydraulics (depending on year), and obviously, a flywheel, clutch, pressure plate, throwout bearing, fork, and bellhousing.

A factory-style swap is certainly the most cost-effective way to gain a gear in an otherwise-stock C10—specifically a 700R4 or a later 4L60, as the parts to interchange won't need to be custom. Simply find a parts rig with the transmission you're after and collect all the drivetrain-related parts.

But to really get the most out of your truck, you should consider swapping in a modern overdrive transmission—especially if you intend to run a later-model engine, such as an LS V-8.

The addition of one (or several) overdrive gears is a real benefit if you intend on driving long distances, and having more gears simply means more flexibility in what your truck can do.

The squarebody truck offers quite a bit of room under the cab because it had to fit several transmission options from the factory, and as such, you can fit a number of different gearboxes in one of these trucks without much floor interference.

GM took the overdrive model it created with the 700R4 and made

If a manual swap is in the cards, be sure to get all the related parts from the donor rig for the job—even if you don't intend to use them all. Some of these components can be hard to track down (and expensive once you find them), so you don't want to discover that you left behind something after the fact. This includes the Z-bar, pedal linkage, return springs, and the pedals themselves—preferably all off the same donor truck.

The factory C10 transmission crossmember bolts both to the top of the frame and the bottom of the frame. The upper bolts drop down from the top, and if your cab bushings are worn, chances are you'll need to remove the cab mount bolts and lift the body slightly to get the bolts out and remove the crossmember. Some builders will simply pry up on the floor to make clearance.

it even better with its later-model units—and just about all of them are good choices for C10 use. Which specific later-model trans is right for you depends on your goals for your truck, as well as the other components you've already installed.

4L60/4L60E/4L65E/4L70E

The 4L60 transmission was an evolution of the 700R4, introduced in 1992. It became the 4L60E in 1997, sharing a lot of the same design, but for the addition of some electronics that will need to be run by a transmission control module (TCM).

These all have four forward gears, and the later models were designed specifically to work with LS powerplants. This is a good option for a C10, as its physical dimensions aren't different from the 700R4, which already fits under the cab. Overall length is 27¾ inches, just like a 700R4. The transmission mount is located in the same place as well, so the stock 700 crossmember out of a 1982 or later rig will work with the 4L60 and 4L60E.

There were two versions of the 60: an early one built from 1992 to 1996, and a late one built from 1996 to 2010. The main difference is in the bellhousing, which is removable on the later transmissions.

In 1998, GM upgraded the 60 with a 300-mm input shaft for use behind the LS engine. It also included a bellhousing bolt in the 12 o'clock position at the upper rear of the engine. Earlier 60s can be used behind LS engines with the addition of a special pilot spacer and dual bolt pattern flexplate—but the LS versions have upgraded internals and can handle more torque. They're the better choice for LS engine use.

The 4L65E was introduced alongside the 2001 6.0 LS engine and are fitted with a converter that is specific to that generation of engine. These transmissions are stronger thanks to some revised internals, but they require a different torque converter than the 60.

The 4L70E is visually nearly identical to the 60, but it is a nearly complete redesign internally. These are the toughest of the bunch, and the ultimate version of the 700R4.

4L80E/4L85E

The 4L80E is an electronic 4-speed version of the TH400. It's

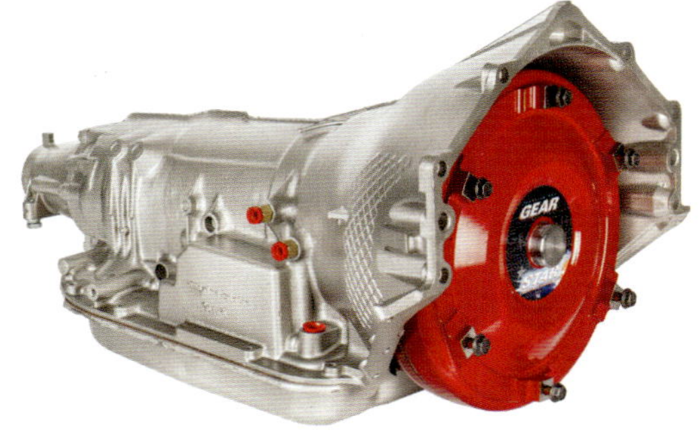

The 4L80E is a great swap option, as it's fairly close in dimensions to the TH400. There are several versions of this transmission, and they can be used behind both Gen II and LS V-8s. If towing and hauling are in the cards, this is a good option. Gearstar offers these transmissions in several configurations, with versions capable of living behind 800 hp. (Photo Courtesy Gearstar)

Gear Ratios and Measurements										
Transmission	First	Second	Third	Fourth	Fifth	Sixth	Overall Length	Bellhousing to Transmission Mount	Input to Transmission Mount	Output Splines
4L60-range	3.06:1	1.62:1	1.00:1	0.69:1	—	—	27¾ inches	22⅜ inches	—	27
4L80E-range	2.48:1	1.48:1	1.00:1	0.75:1	—	—	31½ inches	30⅜ inches	—	32
6L80-range	4.03:1	2.36:1	1:53:1	1.15:1	0.85:1	0.67:1	30.85 inches	25.409 inches	—	32
Tremec TKO 500	3.27:1	1.98:1	1.34:1	1.00:1	0.68:1	—	—	—	—	—
Tremec TKO 600	2.87:1	1.98:1	1.28:1	1.00:1	0.64:1 (or 0.82:1)	—	30.4 inches (input to output)	—	22.1 inches	31
Tremec Magnum/Super Magnum	2.66:1 (or 2.97:1)	1.78:1 (or 2.10:1)	1.30:1 (or 1.46:1)	1.00:1	0.80:1 (or 0.74:1)	0.63:1 (or 0.50:1)	33.5 inches (input to ouput)	—	26.5 inches	31

just as stout as its predecessor, being used from the factory in 3/4- and 1-ton trucks starting in 1991. Again, like the 4L60E, it will need a TCM to control its shift function, but the aftermarket has that covered.

The 4L85 is a stronger version of the 80, originally designed for rigs that were destined for heavy towing. As such, it has additional clutch packs.

If your truck had a TH400, you'll likely be able to get a 4L80E to fit under the trans tunnel—but be warned that this transmission is slightly wider and 4 inches longer than the TH400, and the rear transmission mount is about 1½ inch farther back than it is on the 400, so some fabrication will be required to make it work.

6L80E/6L90E

The 6L80 is a complete departure from the transmissions that came before, as it has six forward gears and was designed from the outset to be controlled electronically. Despite having more gears, these units are actually fairly short in length, but they're physically bigger overall, which could potentially lead to some floor and tunnel modifications in your C10.

Adding to its complexity is the fact that the TCM is internally located, which means it will need to be tuned to your project. And you won't be able to mate it up to anything other than a Gen IV engine—but if you're installing an engine and transmission package out of a wrecked 2010 Silverado, that's not a problem. However, since the paddle shifters that controlled manual up and down shifting were part of the donor vehicle's body control module, you'll be stuck with "D" only—

no manual options, at least at the time of this printing. With the popularity of overdrive swaps, it's only a matter of time before that's solved by the aftermarket.

Could you make one of these work in your C10? Sure. Several companies make kits that can make it a reality, and it will fit under the C10's floor hump, if only barely. Then again, if you want dual overdrives and don't mind a manual transmission, a T56 may be a better option.

Tremec TKO 5-Speed and T56 Magnum/Super Magnum 6-Speed

If rowing your own is your idea of fun, there's no better choice than a modern manual overdrive transmission in your C10. For our purposes, there are two great options: the Tremec TKO and the T56 Magnum/Super Magnum.

The TKO is a beefed-up version of the 5.0 Mustang's T5 5-speed, now capable of living behind up to 600 ft-lbs of torque.

Then there's the T56, Detroit's go-to 6-speed, with versions of it used in fourth-gen Camaros and C5 and C6 Corvettes, Dodge Vipers, and Shelby GT500s.

If you're looking for a stout performance transmission with great flexibility, either of these is a great choice.

The Magnum and Super Magnum have three different shifter locations direct from the factory. For a C10 with a bench seat, using a mid-mount or front-mount shifter is key, and these aftermarket T56s allow you to do that easily. OEM T56s (say, from a GTO or CTSV) don't allow the same flexibility without disassembly and internal modification to the mainshaft. That makes the Magnum series—which were designed as swap-friendly, aftermarket transmissions—the units to use, especially in a C10.

With each of these Tremec transmissions, a custom crossmember will be required for use in your C10.

Tremec's T56 Magnum and Super Magnum share the same basic overall design with some minor differences: The VSS plug on the Super is a GM style, while the Magnum uses a Ford plug. The Super also offers a different speed sensor signal, which makes it more compatible with GM's LS-engine ECUs.

The main problem with T56 installs in trucks has typically been related to shifter location and bench seat interference. The Magnum series solves that with three different shifter location options—but the factory shifter will only mount in the rearmost two. American Powertrain's White Lightning Midshift kit, part number SHWL-20200, moves the shifter forward farther, which puts it just about in the factory location for a 4-speed rig. This is a must-have item for T56 Magnum and Super Magnum transmissions in a C10 with a bench seat.

Two different Magnum transmission gear ratios have been available from Tremec, adding to that transmission's flexibility, but installing either one in an otherwise-stock C10 isn't advisable unless you have a relatively steep rear gear ratio from the factory.

The 12-bolt in my C10 had a factory 2.76 ratio, which isn't compatible with anything past the 1:1 ratio of fourth gear in a Magnum. We'll get to that in chapter 10.

T56 Super Magnum Installation

1 *Summit Racing sells a complete, new T56 Super Magnum (part number NAL-19352208) that can live behind engines making up to 700 hp. This transmission is the 2.66:1 first-gear unit, which is a good fit for a street-driven rig. It comes with a Tremec shifter that can be run either forward or backward in the rear shifter location, making install fairly easy for most builders.*

2 *In addition to the transmission, Summit also sells an attachment kit for LS engines (part number NAL-19301625). It includes an LS7 clutch, pressure plate and flywheel assembly, an LS1-style slave, a roller pilot bearing, an aluminum bellhousing for LS, and all the fasteners to complete the job. This is a great option, as it takes some of the guesswork out of which components will work with the Super Magnum.*

3 *After cleaning the inside of the crank with a piece of sandpaper to clear it for the pilot bearing, the flywheel is the first part of the install. Torque specs on the 15-mm fasteners are 74 ft-lbs, done in several stages. Thread-lock compound is a must here.*

4 *An impact socket that's the same diameter as the pilot bearing is the best tool for installing the bearing. Tapping it in with a hammer makes quick work of it.*

5 *The clutch plate is next. Use a plastic alignment tool to be sure it's centered correctly. The tool's splines mate to the clutch, while the nose seats in the bearing and holds it centered to the crankshaft. Be sure to clean off any handprints or oil from the flywheel with brake parts cleaner or lacquer thinner prior to install.*

6 *The pressure plate bolts to the firewall with the supplied hardware from the kit. The torque spec here is 52 ft-lbs.*

7 *The bellhousing bolts to the transmission next, with the bolts torqued to 37 ft-lbs. After that is the slave cylinder, which is held in place with two 10-mm bolts torqued to 71 in-lbs.*

8 After removing the plastic alignment tool, the transmission should slide right into place, albeit with some wiggling, jiggling, and adjusting of angles. It's important to get it seated by hand, not with the bellhousing bolts. Attempting to pull the transmission to the engine using the bellhousing bolts could easily damage the transmission. Torque is 37 ft-lbs. Note that I've removed the shifter to clear the floor for installation.

9 The key to getting the Magnum or Super Magnum to fit properly in a C10 is in this steel Hooker Blackheart transmission mount (part number 12646HKR). With the optional additional bracket, it places the rear of the transmission in the right place with respect to driveshaft angles when the matching engine mounts are used on a truck that's been lowered. You could build your own unit, but this one is ideal for air-ride trucks, as it allows the exhaust to tuck up into it. It also works with 700R4, 4L60, 4L80, TH350, TH400, and 2004R automatics.

10 With the engine mounts bolted in place, the transmission mount is next to be installed—but not until you have proper floor clearance for the T56. The floor pan interferes with the rear upper part of the transmission housing behind the shifter, so clearance needs to be made before it can be installed.

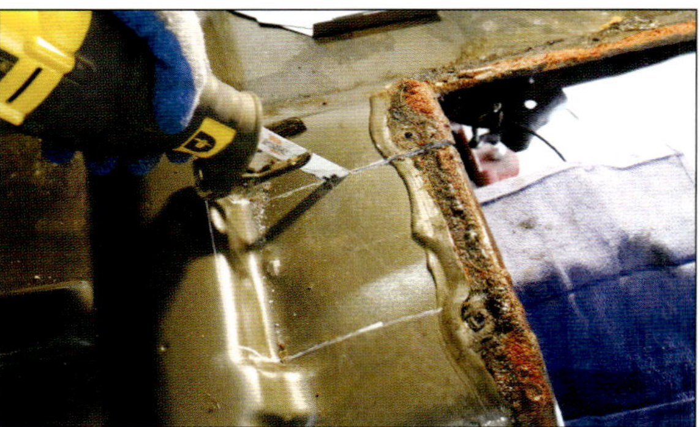

11 I elected to cut the floor where the transmission was hitting it and make a new, additional removable panel out of 18-gauge steel, much like the 4-speed hump already in the truck.

12 Light-gauge steel is great for mocking up a cover. Then, simply transfer the design to thicker steel, paint it, and bolt it in place. The patch should sit as low as possible while also providing at least 1 inch of clearance over the top of the transmission.

13 *Using the front pocket of the T56 Super Magnum and the American Powertrain White Lightning shifter puts the shift knob in just about the right spot—a few inches back from the factory location, which for a 4-speed truck was pretty far forward. This spot will allow for a shifter that sits back from the dash, even in first/third/fifth, but won't hit the seat in second/fourth/sixth.*

14 *Lokar's 16-inch double-bend shifter, part number MSL6B2, is just the ticket here, as it clears the seat even with the seat slid forward for shorter drivers. It's tall enough to be comfortable in a truck, and it's also round, so a factory 4-speed rubber boot and retainer ring will slide down over it. If you want a vaguely stock look even with that 6-speed knob, using the truck shift boot is the way to get it.*

Hydraulic Clutches

Something else to consider is that while the TKO can be set up with a mechanical clutch (as you'd see in all C10s prior to 1985), the Magnum requires a hydraulic clutch—and that can present a problem.

In 1985, GM switched from a mechanical clutch assembly to a hydraulic one. If you have a later truck, you're in luck—the stock hydraulic clutch master cylinder and firewall mount will work with a more modern overdrive manual transmission. But anything earlier will either need to be swapped or converted to use a hydraulic master cylinder.

Magnum and Super Magnum truck swaps have three options: source a stock hydro setup, build something from mixed and matched hydraulic parts, or go through a company such as American Powertrain, which takes all the guesswork out of swapping to a juice clutch via its HydraMax clutch system. That's what

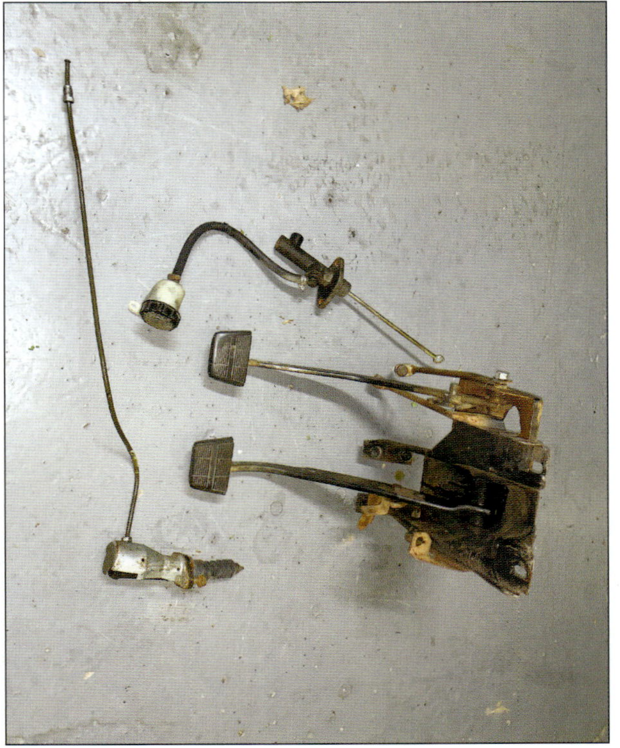

In the past, the trick for squarebody owners was to simply source the 1985 and newer hydro clutch from a wrecked truck and install that in an earlier rig, as it bolts in. But in recent years, prices for factory hydraulic setups have shot to the sky. Most of these used setups will be expensive, and they likely aren't going to be ready to go out of the junkyard anyway—you'll need a new master, maybe new lines, etc. If you can find a cheap setup that's in good shape and is complete, buy it! (Photo Courtesy Joshua Jackowski)

I did, and the swap was surprisingly simple using my factory mechanical clutch parts. However, if you have or can locate a factory setup, it can be used here with good results—and you can add it to an earlier truck with some careful measuring from the donor rig, just to be sure that the master cylinder and pushrod are located in the proper, stock location.

Hydraulic Clutch Installation

1 *Squarebody C10s have great underdash access—after you pull most of the dash apart. To get started on a hydro clutch swap, you need to pull the gauge cluster out of the truck. That starts with this plastic bezel, which is held in place with a handful of Philips-head screws around its perimeter. You'll need to remove the knob from the wiper switch and pull up the rubber grommet at the steering column to get this bezel off.*

2 *The steering column runs underneath the brake and clutch pedal box assembly, so it needs to go as well. Pulling the column completely out of the truck makes the most sense here, as otherwise it will be in your way. Two bolts at the steering box and one bolt farther up the steering shaft should be removed first—this makes the column itself shorter and easier to remove. There are five bolts at the firewall plate, removed from under the dash, and two large nuts that hold the assembly to the dash of the truck. Remove all of that, unplug the wiring harnesses, and the column will come right out.*

3 *The two nuts that retain the steering column to the truck also hold the front of the pedal box in place. The remaining bolts are actually studs that pass through the firewall and serve as mounts for the brake booster. Since the brake booster is coming off, this is a great time to clean it up for reinstallation later.*

4 *With the booster removed, you can unhook the clutch and brake linkages from the pedal assembly and wiggle it out from under the dash. Be sure to unplug the brake light switch as well as the clutch safety switch. You can also remove the large clutch spring that's part of the assembly, since the new setup won't need it.*

5 Years of use can put a heavy strain on the clutch and brake pedal pivot bushings and steel sleeves. GM part number 6264951 is the proper sleeve to replace a worn original, and they're still available from several suppliers. A new set of plastic bushings—at the very least—is a must if you're already pulling the clutch pedal assembly out of the truck. Mine was so heavily worn that it was bent to the side and catching on the high beam switch on the floor.

6 A long center bolt runs through the pedal assembly on these trucks, holding both the brake and clutch pedals in place. Removing it frees both pedals, allowing you to replace the pivot sleeve and bushings. Be sure to apply some white grease to the assembly before reinstallation.

7 The heart of this system is the HydraMax hydraulic clutch from American Powertrain. It uses a special, adjustable bracket that can be oriented in a number of different ways to achieve the proper clutch pedal geometry for good alignment. It comes with everything you need, including the option of adding the slave cylinder for the T56.

8 At first glance, mounting a clutch master looks like a chore, but there's one great place that's already set up and ready: the factory speedometer cable hole. Situated between the brake booster and the wiper motor, it is in direct alignment with the factory clutch pedal, and the hole is already big enough to allow for some adjustment in the placement of your clutch rod.

9 Here's another look at the alignment of the pedal to the factory speedometer cable hole: Note the brake pedal and its factory hole to the right, with the clutch to the left.

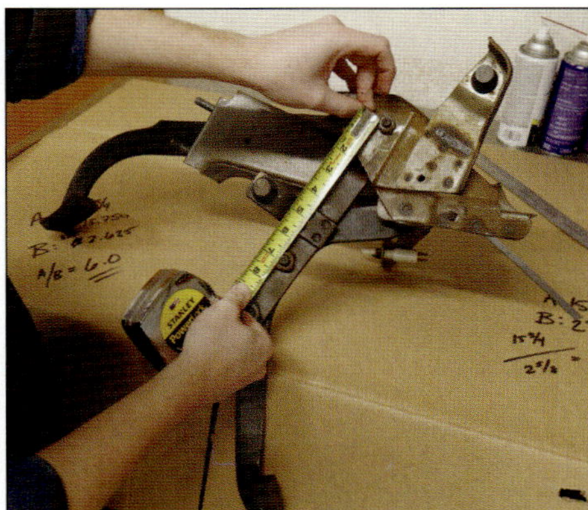

10 Achieving proper pedal geometry is key to getting good clutch operation and feel with a hydraulic clutch system. Since I'm not using the factory mechanical linkage, it means drilling a new hole, and that requires some math: the overall length of the pedal from fulcrum to center of pedal pad is 15¾ inches. American Powertrain recommends a pedal ratio of 6:1, which meant my new hole needed to be 2⅝ inches down from the fulcrum of the pedal.

11 *The HydraMax comes with two steel plates that sandwich the firewall and provide a mount for the adjustable master cylinder bracket. Installing this is as simple as drilling the holes and bolting it up. If you find that the firewall flexes with clutch pedal operation, you can fabricate a pair of steel straps that connect from these fasteners and tie in to the brake pedal mount assembly under the dash.*

12 *It's best to loosely bolt up the complete assembly to check for proper alignment through the clutch pedal travel. Once you're satisfied, cinch everything down. Be sure the clutch rod doesn't rub on anything, and if it does, correct it before going any further.*

13 *Two locknuts serve as a solid pedal stop, which will stop you from overextending either the master cylinder or the slave cylinder by too much pedal travel. Here I've set up travel to be 1 inch at the master, which should give about 6 inches of travel at the pedal pad.*

14 *The key to this system is the adjustable bracket: keeping that 6:1 ratio at the pedal may mean that you'll be mounting this master cylinder at an angle. The bracket allows you to do that, keeping installation simple while maintaining the integrity of your clutch operation.*

15 *I made a little steel bracket to move the clutch fluid reservoir up and away from the brake booster. American Powertrain ships this kit with a couple of screws and fittings to allow a remote mount. All that's left is to install the supplied line, connect it to the transmission, and bleed the system.*

Driveline

Depending on the year and the configuration of your truck, you may have either a stock one-piece driveline or a two-piece driveline. In either case, it's unlikely that you'll be able to reuse your stock piece if you intend to swap transmissions. Either your overall length will be different or the spline count of the new transmission won't match what came out of your truck. You'll likely need either new driveline parts or a completely new driveline.

GM's engineers knew what they were doing when they determined driveline type for each specific truck. Trucks with two-piece drivelines had them for a reason—likely because in that application, for whatever reason, a one-piece shaft would deflect at a certain speed and break parts. Think of your driveline acting like a jump rope and you get the idea. Yes, they can do that, and no, the results aren't pretty.

These trucks came with both types of shafts—one-piece and two-piece—depending on the year of and options of each specific rig. For simplicity's sake, most builders prefer one-piece drivelines, but it pays to consult with a driveline shop before making the swap. They can help you spec out a shaft that will suit your needs—either through building something custom or shortening a longer shaft from a different rig.

Measuring for the proper driveshaft length is also critical because no two aftermarket setups are exactly the same—there aren't off-the-shelf solutions here. Most companies have specific requests when it comes to measurements, typically starting with the distance from the rear transmission tailshaft housing to the U-joint mounting surface of the differential yoke. Additionally, you'll need to know the distance from the tailshaft itself to the yoke. Measure two or three times to be sure you get these numbers right before you submit them to your driveline shop.

Speedometer

Modern transmissions—specifically those that are controlled with a computer—may or may not have a provision for the cable-driven speed-

Single-Piece Driveline Swap

The factory two-piece driveline is a stout piece, but if you're looking to swap over to a single-piece unit on a lowered truck, you'll need to remove the factory carrier bearing support from the frame. This is easiest when the bed is off the truck, as you'll be able to access the rearmost two of its four mounting rivets from above. As with the rear suspension, center-punching and drilling the heads of the rivets is a good way to start removal, followed up with the blade from an air chisel. ■

My short-bed's original driveshaft was a two-piece unit with a center-mounted carrier bearing. This won't work with the T56 conversion, so I removed it and the carrier bearing mount that was riveted to the frame. Since the truck is considerably lower than stock, a new one-piece shaft would interfere with the bracket.

Here's the new driveshaft, built locally at Driveline Service in Portland, Oregon. It's 57$^{13}/_{16}$ inches from front to rear, uses the 31-spline slip yoke for the T56 Magnum and Super Magnum (which is the same as a C6 Ford unit), and has the stock-style 1330 U-joints that came in this truck.

---

ometer that came factory in your truck. If you want to keep the stock interior look with the stock interior gauges, that presents a problem because the modern transmission and the factory gauge likely won't interface.

You can change the gauges to something custom, such as Dakota Digital's C10 gauge package, or if you're dead-set on keeping that factory speedometer, there's a plug-and-play solution in Speedhut's Speedbox.

Speedhut's Speedbox is a genius little solution to a significant problem. It uses both a vehicle speed sensor (VSS) input from a modern electronic transmission as well as a GPS signal to spin an electric motor, which connects to a stock-style cable to run your original speedometer. It comes from Speedhut with the drive cable, all the wiring, and the GPS antenna. It's also great for those who used the factory speedo dash hole to mount a clutch master cylinder.

The wiring is simple: one keyed hot, a ground, a VSS signal wire, and one constant hot to keep the unit synced to the satellites above. The unit primarily uses the GPS signal to calculate your speed, with the VSS as a secondary source. It can also be hooked up with just one or the other signal sources.

The only tricky part of installing the Speedbox is figuring out where you want to mount it. There's a great spot on the driver-side kick panel, tucked up behind the parking brake assembly. A couple of self-tapping screws hold it in place—this location makes wiring easy, and the speedo cable is just the right length for this spot.

Mount the magnetic antenna someplace where it can see the sky—it won't acquire signal through metal, so the hood or the roof is best. You can also put it on top of the dash for a cleaner look.

REAR AXLE

All Chevrolet and GMC pickups from the square era have live rear axles as standard equipment. The 1/2-ton versions of the trucks were equipped with one of two versions from the factory, depending on model year: the 12-bolt and the 10-bolt. If you're building a 1/2-ton from 1973 to 1987, it'll have one of these two units behind the driveline. That's good, as parts are plentiful, and both are fairly solid performers even in stock trim. However, they can be made better with the addition of upgraded parts.

Bolt Count

How do you tell what rear axle you have? The simplest way is to reference what year truck you have. If it's a 1981 or earlier, you should have a 12-bolt. Later trucks will generally have the 10-bolt, but not always. Identification is as simple as counting the bolts that hold the rear cover to the housing: 12 bolts hold the 12-bolt cover in place, while 10 bolts hold the 10-bolt cover to the housing.

The bolt count actually refers to the number of bolts that secure the ring gear to the carrier, but that's not something you can see from outside the assembly, so the rear cover count works for quick identification purposes.

An even quicker way to tell what you have is to look at the 6 o'clock position of the rear axle housing from the back of the truck. If there's a single bolt there, you have a 10-bolt. If there are two, one on either side of that 6 o'clock spot and spaced out parallel to the ground, you have a 12-bolt. No counting required.

Why does this matter? The 12-bolt is thought to be a stronger axle overall, so if you have performance aspirations for your rig, such as drag racing or off-roading, the common thought is that a 12-bolt is the axle to have—at least in terms of factory-style solutions. In reality, both units are stout pieces.

The 10-Bolt

Standard starting in 1982, the 8.5-inch 10-bolt features a 1.625-inch pinion shaft diameter with either

Most of the later (1981 and newer) squarebody trucks will feature a 10-bolt axle, which can be quickly identified by having only one bolt at the 6 o'clock position. Contrary to popular belief, these 10-bolts are stout units that can take a pretty decent amount of punishment.

28- or 30-spline axles. The axles are retained in the carrier with C-clips and a large center pin. The 8.5-inch nomenclature refers to the ring gear diameter. These were used in pickups up until the late 1990s, and they're relatively strong, although they're frequently frowned upon thanks to the weak reputation of GM's lesser 7.5-, 7.625-, and 8.2-inch 10-bolts used in other models. Those axle assemblies frequently failed behind any significant horsepower, and their similar name (and same number of cover bolts) have soured builders on the stronger 8.5- and 8.6-inch 10-bolt units as well.

That said, the 8.5-inch 10-bolt used in squarebody pickups isn't going to live long past about 400 hp, which is not a lot in today's world of high-horse LS conversions. Upgraded carriers, beefier 30-spline axles, and improved ring and pinion sets can be added from the aftermarket to bring an 8.5 up to a much more stout level.

The 12-Bolt

The 12-bolt was introduced in 1964. It features an 8.875-inch ring gear and, in truck applications, a 1.438-inch pinion shaft diameter. Like the 10-bolt, it uses C-clips to retain the axles in the carrier.

The car 12-bolt features a different rear cover than the truck version, which makes identification pretty easy. Note that internal parts between these two axles don't interchange.

These axles are thought to be stronger alternatives to the 10-bolt, but in reality, either one can be built to an acceptable level of strength for use in a C10. All the same performance parts alternatives apply to the 12-bolt, just as they do to the 10-bolt: axles, carriers, rings and pinions, etc.

One important note is that car and truck 12-bolts are not the same. Car units are significantly stronger than their truck counterparts because they have a much larger pinion bearing diameter. They also use a wider, stronger internal carrier, and they mount the pinion higher on the ring gear, which if you're really being picky, is better as it provides less parasitic loss and greater power delivery to the wheels.

However, swapping a car 12-bolt into a truck is not a simple process, as everything from the axle bolt pattern, spring mounts, overall width, and U-joint are different. An easier swap is from a 10-bolt to a truck 12-bolt because the only real dimensional difference between the two is in the pinion U-joint. All truck axles in the squarebody years are the same width, and they mount to the rear leaf springs in the same way. As such, if you buy a truck with a growly 10-bolt, you can swap in a 12-bolt from an earlier truck fairly easily—and vice versa.

Heavy-Duty Units

The 3/4-ton and 1-ton trucks in this era came with GM's corporate 14-bolt axle. It's an eight-lug setup (versus the five-lug 1/2-ton two-wheel-drive and six-lug 1/2-ton four-wheel-drive rigs), and most of

The 12-bolt truck axle is arguably stronger than the 10-bolt. But that reputation comes from the car version of the 12-bolt, which has a much larger pinion shaft diameter than its truck counterpart. Even so, these are also strong units that will stand up to abuse when in good operable condition.

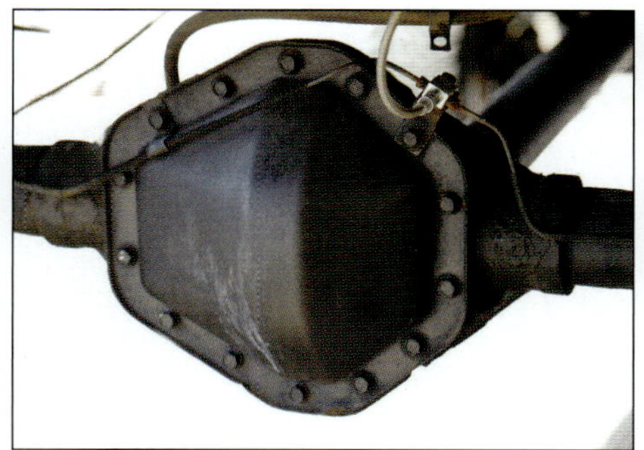

If you have a 3/4-ton or 1-ton rig, you probably have this monster of an axle underneath it. The corporate 14-bolt, as it's known, features some very heavy-duty components that make it ideal for towing and hauling.

If you don't know what gear ratio your C10 has, the axle tube can shed some light on things. The passenger-side upper tube will have a stamping in it, typically about halfway between the pumpkin and the brake backing plate. Look for three letters. In this case, RAJ translates to a 2.76:1 open rear axle. But that only applies to an axle that has never been modified.

these axles are a full-floating design. This means that the axles aren't used to hold up the weight of the truck, but instead are only used to transmit torque, and they do so via a bolt-in hub at each wheel. This is a heavy-duty solution with a 10½-inch ring gear diameter and 1¾-inch pinion, and it's designed for heavy hauling. Interestingly enough, the ring gear is fixed with only 12 bolts—it's the rear cover in this case that generated the name.

In 1981, GM introduced a semi-floating 14-bolt axle that used C-clips like the 1/2-ton 10- and 12-bolt units. It can be identified by a lack of bolted-in axle shafts at the brake drum. A Dana 70 was also used in certain dually trucks and was optional in others. Not much typically goes wrong with these heavy-duty units, other than things like bearings and seals that wear out over time and heavy use.

What's My Gear Ratio?

Want to know what gear ratio you have in your truck? Here's a quick procedure to help you.

1. On a level surface and with the front wheels chocked, jack up the rear axle with a floor jack until both wheels are off the ground. Make sure the truck's in neutral and the parking brake is not set.
2. Spin one tire and watch the other side. If the other tire spins in the same direction as the one you're turning, you have a Positraction axle. If the other tire spins in the opposite direction, you have an open diff.
3. If you have an open diff, set the truck back on the ground and move the jack under the axle, just behind the drum brake backing plate. Jack up the one side until the wheel is off the ground, leaving the other in contact with the ground. If you have a Posi diff, leave the jack in the center with both wheels in the air.
4. Find a way to mark both your tire and the driveshaft. A piece of tape is a good solution. Be sure to use a jackstand or two as a backup to your jack when you're getting under the truck.
5. With both the tire and the pinion marked, spin the tire one full revolution, from 12 o'clock to 12 o'clock using your tape mark, while counting the number of revolutions of the driveshaft tape. The resulting numbers should be your ratio. For example, if your driveshaft turns 3 ¾ turns for the one wheel revolution, you have a 3.73:1 ratio. ■

In my case, the driveshaft spun 2¾ revolutions for the one wheel rotation, which added up with the factory stamping on the axle tube: for a 2.76:1 ratio.

Checking Gears

Both the 10-bolt and the 12-bolt came stock with a variety of gear ratios from the factory, ranging from 2.56:1 to 4:56:1. There is a code stamped in the top of the axle tube on the passenger's side of the truck that can shed some light on what your truck might have had when new, as well as a build sheet or SPID, but that doesn't take into account what might have been swapped into the housing after the factory built the truck.

Also keep in mind that due to the sheer number of trucks produced, complete axle swaps from junkyard rigs were common over the years when these trucks were simply used rigs. There's no telling whether or not the original gears are still in the housing, and there's also no telling whether or not the housing in your truck is the one it had from the factory.

When it comes to gear ratios, there are two sure-fire ways to tell what you have: pull the cover and count the teeth on the ring and pinion or check by rotating a tire and counting the pinion rotations.

It's likely that you'll end up with a set of numerically lower gears in your factory truck because ratios like my 2.76:1 were common in the 1970s and 1980s for lowering fuel consumption at higher speeds. But unfortunately, that sort of ratio is awful from a performance standpoint, so you'll want to consider a rear gear swap if performance is on your mind—especially if you're adding an overdrive transmission, as I did.

Swapping gears is a science in a GM rear axle, as it requires careful shimming to set up a proper contact patch between the ring gear and the pinion gear. A crush sleeve is part of that adjustment, which can't be reused once it's been crushed. But don't let any of that scare you away; swapping gears on a 10- or 12-bolt isn't that complex of a process, especially if you set yourself up with the right parts and the right tools to do the job.

Two-Tire Fire

When you go to mash the loud pedal, the last thing you want is for one tire to go up in smoke. Getting the other side to join the party requires a limited-slip differential, a locker, or a spool.

Limited Slip

Several companies make clutch-style limited-slip differential units for GM rear axles, and GM offered them from the factory as well.

In the aftermarket, two of the major ones are Auburn Gear's High Performance Series differentials and Eaton's Posi Performance differentials. Both units use clutches that link the right and left wheels together when under power but can slip to allow the rear wheels to turn at different rates, as when going around corners.

The main difference between the two designs is in the clutches:

Auburn's limited-slip unit is another good choice for a street-driven rig because it offers long life and great grip. The main difference here is in clutch design, with the Auburn using a cone-style friction surface for its positraction action. (Photo Courtesy Summit Racing)

the Auburn uses cone-style clutches that push against the differential case, while the Eaton uses a flat clutch pack. I've run both, and my preferred unit is the Eaton because it's more easily rebuildable on the rare occasion that the clutches wear out. The Eaton also allows for more tuning via swappable spring packs to either increase or decrease the clutch bias. The Auburn, on the other hand, offers great clutch grip, quick operation, and less possibility of clutch chatter.

Eaton's Positraction is a great street unit, thanks to smooth operation and long life. The bias is adjustable via different springs, and the carbon friction discs can be replaced if they wear out, restoring it to operable condition. This is a 3-series carrier (for 2.76 to 3.42 gear ratios) specific for truck 12-bolt axles (part number 19587-010).

Either one is available for 10-bolt and 12-bolt axles, and either one is good choice for a street-driven performance vehicle.

Locker

A locking differential does just what it says: via mechanical, electronic, or compressed air systems, it locks the rear wheels together. These remain locked in most circumstances. However, they unlock when needed, such as when going around corners.

These units tend to be more expensive than limited-slip units, but they're less likely to wear out over time, as there are no clutches to slip. The downsides are in price and noise. Certain units, like Detroit Lockers, tend to clunk when operating around corners.

Factory units, sold as RPO G80 through the square years, are known as Gov-Lock units. These are a sort of hybrid design between a limited-slip

If you want to be sure you have both tires pushing when you need them, a locker might be your best bet. This is a Detroit Locker, which acts like a spool until you turn a corner. These are some of the best units for big-power street applications, but they do tend to clunk and make noise during use. (Photo Courtesy Summit Racing)

Spools lock the left and right wheels together mechanically, so they cannot turn at different rates. This is great for straight-line acceleration, but it will make for some interesting cornering, especially in a truck that has no weight in the bed. These are best left to the dragstrip. This one is from Strange Engineering. (Photo Courtesy Summit Racing)

and a locker—under 25 mph and when wheel spin is detected, the unit locks up and both tires get power. Above that speed, the Gov-Lock unlocks to allow the rear wheels to operate at different speeds. These work well when they're in good condition and when used for their intended purpose—regular driving. They are not for performance applications. In fact, they've earned the nickname "Gov-Bomb" for good reason, as they tend to explode when they lock up under high-power conditions, typically destroying gears, axles, bearings, and even differential housings when they go boom.

Another option is Eaton's True-trac, which uses helical gears to achieve power to both wheels. These are generally bulletproof, like a locker, but offer much smoother, quiet operation. Both of these units require no special friction modifiers in the rear axle oil, unlike clutch-style systems.

Spool

Unless racing is the only plan for your C10, a spool isn't a great choice—especially not for a street-driven vehicle. These units lock both axles together at all times, allowing no differential in wheel speed from right to left. That's a problem when going around corners—especially tight corners—as both wheels always have to spin at the same rate, which tends to make the rear hop slightly and can cause understeer (followed by snap oversteer when you hit the throttle). For drag racing applications, there's no better option. These are best left to the track.

Parts Selection

Before choosing the gears, you need to consider a few things. First, what other parts are you planning on using? Where will you be driving this truck most often? And what sort of performance are you looking to achieve?

Many things factor into rear gear ratio selection, but your cam, your transmission, and your preferred RPM range at cruise are all at the top of that list.

Cars and trucks with large-duration cams and high-stall torque converters tend to be happier with numerically higher (functionally lower, or "shorter") ratios, in the 3.73–4.56:1 range. But those ranges, while quick off the line, push RPMs higher at cruising speed unless an overdrive transmission is used—such as the 700R4 or 4L60E automatic or T56 Magnum/Super Magnum manual.

Conversely, cars with stock engine and transmission parts can get great mileage with a numerically lower (functionally higher, or "taller") ratio, such as a 3.43:1 or 3.55:1. These

---

setups offer lower RPM cruising in top gear and are much more friendly with factory 3-speed TH350 and TH400 automatic transmissions, while still offering a better rate of acceleration than the smogger-era 2.76:1 or 3.08:1 ratio that's probably still installed in your C10.

Note that GM offered several different carrier styles for both 10- and 12-bolt rear axle assemblies based upon the gearset range used.

These are referred to as 2-series, 3-series, and 4-series carriers, and the breakdown is: 2-series carriers work with gearsets ranging from 2.29:1 to 2:73:1, 3-series carriers work with gearsets from 3.07:1 to 3.73:1, and 4-series work with 4.10:1 to 4.88:1. The reasoning for this is simple: the lower numerical (functionally higher) ratios require a larger-diameter pinion gear, which requires that the ring gear is

Fear the C-Clip?

Ask any wheeler, drag racer, or road racer about C-clip axles and most will tell you the same thing: you better get a set of C-clip eliminators for positive axle retention, like you'd see in a Ford 9-inch. Pressed-on wheel bearings that retain the axle in the housing are a safety feature—if an axle shaft breaks in a Ford, the axle stays in the car. If a shaft breaks in a 10- or 12-bolt Chevy, that wheel—and whatever's left of the axle shaft—comes out of the housing and then out of the truck, causing all kinds of damage along the way and maybe even causing an accident.

While working on the 12-bolt axle for my project truck, I consulted Dan Suldul of Dan's Gears in Sherwood, Oregon. He's built, fixed, and installed axles and gears for over 30 years, and he's seen his share of mangled parts along the way. The one thing he says he's never seen is a broken C-clip.

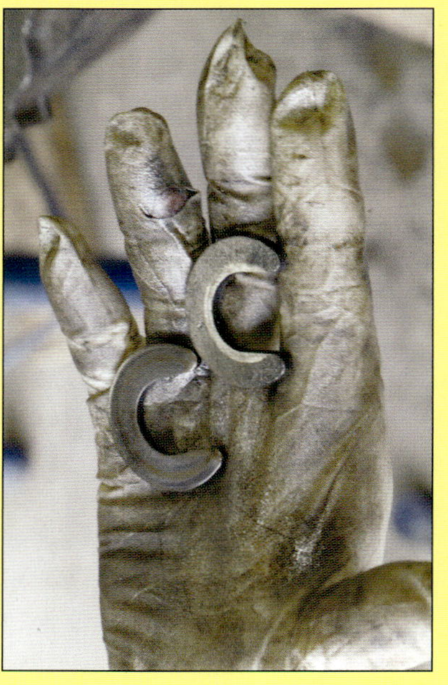

Stock GM axles make use of C-shaped clips for positive axle retention. These slide into the carrier, sit in place at the end of the axle shaft, and are held in place with a center pin. Some builders will tell you to eliminate them, as they can be a weak point in your rear axle assembly—if an axle breaks, it can come out of the housing.

Moser makes a nice C-clip eliminator kit for the 10- and 12-bolt Chevrolet, which consists of a bearing and retainer that press on the wheel side of the axle shaft (as in a Ford 9-inch) and then bolt to the axle housing, which helps to retain a broken axle shaft. This is a smart upgrade. (Photo Courtesy Summit Racing)

That's not to say it can't happen, but it's not common. Factory axles can and do break from time to time under certain high-stress situations, but it's uncommon on a street vehicle.

If everything passes inspection and you don't note any excessive play or clearance around the axles, cross shaft, and C-clips when you have your axle apart, there's no reason to install C-clip eliminators on a street truck. You'd be better served to install upgraded axles, as offered from companies such as Moser or Strange Engineering. These are made of stronger material than the factory carbon steel axles, so they can take much more abuse. You'll also avoid oil leaks around aftermarket C-clip eliminators, which have traditionally been caused by side-loading forces on street vehicles (not an issue on drag vehicles) and have been hard to solve.

If drag racing is in the cards, however, where hard launches on sticky tires is the norm, you might consider an upgrade to eliminators now. Otherwise you may be paying for bodywork—both on you and your truck—later. ■

What's the story with a 2-, 3-, or 4-series carrier? It's all about ratios: a 2-series carrier will require a larger-diameter pinion gear, which requires the ring gear to be spaced farther away from it. This is a 2.76:1 pinion in a 12-bolt.

Here's a pinion for a set of 4.11 gears, which is much smaller in diameter and requires different placement of the ring gear. This is why 2-, 3-, and 4-series carriers aren't interchangeable in most cases.

placed farther away from the centerline of the pinion shaft to make room for that larger pinion gear. As such, you can't mix and match ratios between different series.

The one exception to that rule is to buy thicker gearsets to run 4-series ratios in 3-series carriers. These sets space the ring gear away from the carrier such that the smaller-diameter pinion used in the 4-series sets can mesh properly.

The benefit here is flexibility later: if you want to run 4:11s now for drag racing fun and you want to keep the option to run 3:43s later for better cruising RPM with a 3-speed automatic, a 3-series carrier with thicker 4-series gears designed to fit it is the way to go. Posi carriers cost about $450 without gears. You might as well get the setup that will allow you to run both ratios rather than having to buy a new carrier as well as gears when you decide to swap gears again later.

As for which parts to use, that's up to you, but it's always smart to spend more on better parts when it comes to something as important as your rear axle assembly. I prefer to do this once and do it right.

When it comes to gear choice, your best bet is to search for a gear ratio calculator online and run the numbers for your application, and then follow that advice.

Swapping Gears in a 12-Bolt Chevy

My project C10 still had its factory 12-bolt with original 2.76:1 gears, which, while decently suited to the SM465 4-speed manual it had originally, weren't going to work with the T56 Super Magnum 6-speed that I sourced from Summit Racing for the project. According to Tremec's online calculator, with a 28-inch-tall tire and the engine at 2,000 rpm, I'd have been running 22 mph in first gear, 33 mph in second, and on up to 95 mph in sixth.

Since land speed racing isn't in the cards for this C10, I needed a numerically higher (functionally lower) gear to really make use of the 0.80 and 0.63 overdrive ratios inside the Super Magnum.

After checking Summit's site for what was available for the truck 12-bolt, I ran the numbers again and landed on a 4.11:1 ratio as the perfect solution. Again, at 2,000 rpm, the 4.11s place it at 15 mph in first, 22 in second, and 64 in sixth—much more usable all-around. Here's how to do the swap.

Changing the Gearset

1 *A gear swap can be done with the axle either in or out of the truck. Here, the axle is out and on a stand for easy accessibility.*

4 *With the axles out, it's a good time to check for scoring or discoloration where each axle rides on the axle bearing. If you find any, replace the axle.*

2 *Pulling the rear cover is the only way to drain the gear oil out of a 12-bolt, as there is no drain plug. Note that there's one bolt with a longer shank—this one goes in the hole that supports the brake line bracket. Don't mix this bolt up with the others—be sure it goes back in the same hole, otherwise you may strip its threads on reassembly.*

3 *A 5/16-inch bolt holds the center pin in place. Remove the bolt, then slide out the pin. From there, pushing each axle in toward the brake backing plate will free the C-clips and allow the axles to slide out.*

5 *It's a good idea to mark both caps and the housing with a punch so you can be sure of the original orientation before reassembly. It's best to return both differential caps to their original locations.*

6 With both caps removed, the original carrier can come out. With it will come the carrier bearings, races, and carrier shims. Keep the factory shims organized and segregate them by side—don't mix up the right-side shims with the left-side shims. A large pry bar aids in pulling the carrier from the housing.

7 With the pinion nut loose, drive the pinion in toward the rear of the housing, then remove it completely.

8 Next, drive out the bearing races with a long punch and big hammer. Working around each race helps it come out without binding. One will come out the rear, one will come out the front.

9 After pulling the brake drum backing plates, the next step is to remove each axle bearing. There's one per side. A slide hammer comes in handy here, as these are pressed in place. A couple of good whacks and they'll be out.

10 A couple of cans of brake parts cleaner is all that it takes to clean up a rear housing, assuming there were no broken parts inside. This axle is ready to go back together.

11 Even though the new pinion is going to be fitted with a new pinion bearing, you have to pull apart the old setup to measure which shim is behind the OEM bearing. This will serve as a starting point for your new setup. This slick tool skips the press, instead using a threaded rod and a pneumatic impact wrench to pull the bearing off the pinion without marring it in any way. This is handy, as it allows for repeated install and teardown to find the proper fit without hurting the bearing.

13 This is a 4.11:1 ring and pinion from Motive Gear, sourced from Summit Racing. It's a 3-series gear-set, designed for a 3-series carrier. I chose it for flexibility in gear ratio swaps later because a 4-series carrier would limit me to 4:10 and higher ratios.

12 Ratech's kit (part number 3005K) comes with everything you need to swap a set of gears in a 12-bolt truck axle, from the marking compound to all the seals, bearings, bolts, and races.

14 The original pinion had a 0.030-inch spacer between it and the pinion bearing. The Ratech kit comes with a 0.031-inch spacer, which is a good place to start. With the spacer installed, the bearing needs to be pressed on the pinion.

16 The heart of a performance axle is the differential. This one is a 3-series Eaton clutch-style limited-slip differential, and below it is the Motive Gear ring gear for the 4.11s. Note its thicker design to work with the 3-series carrier.

15 Next up is to install the new bearing races from the Ratech kit. These are best installed using an aluminum-headed driver because that won't damage the race surface when you hammer it into place.

17 Once you're certain that both the ring gear and differential are clean and the surfaces are true, the ring gear can be installed on the carrier. Tighten the bolts in a crisscross pattern to 55 ft-lbs, and be sure to use a thread locker, such as Loctite.

18 Next, it's back to the press to install the carrier bearings—one per side, pressed into place until they stop. No shims needed here.

19 After sliding the pinion bearing into the housing from the back, tighten it without the crush sleeve in place—but only until you start to feel drag on the bearing when you spin the pinion shaft. The idea here is to achieve zero play in the bearings to ballpark the setup of the gears.

21 Setting the carrier in place with the shims, bearings, and races can be a bit of a challenge because everything seems to want to fall out of place. Take your time and watch both sides as you go.

20 Here's where the original carrier shims come into play. From the factory, this 12-bolt had a larger shim opposite the ring gear than it did on the ring gear side of the carrier. For initial setup, the best bet is to attempt to retain those same shim measurements to get into the proper ballpark for gear setup. The OEM shims are one-piece cast-iron pieces, which some prefer to stacked-up smaller shims. If they're in good shape, there's no reason you can't reuse the original iron pieces. Otherwise the Ratech shims from the install kit will do the job.

22 Here's an old trick to get into the ballpark of proper setup with a 12-bolt: If the carrier drops all the way to a seated position, it'll be too loose and will need more shims. If it can't be driven in with thumps from a deadblow hammer, it's too tight and needs fewer shims. If the hammer drives it in place, you're on track. The idea here is to get as much preload as you can, i.e., as many shims between the case and the carrier as you can get to fit.

23 With the carrier caps torqued to spec, you can paint on the gear marking compound that comes in the kit, and then spin the pinion to check the contact patch of the ring gear to the pinion gear.

24 This pattern is about as good as it gets—right on the money, right out of the box. If the pattern is weighted more toward one side or the other (heel or toe of the gear), add and subtract shims from the carrier to center up the contact patch. Adding or subtracting from the pinion gear moves the patch up and down, from crown to root of each gear tooth.

25 With the contact patch set, the carrier needs to come back out so you can install the pinion crush sleeve and oil seal. Everything comes apart the same way it went together—be sure to note which shims went where.

26 GM's 10- and 12-bolt use a crush sleeve to set the pinion preload. This sits in behind the pinion yoke between the inner and outer bearing, and "crushes" when the pinion nut is tightened, setting and holding the proper preload in the process. It's a one-shot deal—there's no reusing one of these once it's crushed too far.

27 The crush sleeve takes approximately 300 to 400 ft-lbs to crush properly, so a heavy-duty impact and a lot of PSI to run it is really the best way to do this job, while stopping frequently to check and not overshoot the proper preload spec: 14–19 in-lbs of rotational force. Be sure to install the oil seal before torqueing the pinion nut, and use threadlock compound here as well.

28 With the carrier reinstalled and the caps torqued to 60 ft-lbs, double-check the contact patch to be sure nothing has moved with regard to the setup.

29 Finally, using a dial indicator, check the ring gear backlash to be sure it's within spec. For a 12-bolt Chevy, it should read between 0.006 and 0.010 inch.

30 Driving in the new axle bearings is best done with an aluminum driver and hammer. They'll come up tight when fully seated.

31 In colder weather, it's particularly important to grease the wheel bearings and the seal before installing that seal. This helps ensure that the new bearings are lubricated until the gear oil can warm up enough to make it down the axle tubes.

32 *With the axles slid in place, the C-clips can be refitted. Once they're in place, pull out on each axle to seat them in the new differential. A magnet helps to get them oriented correctly.*

33 *Finally, the cross shaft can be installed, which keeps the C-clips and the axles tight in the housing. The new differential comes with a new 5/16-inch bolt to retain the shaft.*

34 *A quick shot of primer and paint and the axle is ready for reinstallation in a C10. Be sure to fill it with the proper GL5 mineral-based oil and 4 ounces of GM friction modifier before heading off down the road, and follow the gear manufacturer's instructions for proper gear break-in.*

Breaking in New Gears

You have a new Posi and a new set of gears to wake up your rig's performance in a big way. The first thing to do is go melt some rubber, right? Wrong.

It's important to properly break in a new set of gears for the life of the axle. Just getting out and hammering on the truck can damage those new gears and possibly void any warranty you had on the parts.

The best bet here is to run through a good break-in procedure as recommended by your gear manufacturer. Here are some of the basics:

Heat is the enemy of a new gearset. So drive the first 15 to 20 miles at between 15 and 55 mph, and then stop to let the diff cool before you continue. The idea here is to let the surfaces mate together properly without breaking down.

It's best to keep speeds below 60 mph if at all possible, at least for the first 100 or so miles. After 500 miles, swapping the gear oil is a good idea, as it will remove any metallic contaminants generated when the gears broke in.

You'll want to hold off on towing until after those 500 miles have passed, and again, you'll want to stop frequently—every 15 miles or so—for the first 45 miles of towing.

After that, it's time to go try out that all-new two-tire fire.

BODY, TRIM, AND INTERIOR

When it comes to body modifications on C10s, there's really no limit to what you can do. It all comes down to personal preference and skill level.

There have been a lot of hot trends in trucks over the years from roll bars and KC lights in the 1970s to heartbeat graphic paint in the 1980s and billet steel wheels in the 1990s. Once you start looking around, you'll see custom trucks dating from all these time periods. But today, one of the hotter trends is custom trucks with patina—trucks built with OEM-spec trim and colors that are either legitimately worn or made to look old but built with all-new parts underneath.

Whatever you choose to do, the parts are available to make your truck fit into just about any style category you choose.

Common Body Modifications

Stock trucks do look great—a lot of builders will tell you that GM just did this design right. However, personalization has always been an American car builder staple, and there are many things you can do to a squarebody Chevrolet or GMC to update its look.

Glass

These trucks were praised for their greenhouses in 1973, and current builders are expanding upon that. Many high-end trucks now feature custom glass that eliminates trim and makes a squarebody's greenhouse look much more modern. If you really want a clean look to your C10, you should consider flush-mount front and rear glass and one-piece side glass.

Classic Industries, Brothers, and One Piece Products all sell complete, one-piece side glass kits that eliminate your C10's factory wing windows, instead replacing them with solid side glass that runs from the

One-piece side glass is a hot trend in today's C10 world, which eliminates the truck's wing windows in exchange for a larger piece of glass. These kits, which are offered by One Piece Products, come with all the mounting hardware and only require some minor modifications to the door for fit. That said, there is some cutting involved, so this isn't an easily reversible modification. But if a clean look is what you're after, it's hard to go wrong here. (Photo Courtesy Kevin Whipps)

Several companies make flush-mount glass for C10s, but they vary in quality and fit. Fesler is known for having a good-fitting product that requires little to no bodywork, and it's DOT approved. This glass does away with the factory-style glass seal, instead being held in place with a frit band, primer, and super adhesive urethane, like a modern windshield. It uses no exterior trim. (Photo Courtesy Fesler)

Fesler's rear glass also brings a clean look to the rear of a C10 cab, again fitting flush to the surface and mounting in place with glue rather than a factory weatherstripping. They sell both the windshield and rear glass together in a kit—both are sold as requiring no body modifications, and both include a green tint, as per factory glass. Fesler recommends professional installation of these units. (Photo Courtesy Fesler)

glass kit from Fesler, which ships as a complete kit for both front and rear. These kits are made by Pilkington, which has a long history of manufacturing OEM glass. The kits stand out on C10s because they eliminate the factory weatherstripping, instead gluing in place like a modern windshield and leaving a very small gap between the glass and cab.

Roll Pans

Another option for a smooth look is to remove the factory bumpers and install roll pans in their place, which isn't challenging to do. These pans are available for both front and rear (both in fiberglass and steel) and can be installed several ways, ranging from welding to bolting. Regardless, paintwork will be required here, and how you intend to install them will dictate just how much paintwork will be needed, and whether or not it will include fenders and the bed as well.

Fiberglass parts will be less expensive overall, but steel will last longer and can be welded in place for a more permanent solution. Either one will achieve the same bumper-free result.

Tailgate Handle Relocation

Classic Industries offers a complete tailgate handle relocation kit, which allows a builder to remove the exterior tailgate handle and move it inboard, located inside the bed rather

front of the door to the rear, pretty much exactly like what came in a 1988–1997 C/K truck.

There are a number of benefits here, but the main one is in having a custom look that's generally subtle—most average onlookers won't notice something like this, but truck people will, and they'll want to know how you did it.

The install is straightforward and doesn't require major modification, save for some trimming to part of the internal door structure underneath where the original wing window mounts, some reconfiguring of the door lock mechanism, a few shorter-than-stock door hinge bolts, and a few new holes drilled in the

door. Because of all that, once you swap to this style of glass, it will be hard to swap back to wing windows without either welding up the components you cut or replacing the entire door.

Additionally, you can also source a flush-mount windshield and back

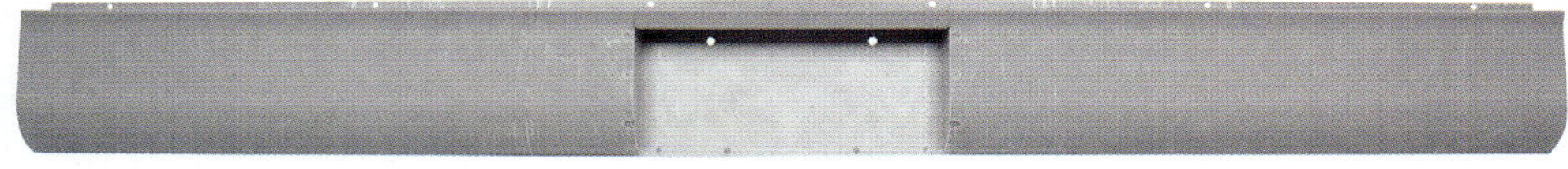

Roll pans have been popular on C10s for decades and for good reason. These pieces can really clean up a C10's lines, and they tend to be cheaper than replacement bumpers, although some might call them dated. They can be welded in place or bolted/screwed—but note that when you run these, there won't be anything to protect your truck's body from parking lot bumps and scrapes. This one is from Classic Industries. It's available with or without the license plate pocket. (Photo Courtesy Classic Industries)

Adding an air suspension system can require more wheel and chassis clearance, which on a C10 is best gained by simply moving the bed up. Here's a fairly extreme example out of SEMA 2018—note all the welds around the wheel tubs to make them fit correctly after having been cut apart and made shorter.

Was this bed cut? How can you tell? Simple: count the stake pockets. Short-bed trucks had four total, while long-beds had six. A savvy builder can remove them, however, so it's not always an exact science. This bed floor has also been raised slightly to make room for suspension modifications underneath. This work was done by MetalOx Fabrications in Peoria, Arizona.

than outside. The process involves some fabrication, but if you don't intend to run a tonneau cover, this is a good way to clean up the exterior of your truck. Note that some cutting and welding will be required, as well as bodywork on the exterior of your truck, where the OEM handle was originally located.

Bed Modifications

If you've slammed your truck down on the ground, you may need to make changes to the bed floor to accommodate raised frame rails and tuck those tires. There are a number of ways to handle this as well, including adding a hump for the rear axle and suspension components. But the cleanest way, and the most popular, is to simply raise the entire bed floor to make the required clearance underneath it.

This is accomplished by unbolting the bed floor, sliding it up, and fabricating a way to fix it back to the bedsides in that new, higher loca-tion—but doing it that way creates some challenges, as the bedsides themselves aren't flat: they have a stamped design that will end up partially covered if you go this route.

If you really want to tackle this correctly, the cleanest option is to section the inside of each bedside the amount you want to raise the bed, removing metal from above the wheel well and from the bedside both fore and aft of the wheel well. Since the C10 features an inner and outer bedside, this solution works well—you just need to work the inner bedside here. But you'll need to be able to cut straight and not too deep to make this work. Since a squarebody bed comes apart into four sections (not including the tailgate), this isn't as challenging as it seems.

Once disassembled, you can take up to 7 inches out of either bedside before the wheel well will touch the bedrail. Note that if you're cutting a long-bed, you'll need to remove the factory mid-mount stake pockets as well. Long-bed trucks have three per side, with one parked right over the top of the wheel well you're about to move up.

All this allows the tire to tuck up much higher, as well as adding a decent-sized amount of space between the bed and the frame. When doing it this way, once everything is welded back together, the factory designs stamped in the inside of the bedside will still be intact.

Yes, this creates a much shallower bed inside the truck, but it also provides more clearance for more extreme drops using welded-in frame components and allows the tire to tuck up almost to the frame rail, which should allow the frame itself to sit on the ground.

Cutting a Long-Bed into a Short-Bed

Builders can fight all day long over whether or not cutting a long-bed is a good idea, but regardless, it's possible to do assuming you have the proper tools and the proper

This was clearly a long-bed at one point, as evidenced by the visible seams where it was welded back together and then worked smooth. The current trend is to show off the seam, which tends to be at the extreme front and rear of the bed, near the stake pocket locations. This is the same bed, again done by MetalOx Fabrications.

Shortening a long-bed into a short-bed also requires removal of 14 inches of truck frame between the cab and the front spring perch—essentially cutting the truck frame in half. One of the cleanest ways to reinforce the area where the two frame sections rejoin is to use the Built by Brooks kit. This is a TIG-welded system in thick plate steel, which indexes off original holes in the frame and squares the frame back up for a clean, strong result. This is essentially a mini-fixture for the DIYer who doesn't have a frame table. Brooks requires 80 percent of the outer plate to be welded in place after installation. If you've decided to cut your frame, you need this kit. (Photo Courtesy Brooks Ekren)

plan in place before you get started. This will require welding skills, bodywork, and a completely level, large workspace.

A long-bed is 93.3 inches from the center of the front stake pocket to the center of the rear stake pocket. A short-bed is 73.4 inches, which rounds out to about 20 inches total that will need to be removed from a long-box to make it a short-box.

The rule of thumb for the bed itself is to remove 14 inches of truck from ahead of the rear wheels, and 6 inches from behind the rear. There are any number of ways you can accomplish this with varied levels of success, depending on if repainting the bed is something you intend on doing as well.

The frame itself needs the same amount of material removed, and there are several schools of thought on how best to cut and rejoin the two sections. A Z-shaped cut with a horizontal section in the middle of two vertical cuts is the strongest method. But unless you're a certified welder, I wouldn't recommend doing this on your own. The weld will be the only thing holding your truck together, so get some help from a pro, or get a kit designed to make the job easier.

All that said, if you want a short-bed, it's a lot easier to just find one—either a frame and bed or just the bed—and start with that before you get out the plasma cutter or cutting wheel and start hacking away on your long-bed.

On top of the challenges of the job, cut beds tend to be worth less than original short-beds, and buyers are now savvy enough to climb underneath and look to see if the chassis has been cut, shortened, and fishplated for strength. Plus, the SPID sticker has the truck's original wheelbase printed right on it in plain sight. It's a dead giveaway.

Cutting the bed also requires cutting down the driveshaft, exhaust, fuel lines, brake lines, parking brake cable, and frame itself. It also requires swapping fuel tanks to short-bed units. If you intend to use your original aluminum and stainless moldings, you'll have to cut them down, too—or replace them with aftermarket pieces for a short-bed.

As of the time of this printing, it might make more sense to simply source an OEM short-bed because they aren't that expensive. However, if these 1973–1987 trucks continue to follow the same trajectory of the 1967–1972s, it won't be that way for long, and cutting bedsides will start to look like a better option.

Replacing Worn Door Hinge Pins

C10 door hinges will sag over time, thanks to the wear in the pivot pins that hold the upper and lower door hinges together. This is easy to see—the door will likely line up with the cab at the beltline until it's opened, but once it's opened, it'll drop. The door itself may also be hard to shut, and it'll likely clunk up and down if you grab it and lift it by the handle end.

Replacing these worn pins isn't hard to do, but it can be a challenge if you attempt it with the doors still installed on the truck. If you need to do this job, I strongly recommend pulling the doors off the hinges but leaving the hinges themselves on the truck. Doing so will make the job much easier. ∎

Reassembling a Torn-Down Truck

Rebuilding a torn-down rig is a simple process. This is where all those little plastic baggies of bolts will really pay off—you won't need to go hunting down any of the hardware needed to get each component installed correctly.

The factory service manual also has all the specs listed pertaining to body gaps, specifically around the doors, fenders, and hood. This is a good place to start, and it really pays to have a second set of hands and eyes to watch panel alignment as everything goes back together, just to keep you from scratching anything—especially if you had any paintwork done while your truck was apart.

Body Gaps

C10s tended to have decent, consistent body gaps from the factory, and there's no reason they shouldn't still be that way with your build. You just need to make them that way.

Factory specs on panel gaps range from 0.16 inch to 0.19 inch, according to the 1980 GM Factory Service Manual. You can use that as a reference and make them tighter or wider, but it's best to shoot for consistency across adjoining panels. Work from the back forward, and don't be afraid to use shims where required to get your gaps into the right ballpark.

The trick to setting up decent panel gaps on a C10 is to work from the door strikers and move forward. This is really only achievable with the truck torn down to a cab on a frame with the doors, fenders, and hood removed and the core support loosely installed at its frame mount.

In some cases, reproduction panels won't fit quite right and will require some massaging, or maybe even some bending, cutting, and/or welding, to get them to fit properly. Therefore, if you're going to be dealing with fresh paint later on, the best bet is to trial fit everything before paint, so any component tweaking or modification won't harm your fresh finish. Do the hammering, twisting, pushing, and pulling prior to new paint.

If you're just reinstalling factory panels, this won't be as important, but it's always a good idea to test fit everything before final assembly.

Replacing Door Hinge Pins with Classic Industries Parts

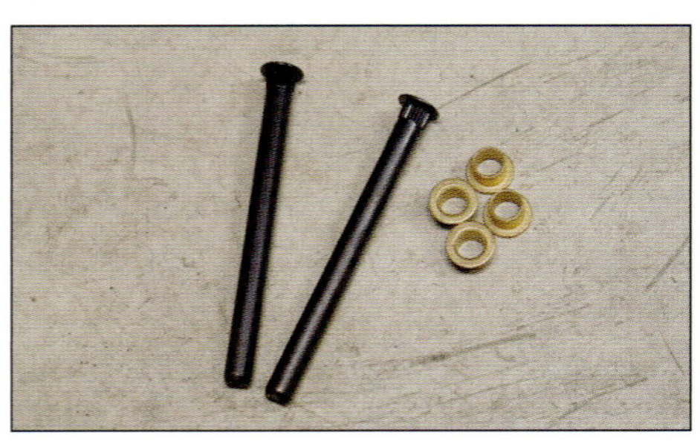

Classic Industries sells a door hinge pin kit (part number C57E) that includes new pins and new pin bushings. Installation is simple if your door is already removed from the truck.

1 *The factory door hinge pins are hardened steel, and they're peened on the end, so you can't just drive them out of the hinge with a punch. Cutting them off with a cutoff wheel is the best option.*

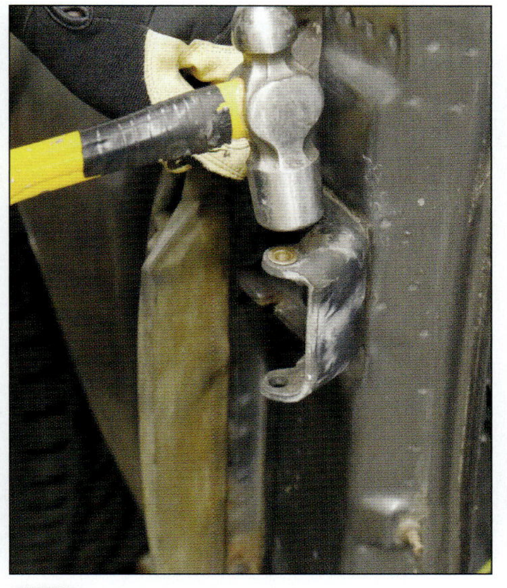

2 *With the old pin out and the hinge disassembled, the new bushings can be tapped into place. The upper goes in from the top, while the lower pushes in from below.*

3 *The final step is to simply drive the new pin into place through the hinge. The last bit is knurled, so tapping it into place with a hammer works best. After that, you can fix the other hinge and then reinstall the door.*

The door hinges provide quite a bit of adjustment fore and aft simply by loosening them where they mount to the cab. This is easiest with an empty door shell with no glass or extra weight inside it, and with the fenders removed from the rig.

All of the mounting hardware is 9/16-inch, and note that each hinge has one bolt that comes from the inside of the cab with its head accessible through a hole in the kick panel under the dash on either side. Be sure to use some tape on your socket and extension to hold them together when you get under the dash to loosen this bolt, and don't remove the bolt entirely because you can easily drop it inside the body, where it will be impossible to retrieve and will probably rattle.

Any in-and-out adjustment with respect to the rocker panel and (ultimately) the fender is handled by the bolts that hold the door to the hinges, while some up/down and fore/aft alignment is handled by the hinge at the cab. Loosen them to get the door to move around. I've had the best luck doing the hinge-at-cab and door-at-hinge adjustments separately.

Ultimately, the goal here is to get an even gap around the door at the roofline, and to have the door line up with the beltline seam on the cab—not too high, not too low, and not too far out from the body when viewed from above.

Once the door is where you want it, move forward to the fender, again

This gap is just about right—but if it were too wide at the back, I'd loosen the hinges at the cab and slide them back toward the striker slightly. The door can also move in and out with respect to the bodyline—as well as up and down—by adjusting the door side of the hinge.

trying to keep the gaps consistent and not too wide. Remember that the factory used spacers to achieve good alignment, and if your truck had them at disassembly, you'll likely need them again, even with new or replacement used parts.

The core support is the final item to tighten to the frame—do this last, after everything else is about where you want it to be, as it does have some adjustment in where it mounts. As the farthest forward component, tightening before the inner or outer fenders are installed will just cause you to fight with it when it comes time to align everything.

Bed Reinstallation

If you have a few friends available to help, you can reinstall the bed without any trouble. If not, a cherry picker and some carefully cut lumber, fastened together in such a way as to grab the bed from the bedrails in the front and rear is all you really need to set a bed back on a truck.

Removing your truck's rear wheels helps, as you won't need to lift the bed up and over them when you go to set it in place. Otherwise, the only special tool you'll need after the bed is sitting on the frame again is a long, skinny screwdriver to help you align each bolt hole. Then drop each bolt in place and have one of those friends stand in the bed and step on each bolt head as you install the nuts and tighten them from below.

Bringing OEM Paint Back from the Dead

Patina is one of the hottest trends in the classic truck world right now. Rigs wearing worn, scruffy original

Even a basic buffing kit, such as this one from Meguiar's that chucks up in a cordless drill, can bring a lot of shine back to matte, original paint. A mid-cut compound will remove some of the top layer of rough paint, leaving behind a smooth—if not thinner—sheen. The traditional key of not burning through the paint isn't as much of a concern if patina is what you're looking for.

paint are bringing more and more attention at shows and at sale time, so if you have a truck that's showing its age, you might want to leave it that way.

Some people think of patina as nothing more than wear, and they might consider the truck's builder to be either lazy or dried up on funds. Others see patina as evidence of the passage of time, and something to be preserved and celebrated.

This is where the "it's only original once" crew clashes head-on with traditional hot rod and custom car builders. Traditionalists will harp on you to paint a rig that's worn out, while builders cued into the modern build trends will scream at you to leave those original bumps, bruises, and scrapes alone.

Trucks seem to be on the front line of this divide, maybe because more of them were used hard when they were new. There are a lot of trucks out there that show wear— more than any type of muscle car or classic—so you'll see more of them built up without fresh, new, perfect paint.

In most cases, a buffing compound and a random orbital polisher will do wonders to put back some shine in original paint that has weathered completely flat. As an added bonus, if that paint is a little thin in places, showing through to primer underneath after a good buffing, the patina crowd will like it even more.

A bigger challenge is fixing rust or body damage, especially if you intend to try to retain a truck's original worn character. Matching fresh bodywork and paint to original, worn components is challenging to say the least, and the results can really vary.

In most cases, trucks weather unevenly, so your new paint will need to be uneven to match, with more fading and flatness up higher and less down lower. If your truck does have a heavier sun fade to it and you end up replacing a door or fender and don't fade it to match, it will stick out. You may as well paint it a different color.

There are many methods to create faux patina to match your OEM parts, and there's really no right or wrong way to do it. If you're interested in some proven methods, check out Kevin Tetz's CarTech book on that subject *Patina: How to Create & Preserve.*

Paintwork on an Original Rig

1 *A lot of squarebody Chevrolet trucks lived hard lives, and even the ones that didn't likely suffered bumps and bruises throughout their past. My truck, while solid, had some body damage on the passenger front fender, some not-so-great paint touch-ups over a wrinkled passenger side door, an aftermarket unpainted hood, and a caved-in driver's door. How do you fix all of that while maintaining the remaining original patina?*

2 *The first step was to pound out the dents in the front fender, smooth out the door, and then prime and sand these pieces to prep them for paint. I reassembled the truck for the final base coat and clear because that would allow for blending into the original paint panels.*

3 *The next step was to tape and prep the panels that would see new paint. Here, master painter Alistair Case has scuffed the paint's surface with a Scotch-Brite pad and has wiped everything down with wax and grease remover in preparation for shooting color.*

4 *In 1979, GM used a bluish-hue zinc coat primer under the paint for rust prevention. The roof of my truck has worn all the way down to it with big sections of blue visible from years of weathering. Case matched that color—the idea being to add in some matching patina to the new panels. He then laid it down on the upper sections of the doors, the bed rails, and a few sections on the hood.*

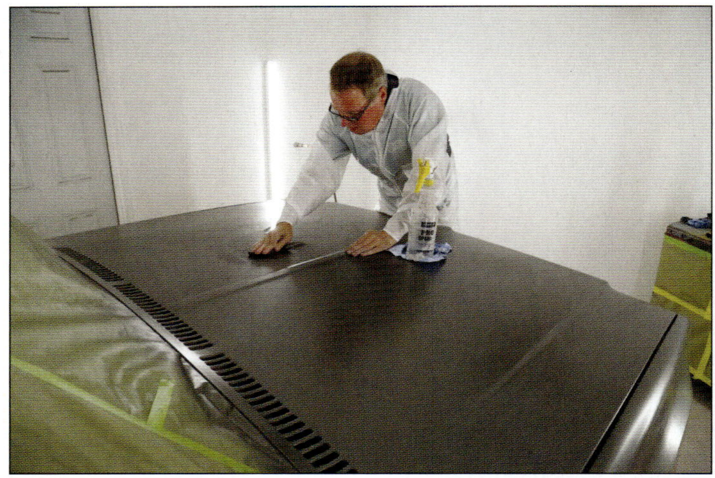

5 *After shooting PPG base coat, Case wet-sanded the areas where he'd sprayed blue with 800-grit paper, bringing the blue through to match the roof. He then followed up with an airbrush to darken some sections to match the roof's unique mottling.*

6 *After a semi-flat clear, the added weathering matches the roof and helps to hide the fact that parts of the truck needed to be replaced.*

Exterior Trim

Nothing takes more of a beating on an old truck than its exterior trim pieces—specifically the side trim and anything relating to the tailgate.

Depending on the year and model of C10, you'll either have extensive side trim, tape stripes, or just a simple body divider. Many higher-level Scottsdale and Silverado trucks had extensive aluminum side trim, and all of it is available in the aftermarket today from companies such as Classic Industries.

Some builders will eliminate all of this trim—and for most of these trucks, that's easy to do, as a lot of the trim pieces are held in place with double-sided tape from the factory— which means not many body holes to fill. Therefore, shaving the trim on one of these trucks is a pretty simple job if you're goal is a clean, not-exactly-stock look.

Most of these trim pieces are made of anodized aluminum, which wears well over time but also will oxidize and fade. Aluminum polish will

If you're intending to use any of your original C10 trim, metal polish is key. These 1979 headlight buckets were fairly heavily worn and oxidized, but a little polish on a toothbrush brought them back to shiny again—they aren't perfect, but it's really hard to tell.

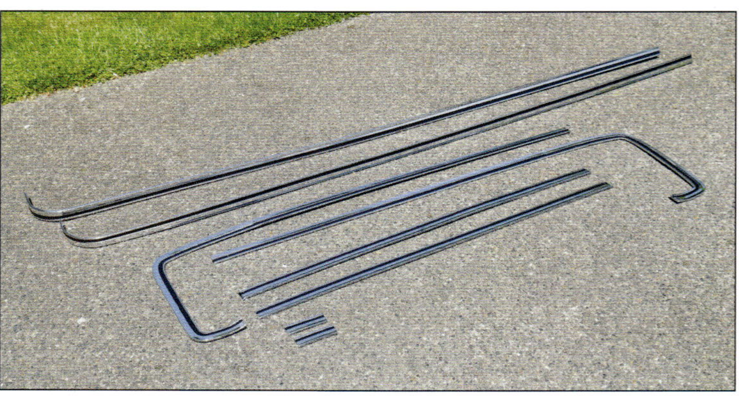

My side trim was broken in a few places and fairly heavily oxidized, which won't polish out thanks to the factory anodizing used by GM. I elected to source a complete upper trim kit for this truck from Classic Industries (part number R1098 for Cheyenne models) because replacing sections piecemeal would cause a mismatch. This trim, made by OEMR, is an exact fit and comes with all the mounting hardware, which makes the installation process easy.

bring back some shine, but that hard anodized coating tends to be a limiting factor in how much shine you can get back from an OEM set of trim.

Of course, if an OEM patina truck is what you're looking to build, that's great—some haze in the trim is probably just the thing you're looking

In addition to the side trim, this truck needed new bumpers as well. This front bumper is from Classic Industries (part number CX1859) and is an exact match for 1973–1980 models without the impact strip that became standard in 1981.

Many C10s came with ugly step bumpers, and mine was no exception. This is Classic Industries' rear bumper for 1973–1980 fleetside C10s (part number T70281), which is arguably much better looking than a step bumper on a lowered truck. Mounting brackets CX1662 hang it off the frame in the factory location. Note that you'll also need to source a factory license plate bracket. Head to your local wrecking yard and look for a Chevy or GMC van bumper. The bracket is the same, and you can score a light for your plate at the same time.

for. But replacing all this trim does really make a visual difference, so if it's in your budget and it fits the style of truck you're looking to build, you should consider replacing your worn, damaged, or missing original units with some aftermarket pieces. I'd strongly advise against mixing and matching stock and reproduction pieces, since the new stuff will always stand out when it's butted-up against an original, weathered piece of aluminum trim. Additionally, even the best reproduction trim won't fit exactly the same as an original piece—hence why NOS parts are so coveted and expensive in the old car and truck world.

Weatherstripping

Keeping water and weather out of your C10 should be a priority, and you can do that by ditching your original, worn-out door seals and window seals.

If your truck showed any evidence of water intrusion—either via a rusty floor, wet carpet or musty smell—you need to solve that problem before you install a nice, new interior. Water can

Door seals are an important and relatively inexpensive component, so you should consider replacing yours to help eliminate wind noise and water intrusion into the cab. These units (part number PW1009 from Classic Industries) push in place over the pinch weld in the doorjamb and are reinforced with a metal strip and have a bead of adhesive already in place inside the groove. Simply push them into place, cut off the excess, and you're done.

Just as important are the inner and outer window channel seals and the window run seal, all of which help to keep the door glass from rattling and water from coming in around the window, either on a rainy day or when you're washing the truck. These simply clip into place inside the door. Classic Industries offers a complete kit (part number CR1063).

come from anywhere, but in a C10, you should take special care to check the windshield seal, the rear window seal, and the door seals at the upper section of the cab.

If the windshield is leaking, replace the seal. Look for seals made by a company called Precision, as they tend to make some of the best fitting C10 seals in the industry—especially for around the windshield and rear window.

Interior

From mild to wild, your C10 is a great canvas for a bunch of interior projects. GM sold these trucks with both bench seats and bucket seats. Today, aftermarket manufacturers have designed a number of bolt-in options for everything from seats to door panels and dash pads, all with a custom look.

Another option is an aftermarket set of buckets, which will offer more flexibility in design and center console configuration. This set from TMI, offered with optional contrasting stitching and several different grommet colors, is designed to be more or less universal, but they do fit in C10 interiors well. (Photo Courtesy Classic Industries)

Some of the most popular trucks in today's custom scene incorporate both a stock look and aftermarket, custom parts. This is Squarebody Syndicate's Syndicate Series 002 truck with a tastefully done interior that looks vaguely stock while also featuring custom finishes, such as rawhide seat covers and door panels, a shortened steering column, a removable transmission tunnel, a subtle roll cage, and more. It all fits well while being unique.

If the stock bench seat isn't for you, you could source a comparatively rare set of factory bucket seats to replace it, along with a center console. These were offered in a low-back configuration until 1977, and they're basically the same as what was offered in Blazers—although they use different mounting brackets, which were unique to the regular-cab trucks. Note that some fabrication will be required because bucket-seat trucks had a welded-in bracket for the inner seat tracks to bolt to. (Photo Courtesy Joshua Jackowski)

Much like the exterior trim, you can source just about every piece and panel for a C10 interior from the aftermarket. So if your rig has worn carpet, holes in the seat cover, or a saggy headliner, you have plenty of options for replacement—or customization, if that's what you'd like to do.

That said, a lot of the character in these trucks lies in their interiors, specifically the dash pad, bench seat, and those round gauges. Swapping worn factory parts with aftermarket replacements is a good baseline for a decent, drivable custom truck while still maintaining some of that original character—and in the process, you can change the color of the interior from stock, which in the 1970s was likely green, tan, or blue.

Changing the Color of Your C10's Interior

On my project C10, I elected to change the color of the interior from gray and white to black using reproduction parts where available and painting other original components where I could.

How to Install the Dash Pad, Headliner, Carpet, and Seat Cover

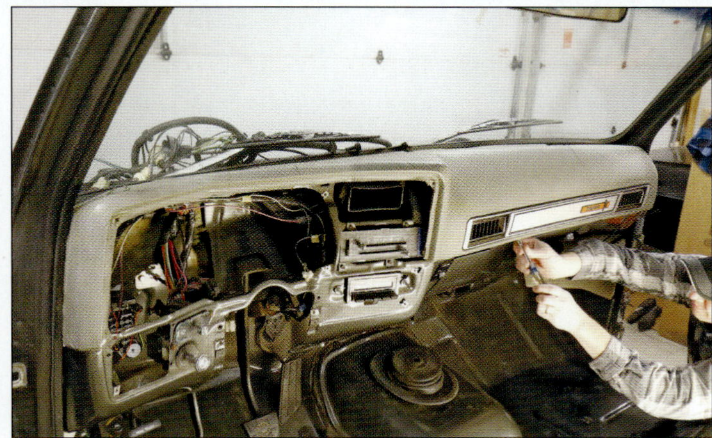

1 *With the gauge cluster and steering column out of the way, the dash pad can come out as well. A row of screws hold the pad in place on the passenger's side, while spring clips pinch it down to the dash frame. With the screws removed, pulling up and back on the pad will free it from the truck.*

2 *The spring clips that hold the dash to the truck need to be transferred to your new dash pad before assembly. Take note of how they're installed in the old dash—fixing them to the new dash requires a push-down, pull-toward-you motion.*

3 *Here's how the dash clips seat in the dash frame, looking up from underneath. You'll need to be sure each dash clip is fully seated, otherwise the top of the dash pad will appear wavy. Once the clips are properly oriented, a solid push is all it takes to get them seated.*

4 *This replacement dash (part number 14009485) came from Classic Industries. After swapping over the factory trim and vents from the old dash, it looks and fits exactly like an original—and it looks way better than the original, cracked dash and today's plastic dash caps that are also available.*

5 *Aftermarket headliners come with sticky-back Velcro that allows them to be stuck in place and then moved around slightly for proper fit. This unit has a plastic backing with a soft, fabric cover, and it's contoured to fit the roof as an original. Classic Industries offers these in a variety of factory colors. Black is part number AH9001.*

6 *The headliner can be installed with or without the plastic perimeter trim, but it looks better with it. Having a small pick tool will make installation a lot easier because it can help align the screw holes and trim. You'll want all the help you can get because you'll be working over your head, which wears out hands fast. I also recommend picking up a stainless steel screw kit from Harbor Freight for use in headliner, door panel, and carpet installation.*

7 *Laying down carpet is next. The key here is to trim off less than you think you'll need to so you don't accidently make it too short anywhere. I use a razor blade because it tends to cut carpet easily. Install your seatbelt and seat bolts prior to laying in the carpet, and simply slice an X over the top of each one, then push them through. This carpet is pre-molded for the 4-speed hump in this 1979. Classic Industries sells it as part number TK16201C3. (Photo Courtesy Katie Pickering)*

8 *This seat is pretty typical of what you might find in a well-used C10. In fact, it's better than most. If keeping the bench is part of your plan, you'll likely need to install a seat cover to match the rest of your interior. Before you go there, however, look for your build sheet underneath the seat, stuffed between the seat springs and foam.*

9 A pair of pliers is all you need to remove a factory seat cover—but you will need to pull the back and the base of the seat apart before you can do this. It's a simple process, as they're just bolted together at the seat's pivot point. A twist-and-pull motion will free these clips. The new cover comes with new fasteners.

10 Measuring and marking the center of the seat and the center of the new seat cover is key to ensure that all the interior pleats are aligned properly. This is also a good time to check on the condition of your seat springs and replace any that are broken—as well as your seat foam.

11 Laying the seat cover flat will help eliminate wrinkles and putting it in the sun will help make it pliable for installation. Doing this on a cold day is a recipe for wrinkles.

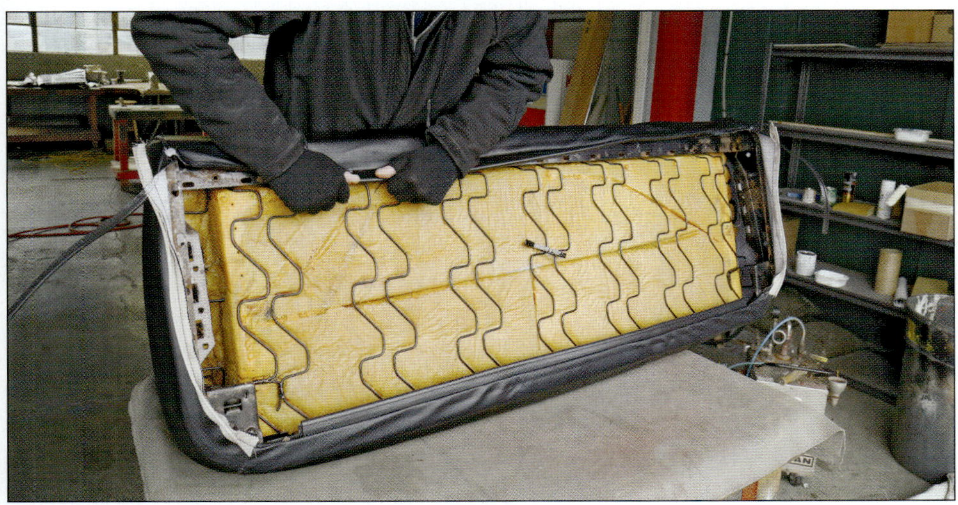

12 After centering the seat cover on the frame using the marks you created on both, pull it tight and start to fasten it with hog rings starting from the center and working out. Keeping everything tight is key as you go.

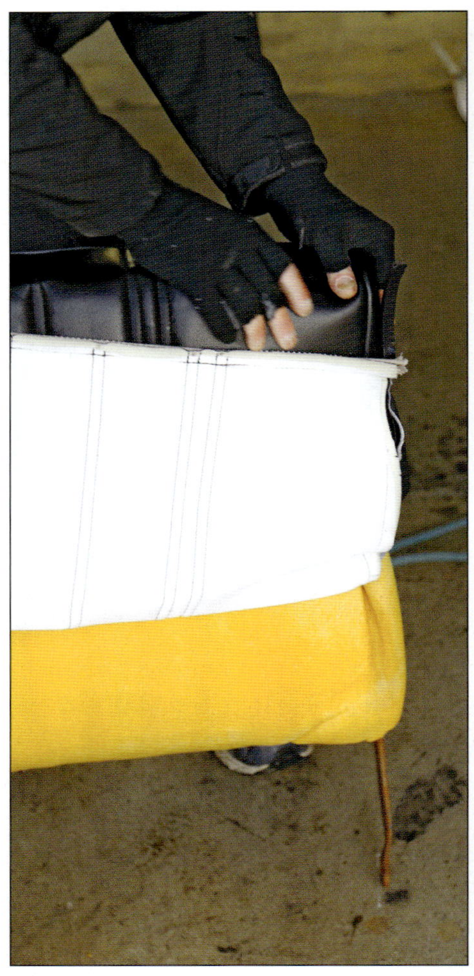

14 *After affixing the seat back and seat bottom together with the factory bolts, this seat is ready to go back into a C10—although it will need some time in the sun to help work out the remaining shipping wrinkles.*

13 *A quick tip for the seat back: turning the new cover partially inside-out will really ease installation, as the new covers tend to fit tight, and they can be a bear to position correctly. This allows you to pull it down tight and then roll the remainder of the cover into place.*

15 *Classic Industries also offers the proper door panels in a number of colors, complete with armrests, lock ferrules, and lock plungers. Install couldn't be easier, as they just hang in place and screw to the door—but note that early squarebody doors take a different panel than some of the later trucks. Also note the correct floor mats here as well, also sourced from Classic Industries. This interior is complete.*

Gauges

The vast majority of C10s came from the factory with a basic gauge cluster that included a large speedometer, large fuel gauge, and either warning lights or gauges for engine temperature, engine oil pressure, and voltage (with a voltmeter—or with an ammeter on earlier squares). Some trucks had a quartz clock. For the trucks that didn't, that area had a blanking plate.

Tachometers were an option on most of these trucks, and when a truck was so equipped, a fuel gauge was relocated from a large right-hand pod down to a lower left-corner pod that would have either had a clock or blanking plate in non-tach rigs.

Most trucks came without a tach, but if you're building a performance driver, you'll really want to have a tachometer, too. They were offered as an option in nearly all the 1973–1987 model years, but you can convert a non-tach truck to run a tach in the factory location if you source a reproduction tach that has the proper font on the face for your pickup.

Stay away from used tachs if possible, as they're often sold in non-operable condition. Companies such as Classic Industries have reproduction tachs in all the different faceplate font options: 1973–1975, 1976–1979, and 1979–1987.

Adding a Tach to the Dash

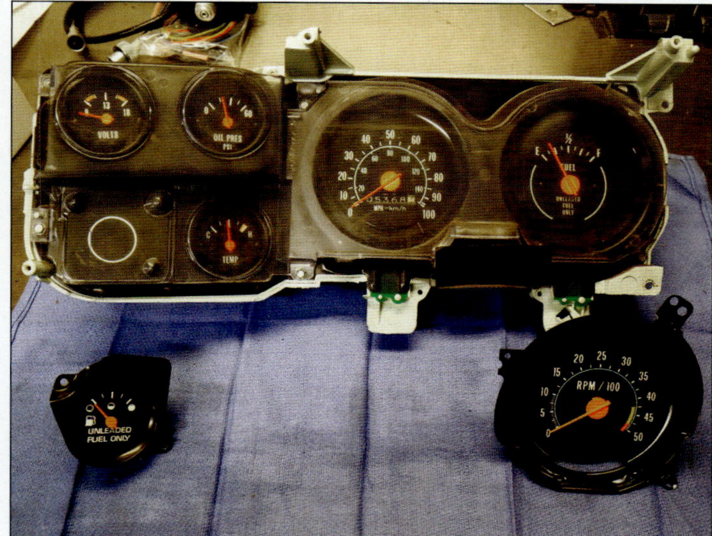

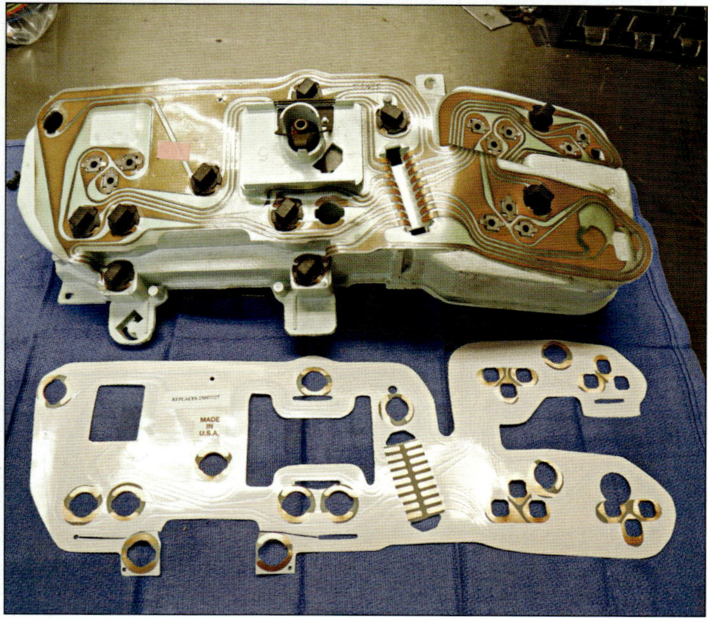

1 It's possible—and not too difficult—to add a tach to a non-tach dash. This truck is a 1979, so it required the later 1976–1979 tach with the color-coded redline and the "RPM/100" nomenclature above the needle. Classic Industries sells this item (part number 5659232). I also sourced an "Unleaded" small fuel gauge (part number T70843). This is a later truck unit, as the factory-style early "Unleaded" gauge isn't yet available in the aftermarket.

2 The other key component here is a new printed circuit (part number 25017327). GM didn't change its wiring harness between tach and non-tach trucks, meaning all you need to do to move your fuel gauge—and make it work—is install one of these printed circuits that reroutes power and signal for a tach-equipped rig.

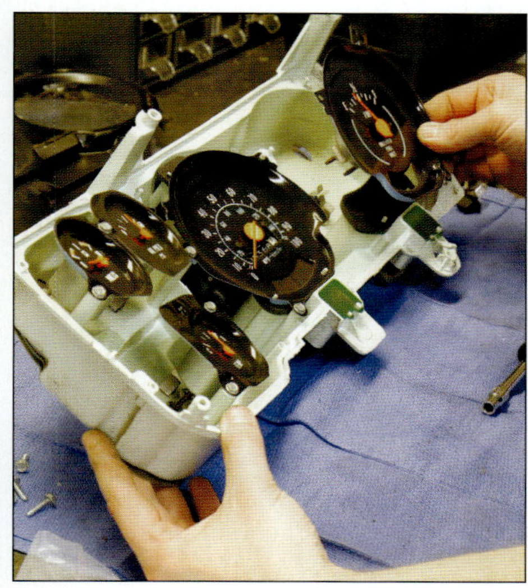

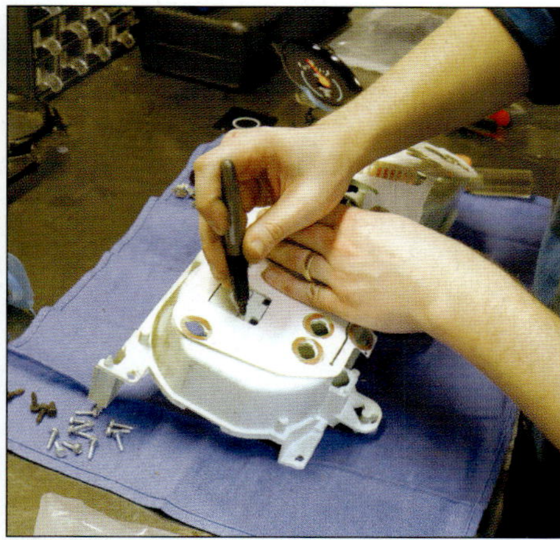

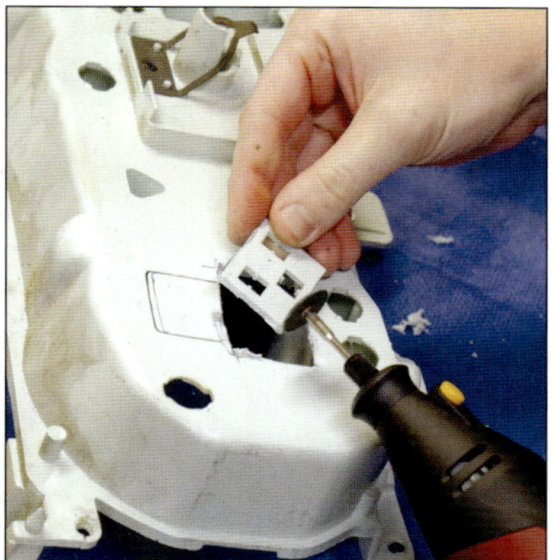

3 Completely tear down the gauge cluster, removing the plastic lens and then all the gauges from the plastic housing. The smaller gauges are held in place at the rear, pinched to the printed circuit with spring clips. Be careful not to break or lose any parts.

4 The plastic housings are different between tach and non-tach trucks, but you can modify a non-tach housing by cutting a relief for the tach, and then cutting and relocating the three holes for the fuel gauge as well. Use the new printed circuit as a guide to mark where to make your cuts. A Dremel tool with a plastic cutoff wheel works well here.

5 This three-holed section used to hold the contacts for the big fuel gauge, but since that gauge is moving to a small corner location, these contacts will need to move as well. The outlined section above also needs to be removed to make room for the tach, which uses its own wiring harness, not the printed circuit.

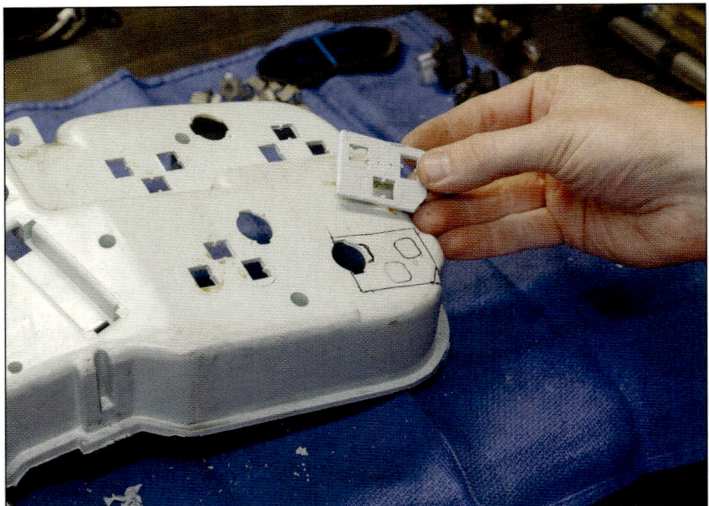

6 *Using the printed circuit as a guide, you can clearly see where the fuel gauge section needs to go. Simply locate and trace around it, and then cut out the plastic so the fuel gauge connector section you've already removed can be epoxied in place.*

7 *Two-part epoxy will fuse this in place and make it function just like a factory tach unit. All that's left (after the proper cure time) is to install the circuit and gauges, and then reassemble the unit with the new gauges.*

8 *You can buy a reproduction tach harness, but you can also make your own using female spade connectors. The white wire here is the tach signal, which in this case gets connected to the blue wire from the Holley Dominator ECU, but it could also be fed a signal from the tach port of an HEI. Black is ground and red is keyed ignition from the fuse panel.*

9 *Here's the final product, ready to be reinstalled in the truck. Some ignition systems may require a tach filter so the tach reads correctly, but it isn't a problem when an ECU is in control of the tach signal.*

LIGHTING

One of the easiest areas to improve on a factory C10 is its lighting system. Originally, these trucks used incandescent bulbs throughout, from the industry-standard sealed-beam headlamps to the smaller 1156, 1157, and 194 bulbs used for brakes, turn signals, reverse lights, and interior dash lighting. Fortunately, that makes stock replacement easy, but they're not the brightest options for your custom C10. Seeing—and being seen—is incredibly important when you're driving a classic truck, so upgrades here are wise.

Now, that's not to say that a factory truck with factory lights is somehow dangerous. It's not. But there are much better solutions out there today that can make a C10 much easier to see at night—and they look better than stock too.

Headlamps

Seeing clearly is key when it comes to building a truck that you intend to use regularly. To that end, it's important to boost the output of the headlights both so you can see as well as possible and so others can see you. Just like a good brake system, a good lighting system is an import-ant safety feature for an older rig on today's roads. Plus, brighter lighting just looks cool.

Headlight Relays

Before you make the choice to upgrade the headlights, you should upgrade your truck's wiring and add relays into the system.

Relays weren't a new technology when 1973 C10s started rolling off the assembly line, but they didn't become standard in any capacity other than horn actuation until the later 1980s.

Relays are important for one key reason: Your truck's original wiring harness routed power for the headlights from the battery, through the positive battery cable to the starter lug, and then through the firewall junction block to the headlight switch in the dash. From there, it routes through the high-beam switch, and then out to the core support, where it plugs into the back of each headlight.

Over that long length of wire, there are a number of wire connections and junctions that cause voltage drop, as well as the switch itself, which must carry the complete load of your truck's headlamps. Voltage drop leads to dim lights.

If you're lucky, you'll only have about 1 volt of voltage drop between the alternator or battery and the headlight plug, but chances are you'll have more, thanks to a bunch of old wire, old connections that

C10s were using old technology for their lighting even by 1973 standards. Today, there's plenty of room for improvement without needing to completely rewire the entire headlight circuit. That said, before you go to the trouble of swapping bulbs and rewiring sections of your truck, make sure your headlights are aimed properly—there are up/down and side/side adjuster screws for each headlight behind the chrome buckets. Find a plain wall, back up 25 feet from it, and use the light pattern your headlights make on that wall to aim them where you want them.

A digital multimeter is a great tool to have to troubleshoot all kinds of wiring issues. Here we're tracking just how much voltage drop the headlights are seeing through the factory wiring harness. The brown wire is the feed for the low-beam circuit on these sealed-beam headlights, while the green wire feeds the high beam. Black is the ground. Checking the output of the bulb is as simple as probing the correct terminal and recording the number. The battery is a solid 12.5 volts, while here at the headlight, we see only 10.7 volts.

A relay like this is fantastic for remote triggering of high-load electronics. You've probably already worked with them on the fuel system and the cooling fans, so installing a set in the OEM headlight circuit should be no big deal, as it all follows the same theory. These are inexpensive from places such as Summit Racing, and they come with a pigtail as well. I like to use 30-amp units along with a 20-amp circuit breaker on the main power feed from the battery. You could also use a fuse, but a breaker will reset, which is a good safety measure if you lose your lights at speed in the dark. When a fuse blows, you're done until you replace it—driving or not.

have likely corroded over the years, and that original headlight switch that gets hot when you use it.

Installing a relay in-line is a quick and effective way to boost light output for not a lot of money, as it only requires two 30-amp relays, two 20-amp circuit breakers, some 14-gauge wire, assorted shrink tube, and a few wiring terminals.

Installing headlight relays will boost even stock headlight output, as they can be wired to pull power directly from the battery. In this case, rather than use the original wiring to handle the current of the headlight circuit, those original wires only need to trigger a relay, which removes all the load from the original headlight circuit, and then pulls power from the battery using a much shorter length of thicker wire, used to combat any voltage drop that might occur.

The main bonus here is brighter headlights, but another plus is that the circuit and the original headlight switch stay a lot cooler, and the increased power to the headlight plugs allows you to run higher-intensity lights without damaging any of the original wiring.

Additionally, doing it this way keeps all the functionality of the original system, including the dash lights, the high-beam indicator, and a headlight warning buzzer, if your system has one.

You'll be surprised just how much of a difference that extra volt or two can make in the brightness of even your stock sealed-beam headlights. Do this swap first, before adding any other headlight parts to your system. You may find that you don't really need to do anything else, depending on your needs.

The nice thing about this upgrade is it's simple and cheap, and it's a great place to start before you swap those OEM bulbs for anything else.

Sealed-Beam and Halogen

Sealed-beam units are so named because they're sealed units, complete with the bulb and reflector sealed inside a glass housing. If the light burns out or breaks, you must remove and replace the entire modular unit. This is what all 1973–1987 C10s had from new—although later examples were higher intensity than earlier ones, but we'll get to that in a second.

Until 1980, all C10s from this generation came from the factory with 7-inch-round sealed-beam headlamps. These headlamps were dual-filament units, so they served as both regular and high-beam units for the C10. They work fine, but it's old technology. Sealed-beam lights date from 1939 and were mandatory in cars and truck on US roads until 1984. Bulb technology has evolved considerably, even in the past decade, so upgrades here are both easy and smart.

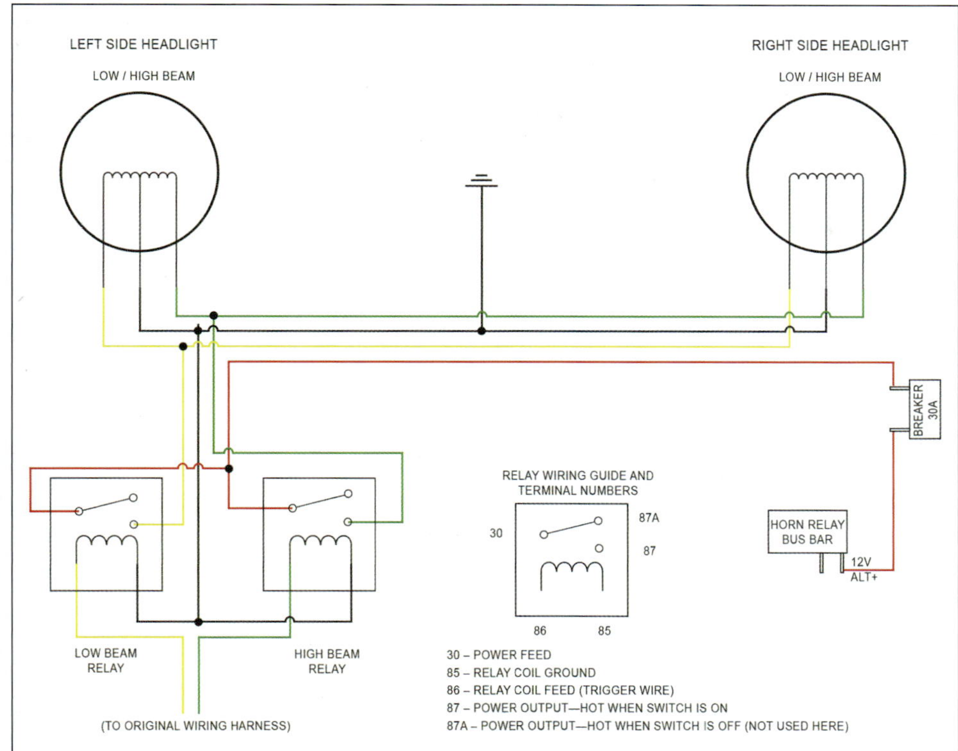

Adding a relay into the system is simple to do while also continuing to use most of the factory wiring. Here, we're using the original wiring to trigger the relay versus actually power the light. A new run of wire that's thicker gauge than what was used originally can then feed power to the relay from the battery, using a much shorter and more direct path. The net result is more usable power at the headlight plug, and therefore brighter lights. (Illustration Courtesy American Car Collector *magazine)*

The basic halogen headlight is a good, inexpensive replacement for a C10. These may be entry-level, but you'd be surprised how bright they can be when powered with charging-system voltage after adding relays into the wiring system. This is a cheap upgrade that does make a difference—especially if you don't know when your headlights were last replaced. (Photo Courtesy United Pacific Industries)

Halogen headlamps came into the fold in Europe in 1962 with the introduction of the H1 design. These lights were too bright for US DOT regulators at the time, so they were not available in the US. However, by 1978, the rules had changed, with brighter headlights becoming allowed in this country and halogen serving as the path to that brightness.

Halogen sealed beams (which are significantly brighter than the old sealed beams thanks to halogen gas and a revised metal reflector inside the light housing) became available in 1978 and were standard in 1979. Chances are that if your truck is still running sealed-beam units, they were likely replaced in the past with the brighter halogen units. If your truck is a 1979, you probably have halogens.

In 1975, rectangular headlamps became legal in the US, but the C10 didn't get a set until 1980. All trucks from 1981–on had either single or dual rectangular lights, typically with the high beams as secondary bulbs to augment the low-beam lights.

If you want to keep things simple, you can purchase high-output sealed-beam headlamps today from places such as United Pacific, Rock Auto, or Summit Racing. They all do a good job of lighting the way for most C10 trucks or really any American car from the era in need of a little more lighting. These are all DOT legal for US roads.

High-Intensity Discharge Lights

High-intensity discharge (HID) lights became widespread in OEM applications in the 2000s and hit the aftermarket shortly thereafter. These lights are fundamentally different in

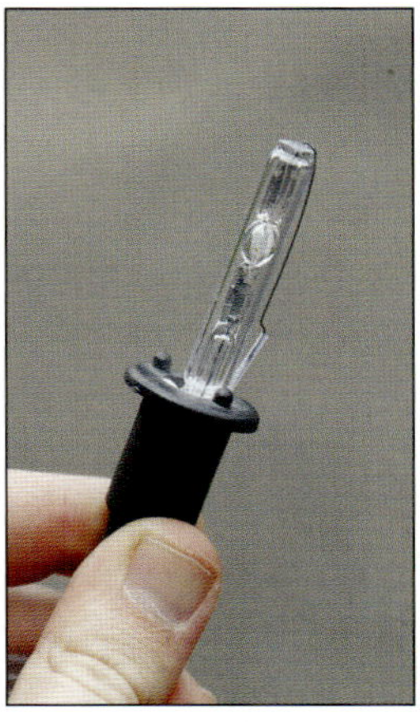

An HID bulb is a much brighter solution than a sealed beam or H4, but it requires using a projector housing that's designed to help control the light's beam. Without it, you'll actually end up having a harder time seeing distances in the dark, and you'll blind other oncoming drivers. Don't install these in a basic, round, H4-style housing.

how they create light, using an electric arc that passes from one tungsten arc to another inside a fused quartz or alumina arc tube that's filled with a noble gas and some other metals and/or salts.

These are known for creating more visible light for the power they consume, so they are in fact much brighter than halogens. But they also require some special lenses to control where the light goes, as well as a ballast to start and maintain the light's arc. As such, these tend to be offered as kits that include everything needed for installation.

An obvious plus here is increased visibility at night, especially of objects in the periphery of the vehicle. Street signs or animals on the side of the road are more visible with lights like these compared to standard halogen or sealed-beam units. Another thing you'll notice about HIDs is their distinct cutoff point, which comes with the focused lens that's required to keep from irritating other drivers with glare. Keep in mind that HID kits may or may not be DOT legal, and there are different

Bringing a Euro Look to your C10

In Europe, the rules for lighting were much different than here in the US, with output being a main concern versus here in the States, where lower power consumption was more important. Still, starting in 1983, some of that Euro influence made its way stateside with Ford's approved petition for replaceable-bulb architectural-style headlights that featured aerodynamic lenses and non-standard shapes. Europe had been doing this for years, so the technology was easy to apply and modify for US roads. The key here was in the replaceable bulb, as it made for less-expensive replacement, at least in theory. It also allowed plastic housings to be fitted in place of the glass units that had come before.

What's that mean for C10 owners? You can remove your old sealed-beam halogen units and convert to a round housing that can take a newer-style halogen bulb, which is the Euro way of doing things. The H4 bulb in a new, round housing has much more potential to light the way and shares the same basic plug design with the original headlights, so they should simply plug in to the original harness. But note that while they're easy to come by, technically, European H4s still aren't street legal here in the US because they're tuned for higher light output than the DOT allows. There are, however, DOT-compliant H4-style bulbs available. They're known as HB2-9003 bulbs.

Companies such as United Pacific Industries offer replacement housings for the 7-inch-round and smaller rectangular headlamps used in all years of C10s. After swapping out the housings themselves, there's a bevy of headlamp options out there with a variety of color tones and temperatures to suit your taste. An H4-style bulb will plug directly into the original harness for your C10, and with the relay mod, it will provide more than enough light for your truck.

Keep in mind, however, that too much light isn't always a good thing—especially if you'd like to steer clear of your local police department. Lighting may not seem like a big deal, but if you're out blinding everyone else on the highway with your high-output headlamps, plan to be stopped and perhaps ticketed for being a nuisance. ■

This housing is specifically for H4-style bulbs, and it measures in at 7 inches for use in round-eye C10s. A number of companies make these, but it's best to buy one from a reputable place, as they do contain reflectors that need to be properly designed to be effective. This one is United Pacific part number A5023-3, which has a glass construction (versus plastic on some other versions) and comes with an H4 bulb already installed. Note that these are sold for "Off-Road Show Use" only. (Photo Courtesy United Pacific Industries)

The next step up in lighting is to move to an H4 bulb, which was designed for use in Europe and is much brighter than the DOT-style halogen sealed-beam setup. The nice thing about these is the wiring plug is the same for H4 as it is for sealed beam, so you can swap over without too much trouble. These are a basic bolt-in solution, but you'll need the matching housing as well. (Photo Courtesy United Pacific Industries)

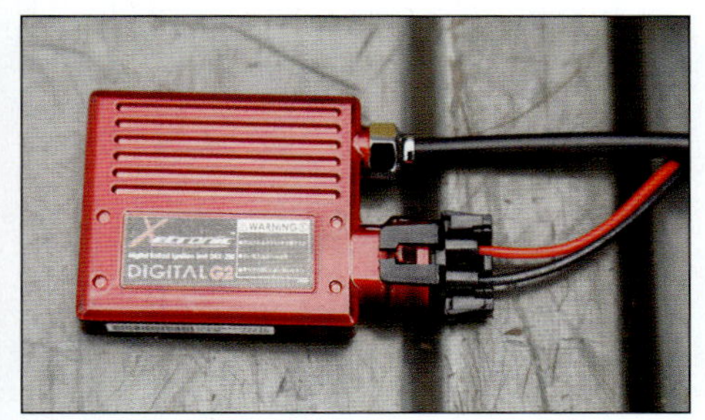

The HID light is created when a carefully measured electric current is passed through several electrodes inside a sealed quartz glass tube. The power needed for maintaining the light in one of these systems is regulated by a ballast, which is required because it can take up to 20,000 volts to light off the arc inside each bulb—but it only requires 12 volts to keep it in operation once lit. The ballast needs to be installed between the headlight itself and switched power from the headlight relay.

tints available, from blue to white to purple, depending on the brightness level you choose to use.

LEDs

Another fundamental lighting shift came with the introduction of LED headlights, which only started to become available in the aftermarket over the past five years. LED stands for light-emitting diode, which is basically a semiconductor that emits light upon a flow of current through it. They don't require much in the way of current to run—significantly less than a standard halogen bulb—and they last much longer and don't get hot while operating.

These are easy to spot, as they don't emit light gradually when powered up: they're either on or off. A lot of modern stoplights are LEDs, as are most city bus taillights. In both cases, they've been chosen because they last a lot longer than other light sources, even under heavy use.

Again, to use an LED headlight in a C10, you'll need a 7-inch-round or smaller square headlight housing assembly that can take an H4-style bulb, and then an LED kit that is configured to plug into that H4-style housing.

These lights produce a very white, bright light, so if you're looking to be seen in all conditions, these

are a good option for you. They do, however, require some special wiring to run, all of which should come in the kit. Again, DOT regulations may not be in your favor here, so consider that before upgrading.

Compared to a standard incandescent bulb, the LED is leaps and bounds ahead in terms of brightness and longevity. For headlight use, something like United Pacific part number 36512 is what you'll need, as it fits in a standard H4-style housing and uses the same type of plug as the H4 or the OEM sealed beam. Note that you may need to clearance your C10's headlight bucket to make these fit, as they include a sizable heatsink at the rear. While the bulbs themselves don't get hot, these heatsinks do, so consider that when installing a set. (Photo Courtesy United Pacific Industries)

Turn Signals and Brake Lights

When it comes to aftermarket C10 brake lights, LEDs tend to be the industry favorite. They're brighter than stock, they use less power, and they can be configured in a variety of ways, up to and including a cascade effect, depending on the kit used.

There are several ways you can apply LED lights to a C10, specifically in the brake light area. First, if you're dead-set on using your original housing, you can simply buy an 1157-style LED bulb for the factory plug and install it. It's a plug-and-play solution, but you're limited in how many LEDs can fit on a standard 1157-size bulb socket, so it's not the best option in terms of brightness. Brighter than stock? Sure, but not as bright as they could be.

If you want an even brighter solution, several companies make retrofit C10 lenses that are already configured with a matrix of LED lamps inside. Some of these can be programmed to have a sequential effect when turned on, which makes them even more visible on the back of a truck.

You can also buy complete turn-signal kits for C10s that plug into the factory wiring harness of the truck and run a panel of LEDs behind the lens rather than an incandescent 1157 bulb. These are much brighter than stock and have that typical LED on/off look that's hard to miss.

Obviously, the brighter your brake lights and turn signals are, the better for your overall visibility. The cool factor that comes with the LED's function is just a bonus.

Note that incandescent bulbs use a thermal flasher to run both the turn signals and the four-way flashers. LEDs draw much less current than the original bulbs, so as such,

If super bright isn't bright enough, a step further is to install custom, multi-LED headlights in the 7-inch-round configuration. This one features a bunch of LEDs, all of which combine to offer a much more piercing amount of light from the front of your C10. They'll also make it stand out. (Photo Courtesy United Pacific Industries)

A conversion bulb is the simplest way to add LED lights to other spots on your C10. They plug into any 1156 or 1157 socket—which means they work for your C10's turn signals, brake light bulbs, and reverse lights. You can find these at your local parts house, or just buy them online, as they're universal. (Photo Courtesy United Pacific Industries)

they don't typically function properly with OEM-style thermal flashers. To solve this problem, you'll also need to replace both the four-way and the turn-signal flashers with digital, timed versions if you intend to run LEDs. Both flashers mount to the factory fuse panel. You can find them from the same vendors who sell LED automotive lighting.

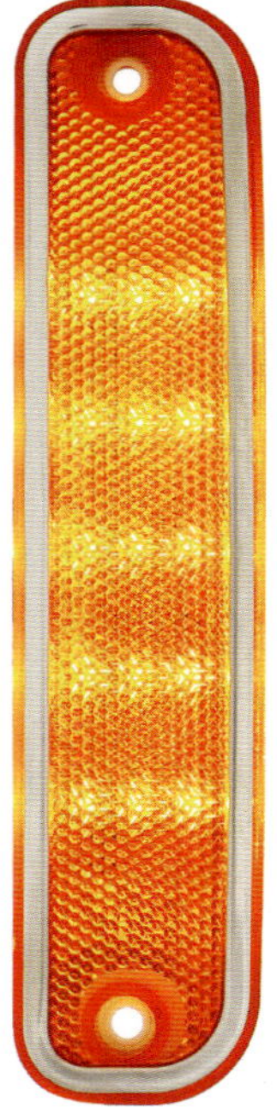

For running lights, there's no reason to go with universal bulbs when you can source direct bolt-in lenses that are already fitted with LED panels inside. This is brighter than just running one conversion bulb, as there is more internal space for LEDs. (Photo Courtesy United Pacific Industries)

Dash Lighting

The dash gauges in a C10 are lit with a handful of small incandescent bulbs, all of which twist in place from behind the gauge cluster under the dash. Replacing them is straightforward, but it isn't the easiest thing to do because some can be tough to reach, and you'll need to get down on the floor and look up behind the dash to see their plugs. Or, if you're willing to take the dash pad out, you can simply remove the cluster assembly to access all of the lighting mounted behind it.

Unfortunately, as is the case with most GM products of this era, you'll probably find yourself doing this job sooner or later, as the little 194-style bulbs used here tend to burn out from time to time, and they can suffer from connection problems between their plastic retainer sockets and the printed circuit on the back of the dash cluster. Adding to that is that all the idiot lights and the turn-signal indicators use the same-style bulb, plug, and connector, and nothing is clearly marked. That makes hunting down a burnt-out dash bulb kind of

a chore if you're trying to do it while looking up from the floor.

Fortunately, 194-style LED bulbs are available as replacements for the older-style units, and they'll add a considerable amount of brightness to your dash illumination. However, installing them will render the dash light dimmer switch inoperable, as it's designed to be used with incandescent bulbs only. But if brighter and clearer is what you're after, LEDs will get you there—and you probably aren't concerned with dimming them anyway. You'll need five bulbs for dash lighting and an additional seven for indicator and warning lights.

One other word of warning: LEDs are bright, and it's easy to go overboard here. If you decide to upgrade from factory 194s, try to source a set with no forward-facing diodes to help even out the lighting across your gauges and eliminate bright spots.

For those of you looking for the brightest brake light available, an LED panel-style unit is by far the best option. This one (part number CTL7387LED from United Pacific) can be set up to come on all at once, or sequentially, in a cascade of light from one side to the other. It contains 56 red LEDs and 12 white LEDs. Several companies make setups like this, all of them brighter than stock lights. This is a bolt-in solution that just requires some basic wiring to hook up. (Photo Courtesy United Pacific Industries)

WHEELS AND TIRES

You'll make a lot of important decisions when building a custom car or truck, which includes selecting wheel design and size.

The look of your custom truck really depends a lot on the wheels that are on it, and getting them sized right is especially important, as custom wheels are hard to return if you get your measurements incorrect. Selecting and ordering wheels is a measure-twice-buy-once scenario. Plus, even a small bit of backspace adjustment can really change the look of your rig, so it pays to verify what exactly you can fit under your C10 considering the other modifications you have made.

The same can be said for tires as well, since what you'll really need versus what you think you want can be two very different things when it comes to rubber. Summer tires look great and perform well in dry times of year, but when the temperature drops and the rainy—or snowy—season rolls in, you'll be spinning those summer tires all over the place, trying to grab traction at every stoplight. This is especially true with pickups because they aren't as well balanced as a car thanks to a lack of weight in the bed. All-season tires are good, but

if you're driving year-round, two sets of tires—one for summer and one for winter—may be the best bet.

It all boils down to this: Measure correctly, choose your rim design wisely, and buy the right tires for how you realistically intend to use your truck.

Wheels

Chances are that if you've built a custom truck, you're in the market for custom wheels. Off-the-shelf rims may or may not work for your application, but before you can measure and know for sure, you have to get up to speed on *how* wheels are measured.

The overall diameter is simple: it's just the measurement of the wheel from tire bead seat to tire bead seat. For example, stock GM truck wheels were 15 inches from the factory for 1/2-ton applications. Some were larger at 16 or 16½ inches on 3/4-ton and 1-ton rigs.

Width is just as simple: it's the measurement from the inner bead seat to the outer bead seat. If you measure from the inner to the outer edges of the wheel, you'll end up with a measurement that's approximately a

1/2 inch wider than the actual wheel. For example, if you measure a 15x7 rim from outer edge to edge, it will read approximately 7½ inches. The true measurement is where the tire bead sits inside the rim.

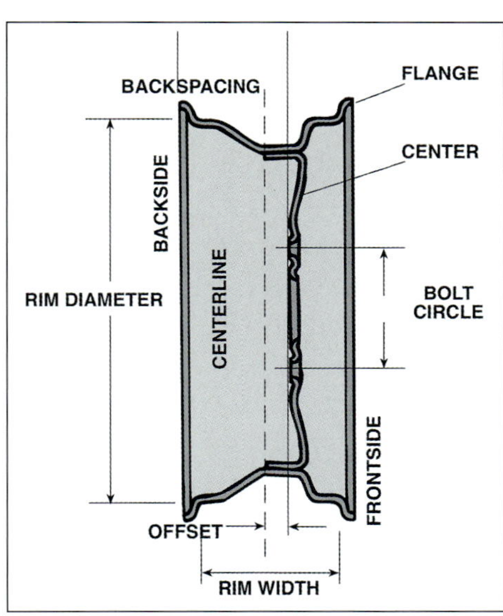

Before you can properly measure your truck for rims, you'll need to understand rim terminology. For a C10, the most important things to consider are the diameter, backspacing, width, and bolt circle. Increasing or decreasing the wheel backspace can allow you to center up a wide rim width in the space available under a C10. (Illustration Courtesy American Car Collector *magazine)*

While all squarebody trucks share one of three different wheel bolt circles, when rim shopping, it's important to verify before you buy—especially if you're picking up a set of used rims. This is a 5-on-5 setup: 5 lug holes, spaced out at 5 inches across. Note that the measurement is from the extreme edge of one mounting hole to the center of the hole opposite. Also note that this wheel is set up for large 1/2-inch wheel studs, as was factory on 1/2-ton two-wheel-drive C10s.

Wheel offset is the distance from the mounting surface of the rim to the wheel's centerline. With many modern aftermarket wheels, this is measured in millimeters, and it can be either a positive or negative number, depending on how far in or out from the hub you want your wheel to sit. Alternatively, the term *backspace* is also used, which is more or less the same measurement, except it's measured from the wheel's mounting surface to the rear bead seat of the tire.

Offset and backspace can really make a big difference not only in the width of rim you can tuck under a truck, but it can also change the look of a truck significantly. Typically, the less backspace you run, the more dish there will be to the wheel, making it look wider when mounted on the truck. Of course, this pushes the wheel from the axle's hub farther from the center of the truck, which then can cause interference problems with the bedside—especially in trucks that have been lowered. All of this illustrates why it's important to measure before you try to buy wheels and tires.

GM's squarebody trucks share several common wheel bolt patterns and lug sizes, which makes sourcing wheels that will bolt up a simple process.

The sheer number of these trucks built over the years, along with a robust aftermarket wheel industry even when these trucks were new, means finding a set of wheels that will at least bolt up to your hubs shouldn't be an issue. The 5-on-5 setup used on C10s is common among other manufacturers as well, which only helps to broaden the selection of wheels available to you in the aftermarket.

A common mistake is to assume that GM car wheels will fit C10s. This isn't true in most cases, save for the 1971–1976 GM full-size cars and 9C1 Police Impala/Caprice, which had the same 5-on-5 pattern. GM cars, specifically from the muscle car era, used a 5-on-4.75 bolt pattern and 7/16-inch lug studs. That means that

your old TorqThrust wheels probably won't fit your C10—unless they came on a C10 originally.

Measuring for Wheels

Variation in the components used means there's no real magic setup you can order and know it will fit—at least not if you intend to run the widest possible rubber for that filled-fender look. Most aftermarket components are engineered to generally be the same in terms of wheel placement, but some front disc brake conversion kits, for example, can change the location of the wheel hub slightly, which will require a different offset or backspacing over a factory rim. The same can be true for rear disc brake kits, which may be slightly thicker than the stock drums, pushing the wheels out farther from the axle flange. To be sure of what will fit, you really just need to measure—especially if you've changed the suspension or brakes from the stock configuration.

Before you can accurately measure for wheels, you need to have any associated body panels installed. In the case of the front wheels, this means the inner fender liners if you intend on running them. Out back, that means the bed needs to be installed, and the axle and front suspension need to be set as close as possible to ride height—which is mostly an option with height-adjustable trucks.

C10s have quite a bit of room underneath them from the factory, which is very helpful for those who'd like to tuck some wide rubber up underneath the fenders.

You don't need special tools to properly measure for wheels and tires, but it really helps to have something that's designed to take some of the guesswork out of the job.

Squarebody Lug Patterns		
Vehicle	Bolt Pattern	Lug Stud Size
1/2-ton 2WD	5 on 5 inch (5 x 127 mm)	1/2 inch x 20
3/4- and 1-ton 2WD and 4WD	8 on 6.5 inch (8 x 165.1 mm)	9/16 inch x 20
1/2-ton 4WD	6 on 5.5 inch (6 x 139.7 mm)	7/16 inch x 20 (same stud size as GM cars)

The C10's rear wheel tubs are both wide and tall, which should allow for a big tire to fit. But note that it does get slightly narrower the higher you go inside the rear wheel tubs, so if your truck is lowered, you'll need to factor that into your wheel measurements.

The stock rims fit the lines of these trucks well, especially when paired with a set of OEM hubcaps to match. These came in several versions, this set being for 1973–1976 trucks. Note that one bowtie has been painted blue for use on an earlier rig—caps from 1967–1972 trucks were steel and featured blue bowties.

Up front is the same story: loads of space, but it gets slightly narrower the higher you go. Also consider that the front wheels have to turn from right to left, which can cause rubbing issues with wider wheels and tires.

Wheel rim size will depend on two things: the look you're after and the size of your brakes. Factory brakes fit fine under a 15-inch wheel. Aftermarket setups, such as this Baer 6-piston caliper and 14-inch rotor, will require at least an 18-inch rim diameter for caliper clearance. Most aftermarket brake parts come with a rim size minimum recommendation.

Stock Wheels and Caps

From stock-style 15-inch steel rims all the way to 22-inch aluminum 10-spokes, you have a huge range of options at your disposal for your C10. The trick is to pick something you think will look good—and will not turn dated or stale quickly.

There's a lot to be said for a stock set of basic steel wheels and factory hubcaps, especially when they're combined with a lowered suspension. Original-style wheels are timeless, and with some custom widths and backspacing, they can really make a C10 look tough—that is, if you steer away from narrow stockers toward something wider to fill up a squarebody C10's cavernous wheel wells.

You can find a number of options for trucks in 15x7 and 15x8 configurations, as both were available over the years in a 4-inch backspace. These rims, if original, will have their size stamped on the inside of the wheel hoop. You can usually find them at wrecking yards or swap meets, and they shouldn't be expensive, as they're common.

If you want the stock look with a custom width or backspace, Squarebody Syndicate's Joe Yezzi suggests Wheel Vintiques 62 Series O.E. wheels. They look like the factory units, and they're available to order in a variety of size options. For stock or slightly lowered rigs, 15x8 in front and 15x10 in the rear is a good place to start, with a 4-inch backspace up front and a 5-inch backspace in the rear.

However, the original stainless hubcaps are getting harder to find—especially as they also fit the earlier 1967–1972 rigs, and many of those truck builders have hoarded them.

In 1976, GM changed its hubcap design to this cleaner version. These were offered on GM trucks through the end of squarebody production, depending on the option group you selected. This is the 3/4-ton variety, which measures 12 inches in diameter.

Bigger can be better when it comes to rims, but you need to factor in ride quality with the rims you choose. The larger the rim, say 22s, the smaller the tire's sidewall will be, which can make a truck ride rough. I don't like rims larger than 20 inches for that reason. If you're all about looks, go for it—but there's a balance between looks and performance that is smart to consider before you go spending a lot of money on a wheel and tire combo.

On first glance, these hubcaps all look more or less the same. They're not.

First, the 1/2-ton versions are smaller. They measure 10½ inches across, compared to the 3/4-ton versions, which are 12 inches in diameter. The 4x4 versions of each are cut out in the center to make room for the locking hub.

A similar cap was used on earlier trucks as well. The 1973–up versions are either painted or stainless and have a yellow Chevrolet bowtie in the center, with a concave face. The 1967–1972 versions are either painted or chrome-plated and have a blue bowtie with a convex face. You'll often find later caps—the ones for the 1973–1975 trucks—done up with blue bowties for the earlier trucks, as the earlier chrome versions didn't hold up as well over time, and the earlier truck guys have adopted the later caps for their own rigs. Newer caps done up as earlier versions are easy to spot, however; regardless of the paint, they still have that concave shape to the face around the bowtie or GMC logo.

For trucks starting in 1976, a different design dog-dish hubcap was used, which is much easier to find because the earlier truck builders don't tend to run them on their rigs. Swap meets and junkyards tend to be the best place to source a set. Don't forget to look at vans too—they ran the same caps.

The truck Rally wheel was an available option starting in 1976, both for two-wheel-drive and 4x4 rigs, and it's another good stock option that tends to look right on these trucks. The rims themselves aren't hard to come by, unless you're looking for a date-coded set, which is probably best left to the resto crowd. The aftermarket has a variety of backspace and rim-diameter options for these wheels, up to and including 22-inch versions from Detroit Steel Wheels.

Beyond that stock look, there are a million combinations out there when it comes to rim design, from spoked forged aluminum wheels through steel smoothies. The real challenge is narrowing down the field.

Tires

Just as the wheels you choose have a big impact on the look of your truck, so too do the tires—in addition to controlling a lot of your truck's handling characteristics. Most builders want to cram as much rubber under the fenders as they can, but getting a balanced, drivable rig is about more than running fat rubber on all four corners. Getting a sizable contact patch with the ground is important, but so is clearance all around the tire. Any tire contact with the body is a bad thing, so measuring first, before buying tires, is key. Fortunately, you can do that at the same time you measure for rims.

Tire height is an important consideration because the overall wheel diameter will impact everything from your speedometer readings to the final drive ratio of the truck. A taller tire will fill up the wheel well of a C10 and will cover more distance per single revolution when compared to a smaller-diameter tire. That manifests in slower number of rotations for the larger tire to maintain a set speed, say 55 mph, than a smaller tire. That's why adding bigger tires will throw off your factory speedometer, which measures revolutions. So you need to consider that when sizing tires—unless you're running a GPS-based speedometer, such as the Speedhut Speedbox, you'll likely need to account for a different overall diameter than stock, and modify your speedometer drive gear accordingly. Depending on your transmission, this can be done by swapping the speedo gear with one that has either more or fewer teeth, or by reprogramming the TCU for a different tire height.

Rubber Selection

When it comes to sizing modern tires, everything you need to know is printed right on the sidewall. For example, from a P275/60 R15, you know it's a passenger car tire (P), the width is 275 mm across the tread (275), the aspect ratio of the sidewall compared to the tread (60), that it's a radial (R), and it's sized for a 15-inch rim (15).

The letters and numbers after that include the tire's load rating (important if you're looking to haul weight in the bed—two digits; and the higher the number, the greater its load-carrying ability), the speed rating, and whether or not the tire is

The tire's sidewall can tell you a lot about the tire, from its width and aspect ratio to its speed rating and load rating. The last three digits here, 99Y, tell you the tire's carrying capacity (99, which decodes to 1,709 pounds) and top speed rating (Y, or 186 mph).

suitable for all weather conditions.

Some tires use an LT rating rather than a P, which stands for Light Truck. These tires tend to be rated to haul more weight, which is obviously a benefit to trucks and SUVs. They also tend to have a stiffer sidewall to accomplish this, which also usually results in a stiffer, bumpier ride. This will be amplified with larger rims and shorter sidewalls.

For C10 use, it's important to pay attention to the speed rating of a tire—particularly when it comes to plus-sized rubber for rim diameters of 17 inches and greater. Remember that while you've probably added a bunch of speed parts and horsepower to your truck, it's still shaped like a truck, which is to say, a brick. How

Tire Speed Ratings (Maximum)		
L: 75 mph		H: 130 mph
Q: 99 mph		V: 149 mph
R: 106 mph		Z: 149+ mph
S: 112 mph		W: 168 mph
T: 118 mph		Y: 186 mph
U: 124 mph		

fast are you really going to go?

The chances are that most high-performance tires will be overkill for your rig. A lot of 20-inch tires are designed and used for high-performance cars, and they tend to be capable of higher speeds than your truck might see. That's not a bad thing, but it may be smarter to try to find a set of H- or V-rated tires in place of Z-rated examples, if you can find them in the size you need. At the very least, they'll be cheaper, so it won't hurt so much to have to replace a pair of them after you grind all their tread off doing smoky burnouts. Tires with H and V ratings are typically sold as "Touring" or "Performance Touring" tires, compared to the "High-Performance" W-, Y-, and Z-rated rubber.

Additionally, the higher speed ratings tend to use softer rubber compounds, which offer increased traction and stopping ability but at the cost of tire life. They'll be more expensive, and they won't last as long. It's a trade-off to consider before making your tire decision.

Beyond that, tire choice is a matter of taste with a range of sizes available for whatever look you're after. I've found the best ride quality with similar overall diameter rubber front and rear, which can sometimes mean different aspect ratios between the front and rear tires.

Measuring for Wheels and Tires

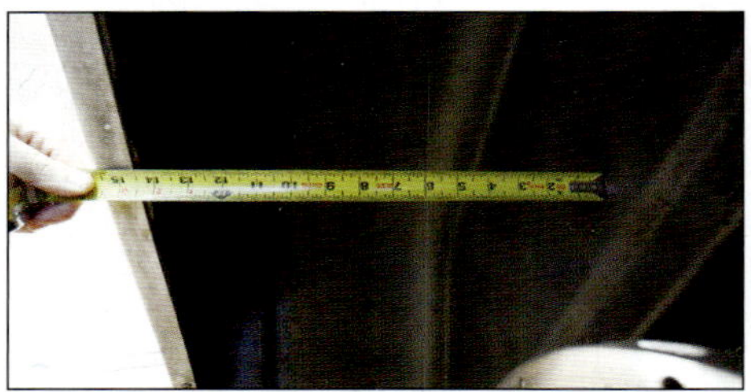

1 *A tape measure is a great way to get a good overall picture of what you'll be working with, at least* roughly. The C10's rear wheel tub size is a massive 14½ inches from the inside wall to the outer lip, which can house up to a 315-series tire with the right rim backspacing and width. Up front is just as wide, but most builders tend to run a narrower tire up front than in the rear.

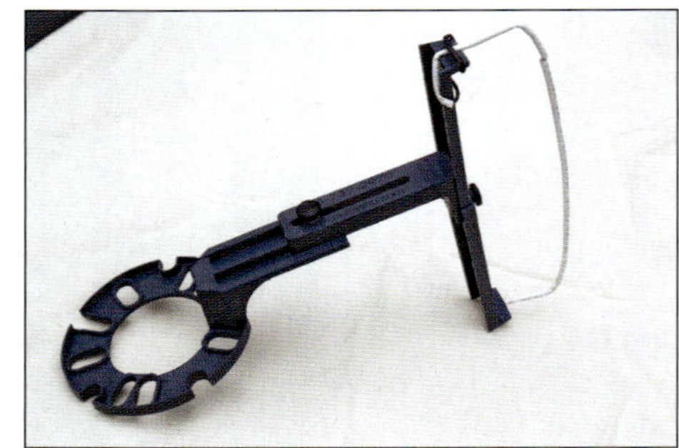

2 *You don't absolutely need a special tool to measure for correct rim size, but it makes the process much easier. This is Percy's Wheelrite,* which mounts to the wheel hub and mocks up a rim and tire. Width, diameter, backspace, and tire size are all adjustable with this tool, which can save you hours of time.

3 *Using a Wheelrite is as simple as bolting it in place and* sliding the adjustment around to get the spacing you're after. It's important to do this at ride height, so a floor jack is the best way to lift the truck here, specifically positioned underneath the axle or front control arm on the side of the truck you're measuring.

4 *The face of the Wheelrite has a marker for rim diameter. All you* need to do is loosen the screw and slide the unit up or down to set the desired rim size for your application. For this truck, I've chosen 20s to clear the disc brakes front and rear.

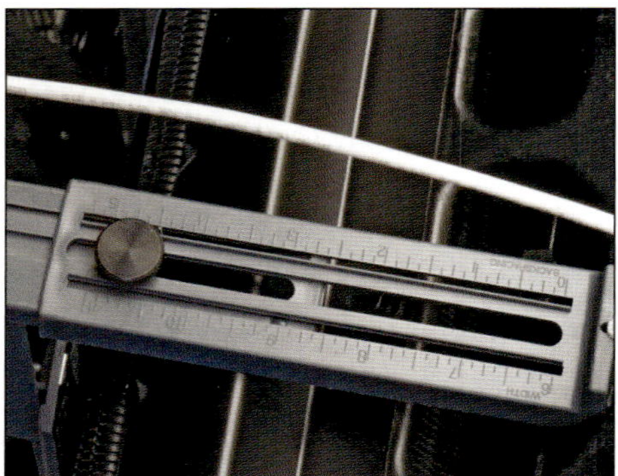

5 *Next is rim width, which is handled (along with backspacing by) the knob at the top. Again,* loosen and slide to get the desired rim width and backspacing.

6 *What I learned here, at least for the rear, is that a 5¼-inch* backspace worked well with a 9½-inch rim. That combination allows for plenty of room around the rim while also allowing the wheel to tuck inside the wheel well. You could go even wider if desired—up to an 11-inch rim with the proper tire.

7 Up front is a different story, as the wheel's travel is more dynamic: in addition to the suspension moving up and down, the wheel and tire need to turn without hitting the inner fender liner. Here an 8-inch rim with a 4½-inch backspace put the rubber right where I needed it when the truck was at ride height and lower. Again, there is more space to play with here if needed.

11 The moment of truth comes when you bolt the wheel and tire combination up to the truck. Here, there's a bunch of clearance around both the front and rear wheels and tires when the truck is at ride height, and each tire still has about a finger's worth of space between it and the wheel well when the truck is aired all the way down—that's important, as it will allow me to move the truck even when its suspension is totally aired out.

8 For rims, I went with American Racing's VN511 salt flat wheels in a polished finish. The sizes are 20x8 in front with a 4½-inch backspace and 20x9½ in the rear with a 5¼-inch backspace. Here they are compared to the 15-inch rims that came on the truck.

9 Baer brakes offers a special template on their website that you can use to check clearance on any set of rims you might be interested in running—or to check to see if a new set of brakes will fit with the rims you already have. All you need to do is download it, print it out, cut it out, and check for clearance between the caliper and the rim itself.

10 As for tire size, many builders will spec out a big and little look, with taller tires at the rear of the vehicle. However, matching rubber, at least in terms of overall diameter, can make for a better ride. So I picked a 28-inch-tall overall tire diameter. For the front, this meant 245/40R20, which measures 27.7 inches in diameter and 9.6 inches wide at the tread. Out back, I stepped up in width but down in aspect ratio to maintain that same rough overall diameter: 285/35R20. These rear tires are 27.9 inches tall and 11.2 inches wide.

12 The key to all of this is to get the right look, power, and handling, and I think I nailed it here for a street-driven rig with an edge. As far as the wheels and tires, there's good clearance all around, but both the front and rear tires are wide enough to fill the wheel wells nicely when the truck is at ride height. All that's left is to go drive it.

SOURCE GUIDE

American Car Collector
  magazine and *Sports Car Market* magazine
P.O. Box 4797
Portland, Oregon 97208
503-261-0555
www.americancarcollector.com
www.sportscarmarket.com

Automotive Interior
  Restorations
3530 SW Multnomah Blvd.
Portland, Oregon 97219
503-997-9596

American Powertrain
3075 Poplar Grove Rd.
Cookeville, Tennessee 38506
931-646-4836
www.americanpowertrain.com

American Racing Wheels
www.americanracing.com

Auburn Gear
400 E. Auburn Dr.
Auburn, Indiana 46706
260-925-3200
www.auburngear.com

Baer Brakes
2222 W. Peoria Ave.
Phoenix, Arizona 85029
602-233-1411
www.baer.com

Built by Brooks
BuiltByBrooks@gmail.com
Instagram: @builtbybrooks

Classic Industries
18460 Gothard St.
Huntington Beach, California
  92648
1-800-854-1280
www.classicindustries.com

Classic Performance Products
175 E Freedom Ave.
Anaheim, California 92801
714-522-2000
www.classicperform.com

Dan's Gears
12040 SW Tonquin Rd.
Sherwood, Oregon 97140
503-692-1547

Dirty Dingo Motorsports
506 E. Juanita Ave. Suite 3
Mesa, Arizona 85204
480-824-1968
www.dirtydingo.com

Eastwood
263 Shoemaker Rd.
Pottstown, Pennsylvania 19464
800-343-9353
www.eastwood.com

Eaton Performance Aftermarket
800-328-3850
www.eaton.com

Edelbrock, LLC
2700 California St.
Torrance, California 90503
800-416-8628
www.edelbrock.com

Fesler Built
866-553-1856
www.shopfesler.com

Flaming River Industries
800 Poertner Dr.
Berea, Ohio 44017
440-826-4488
www.flamingriver.com

Flowmaster Mufflers
1801 Russellville Rd.
Bowling Green, Kentucky
  42101
270-782-2900
www.holley.com

Gearstar Performance
  Transmissions
132 N. Howard St.
Akron, Ohio 44308
330-434-5216
www.gearstar.com

Holley Performance Products
1801 Russellville Rd.
Bowling Green, Kentucky 42101
270-782-2900
www.holley.com

Hooker Headers
1801 Russellville Rd.
Bowling Green, Kentucky 42101
270-782-2900
www.holley.com

Lingenfelter Performance
  Engineering
7819 Lochlin Dr.
Brighton, Michigan 48116
248-486-5342
www.lingenfelter.com

Lokar Performance Products
10924 Murdock Dr.
Knoxville, Tennessee 37932
865-966-2269
www.lokar.com

Meguiar's, Inc
17991 Mitchell South
Irvine, California 92614
1-800-347-5700
www.meguiars.com

Metalox Fab LLC
8615 W. Kelton Ln. Suite 305
Peoria, Arizona 85382
623-308-1170
www.metaloxfab.com

Motive Gear
1001 W. Exchange Ave.
Chicago, Illinois 60609
800-934-2727
www.motivegear.com

MSD
1801 Russellville Rd.
Bowling Green, Kentucky 42101
270-782-2900
www.holley.com

Ratech
11110 Adwood Dr.
Cincinatti, Ohio 45240
www.ratechmfg.com

Redhead Steering Gears
4302 B St. NW
Auburn, Washington 98001
800-808-1148
www.redheadsteeringgears.com

Ridetech
350 S. St. Charles St.
Jasper, Indiana 47546
812-481-4787
www.ridetech.com

Snap-on, Inc.
877-762-7664
www.snapon.com

Speedhut
801-221-1460
www.speedhut.com

Squarebody Syndicate
www.squarebodysyndicate.com
Instagram: @squarebody
  syndicate

Summit Racing Equipment
P.O. Box 909
Akron, Ohio 44309
800-230-3030
www.summitracing.com

Switch Suspension
2340 W. Broadway Rd.
  Suite 105
Mesa, Arizona 85202
800-928-1984
www.switchsuspension.com

United Pacific Industries
3788 E. Conant St.
Long Beach, California 90808
866-327-5288
www.upauto.com

Wilson's Cylinder Heads &
  Machine
16190 SW Farmington Rd.
Beaverton, Oregon 97007
971-570-6009
www.wilsoncylinderheads.com